Five Screenplays

Other works by Harold Pinter Published by Grove Press

THE BIRTHDAY PARTY *and* THE ROOM
THE CARETAKER *and* THE DUMB WAITER
THE HOMECOMING
THE LOVER, TEA PARTY, THE BASEMENT
A NIGHT OUT, NIGHT SCHOOL, REVUE SKETCHES
THREE PLAYS: THE COLLECTION, A SLIGHT ACHE, THE DWARFS
LANDSCAPE, *limited edition*
MAC: A MEMOIR, *limited edition*
OLD TIMES

Five Screenplays

by HAROLD PINTER

THE SERVANT

THE PUMPKIN EATER

THE QUILLER MEMORANDUM

ACCIDENT

THE GO-BETWEEN

Grove Press, Inc.   New York

Contents

*Although Robin Maugham's stage play of *The Servant* was in existence at the time of writing, this screenplay was based solely on Robin Maugham's novel.

To Joseph Losey, Jack Clayton,
Michael Anderson
and Pamela Davies

The Servant

The Servant was first presented by Elstree Distributors Ltd on 14th November 1963 with the following cast:

BARRETT	Dirk Bogarde
TONY	James Fox
SUSAN	Wendy Craig
HEAD WAITER	Derek Tansley
GIRL IN PHONE BOX	Dorothy Bromiley
SOCIETY WOMAN	Ann Firbank
SOCIETY MAN	Harold Pinter
VERA	Sarah Miles
BISHOP	Patrick Magee
OLDER WOMAN	Doris Knox
YOUNGER WOMAN	Jill Melford
CURATE	Alun Owen
LORD MOUNTSET	Richard Vernon
LADY MOUNTSET	Catherine Lacey
CASHIER IN COFFEE BAR	Chris Williams
MAN IN PUB	Brian Phelan
GIRL IN PUB	Alison Seebohm
WOMAN IN BEDROOM	Hazel Terry
GIRL IN BEDROOM	Philippa Hare

Directed by Joseph Losey

The Servant

Exterior. Knightsbridge Square. October. Day.
A quiet square off Knightsbridge. Winter sun. Bare
trees. Numerous parked cars.
At the far side of the square BARRETT *appears. From*
high, see him approach. He stops at the kerb. Cars pass.
He crosses the road. His steps are sharp on the pave-
ment. Looking for a number he passes houses. He stops
at a house, slightly shabbier than the others, discerns
number and goes up the steps. The door is open. He
looks into the dark hall. Silence. There is no door-
knocker. He finds a bell, rings. A faint uncertain ring.

Interior. Hall. TONY's *house. Day.*
From inside the hall see BARRETT *enter and stand.*
The hall wallpaper is dark, of a faded grape design.
There are no carpets, no sign of occupation. Silence.
He crosses to the drawing room door, knocks.

Interior. Drawing room. Day.
From conservatory end of the large empty room see
BARRETT *look round the door. He walks into the room*
and peers into the conservatory. Low down in an old
deckchair lies a body.

Interior. Conservatory. Day.
BARRETT *approaches, stops a little way from the*
body, regards it. He bends over TONY.

BARRETT. Excuse me . . . (TONY *starts up.*) My name's
Barrett, sir.

TONY *stares at him, clicks his fingers.*

TONY. Oh God, of course. I'm so sorry, I fell asleep. We've got an appointment.

BARRETT. Yes, sir.

TONY. What time?

BARRETT. Three o'clock sir.

TONY. Well what time is it now?

BARRETT. Three o'clock, sir.

TONY. Too many beers at lunch, that's what it is. Do you drink beer?

BARRETT. No I don't, sir.

TONY stands.

TONY. Come upstairs. We can sit down.

They move to the door.

Interior. Hall. Stairs. Day.
They walk up the stairs.

TONY. I'm just back from Africa. I'm quite liking it. What do you think of the house?

BARRETT. It's very nice, sir.

TONY. Needs a lot done to it of course.

Interior. TONY's bedroom. First floor. Day.
Winter sun striking across floorboards. The room is empty but for two chairs. The door is flung open. TONY comes in, followed by BARRETT. His words gain a slight echo in the room.

TONY. Damn lucky to get this place, actually. Little bit of wet rot, but not much. Sit down.

BARRETT. Thank you, sir.

BARRETT sits. BARRETT's chair is in the centre of the room. TONY, while speaking, moves about the room, almost circling the seated figure.

TONY. Well now, this post. What's happening is this . . . I'll be moving into this house in about . . . two or three weeks and I'm all alone at the moment, so I'll be needing a manservant, you see. I've seen one or two chaps already but they didn't seem very suitable to me somehow. What . . . you've had experience at this kind of work have you?

BARRETT. I've been in service for the last thirteen years, sir. The last few years I've acted as personal manservant to various members of the peerage.

TONY. Oh.

BARRETT. I was with Viscount Barr until about five weeks ago.

TONY. Oh Lord Barr? My father knew him well. They died within a week of each other as a matter of fact. So you're free?

BARRETT. I am sir.

TONY *stands at the front window.*

Exterior. Gardens in the square. Day.
The gardens in the square, seen by TONY *from the window.* BARRETT's *reflection in the pane.*

Interior. Bedroom. Day.
TONY *turns.*

TONY. Do you like the work?

BARRETT. Oh I do, sir. I do very much.

TONY. Can you cook?

BARRETT. Well it's . . . if I might put it this way, sir, cooking is something in which I take a great deal of pride.

TONY. Any dish in particular?

BARRETT. Well, my . . . my soufflés have always received a great deal of praise in the past, sir.

TONY. Do you know anything about Indian dishes?

BARRETT. A little, sir.

TONY. Well, I know a hell of a lot.

TONY *sits in the other chair.*

You'd have to do all the cooking here.

BARRETT. That would give me great pleasure, sir.

TONY. I could have got a housekeeper of course, to look after the place and run the kitchen, but quite honestly the thought of some old woman running about the house telling me what to do . . . rather put me off.

BARRETT. Quite, sir.

TONY. Now apart from the cooking, I'll need . . . well, everything . . . (*He laughs.*) General looking after . . . you know.

BARRETT. Yes, I do, sir.

Interior. Restaurant. Night.
Small, elegant restaurant with dance floor. The band playing. Dancers. SUSAN *swings into close shot over* TONY's *shoulder.*

SUSAN (*laughing*). Brazil?

TONY. Yes. In the jungle.

The music stops. They go back to the table.

TONY. Waiter! We've got to clear the jungle first.

SUSAN. What? just you?

TONY. No! It's a giant development. They're going to build three cities.

SUSAN. Are they?

TONY. Mm. Gigantic project. Matter of clearing hundreds of miles of jungle.

HEAD WAITER. Sir?

TONY. I'll have another bottle, and by the way, this one's corked.

HEAD WAITER. I'm very sorry, sir.

SUSAN. You're corked.

TONY. Now listen, I'm telling you. . . . First we have to build the cities. Then we've got to find the people to go and live in the cities.

SUSAN. Where are you going to find them?

TONY. From Asia Minor. Thousands of peasants, you see. They're having a pretty rough time of it in Asia Minor and this'll mean a new life for them. Anyway he wants me to help arrange the whole thing. It's going to cost millions, millions.

HEAD WAITER *returns with bottle. Pours.* TONY *sips.*

TONY. Fine. I'm having lunch with him next week.

SUSAN. Where? In the jungle?

TONY. Either here or in Paris, actually. Anyway there's no hurry. I could do with a rest.

SUSAN (*laughing*). A rest from what?

TONY. No. Seriously, what do you think of the idea?

SUSAN (*lifts her glass*). Cosy.

Interior. Drawing room. Bare floors. Night.
TONY *and* SUSAN *lying on the floor, coats as a pillow, a rug over them. A small electric fire plugged in. Night light from window. They kiss.*

TONY. Want to go there?

SUSAN. Where?

TONY. The jungle.

SUSAN. Not now.

TONY. No, not now.

He kisses her.

SUSAN. Batchelor.

She kisses him.

TONY. Oh by the way, I forgot to tell you. I've found a manservant.

SUSAN (*laughing*). What?

Interior. Hall and stairs. Day.
Looking from top of stairs down into empty hall. Voices ascend from kitchen.

BARRETT. Very good idea, sir.

They appear in hall, look up the stairs.

What about the landing, sir?

TONY. White.

They begin to walk up the stairs.

Interior. First landing. Day.
TONY *and* BARRETT *come up the stairs.*

TONY. Well perhaps a little blue here and there . . . but I think the overall colour should be white.

BARRETT. Mandarin red and fuschia is a very chic combination this year, sir.

TONY. Not overall, surely?

BARRETT. No, no, no. Not overall.

TONY. Just a wall?

BARRETT. Oh yes, just a wall, sir, here and there.

Interior. Bedroom. Day.
They enter and look about. TONY's *personal bathroom and dressing room in background.*

TONY. You're very knowledgeable about decoration, Barrett.

BARRETT. Well, it makes all the difference to life, sir.

TONY. Oh. What does?

BARRETT. Tasteful and pleasant surroundings.

TONY. Quite right.

Interior. Top Landing. Day.
TONY *and* BARRETT *arrive on landing.*

TONY (*pointing*). That's your room. Wait a minute, what's that?

They open door of a small room.

Interior. Box Room. Day.
They enter. It is small, ill-lit.

TONY. Box room.

BARRETT. Always do for a maid, sir.

TONY. Oh we'll have a cleaning woman. D'you think we'll need a maid?

BARRETT. They can be useful, sir.

Interior. Hall. Day.

Decorators all over the house, plasterers, painters, etc.
The workmen set up plank on two ladders. BARRETT
coming downstairs passes them on his way to the
kitchen.

BARRETT. Mind the paintwork.

He looks in through the dining-room door.

Interior. Dining-room. Day. Sheets on the floor.
Painters on ladders.

BARRETT. Is everything going all right?

WORKMAN. Yes, thank you.

BARRETT. Yes, well I'll be glad if you'll tell me of any problem so we can correct it before it becomes a fault.

The two painters look at him, then at each other.
BARRETT *exits.*

Interior. Conservatory. Day.
TONY, *smoking, is sketching a design for the garden.*
BARRETT *enters from drawing-room and puts tray*
down.

BARRETT. Lunch, sir.

TONY. Ah that's nice.

BARRETT. No trouble, sir.

TONY. How are they getting on?

BARRETT. I'm keeping an eye on them.

TONY. Are you? You might bring me a lager.

BARRETT. I was just about to, sir.

TONY (*sitting to salad*). I'm ready for it.

BARRETT. Sir . . .

BARRETT *goes, leaving* TONY *eating.*

Exterior. TONY'*s house. Night.*
High shot of sports car slowing to halt. TONY *and*
SUSAN *get out, go up steps.*

Interior. Hall. Night.
House well lit and carpeted. Furniture rather too large
for the rooms. It has come from TONY's *family house.*
BARRETT *opens the door, inclines his head.*

TONY. This is Barrett, Susan, Barrett . . . my fiancée
. . . Miss Stewart.

SUSAN. Hallo.

BARRETT. Good evening, Miss Stewart. Shall I take your
coat?

SUSAN. No, I'll keep it on, thanks.

TONY. In here.

Interior. Drawing-room. Night.
They come in. She looks about.

TONY. Do you like it?

SUSAN. Mm. It's beautiful.

BARRETT. The simple and classic is always the best, Miss.

She looks at a heavy ornament.

SUSAN. Is this classic? This isn't classic, it's prehistoric.

TONY. We've always had it and I like it. Barrett let's have
a drink.

BARRETT. Yes, sir.

SUSAN. Vodka on the rocks.

BARRETT. The usual, sir?

TONY. Thank you. Which one d'you want?

He gestures to armchairs.

SUSAN. This one.

TONY. My mother's favourite.

BARRETT *serves the drinks and exits.*

TONY. He's been a wonderful help, that chap. Wait till you
taste the food. Honestly, I've never been more
comfortable.

SUSAN. Never?

TONY. I don't have to think of a thing.

SUSAN. Does he give you breakfast in bed?

TONY. Of course.

She smiles faintly, stands, walks about.

SUSAN. Have you checked his criminal record?

BARRETT *appears at the door.*

TONY. Yes, Barrett?
BARRETT. You will ring, sir, when you'd like dinner served.
TONY. Yes, I will.

BARRETT *goes.*

SUSAN. Why didn't you get a housekeeper?
TONY. Oh, women are no damn good. They can't cook.

He seizes her, kisses her, pulls her on to sofa.

Interior. Dining-room. Night.
TONY *and* SUSAN *sitting at dinner.* BARRETT *with wine. He wears white cotton gloves.*

SUSAN. The whole place needs brightening . . . more variety you know . . . colour.
TONY. Oh. Do you think so?
SUSAN. Yes, and tomorrow I'm going to organize a proper spice shelf for the kitchen.
BARRETT. Would you like to taste the wine, sir?
TONY. Thank you.
SUSAN. What ducky gloves.
TONY. Barrett's idea. I like it.
BARRETT. It's Italian, miss. They're used in Italy.
SUSAN. Who by?

TONY *tastes wine.*

TONY. Excellent.
BARRETT. Just a Beaujolais sir, but a good bottler.
SUSAN. A good what?
TONY. Bottler.

BARRETT *slightly inclines his head and goes.*

Interior. Kitchen. Night.

BARRETT *sitting alone on chair in kitchen, smoking, picking his teeth.*

Exterior. House. Day.
TONY *running in pouring rain up steps of house.*

Interior. Hall. Day.
TONY's *wet feet. He takes off his raincoat.*

Interior. Kitchen. Day.
BARRETT *pouring salt into bowl of warm water.*

Interior. Drawing-room. Day.
TONY *sitting in library alcove.* BARRETT *undoes his shoes, takes socks off.* TONY *puts feet in bowl.*
TONY. Oh, is this necessary?
BARRETT. Better to be safe than sorry, sir.
TONY. You're too skinny to be a nanny, Barrett.

BARRETT *looks at him.*

Oh, come on, don't sulk, I didn't mean it.

He squiggles his feet.

Oh . . . oh . . . splendid!

Interior. Drawing-room. Night.
Close shot of SUSAN's *feet. Pull back to show* TONY *lying on carpet, smoking long, thin cigar.* SUSAN *sitting in chair. Record player on. The record plays throughout the scene.*
GIRL SINGING ON RECORD
Now while I love you alone
Now while I love you alone
Now while I love you
Can't love without you
Must love without you . . . alone.

SUSAN. Any news from your new frontier?

TONY. No, no, there isn't actually. Well, as a matter of fact he had to go over there and do various things, you know, make various arrangements. Heads of Government and all that.

SUSAN. Heard from him?

TONY. Yes, I mean of course the whole idea's in a very preliminary stage.

He puffs. Silence.

Still I'm quite happy at the moment, . . . aren't you?

SUSAN. Mm.

TONY. I can manage for a good few months. Oh, Barrett has installed my new abstract in the garden. Looks very chic doesn't it?

SUSAN stands, looking through the conservatory into garden. Turns back, goes to him, kisses him. He pulls her to the floor with him, kisses her. The record continues.

GIRL SINGING
. . . Leave it alone
It's all gone
Leave it alone
It's all gone
Don't stay to see me
Turn from your arms
Leave it alone
It's all gone
Give me my death
Close my mouth
Give me my breath
Close my mouth
How can I bear
The ghost of you here
Can't love without you
Must love without you . . .

. . . Now while I love you alone

> Now while I love you
> Can't love without you
> Must love without you
> Now while I love you alone
> Now while I love you alone
> Now while I love you
> Can't love without you
> Must love without you . . . alone.

TONY. That mouth! (*She kisses him.*) Why don't you come and stay?

SUSAN. For a weekend? . . . A long weekend? . . . Or a couple of weeks . . .?

TONY. Marry me.

They embrace. She rolls on top of him. A concealed door opens in the library alcove. BARRET *comes in. They look up. Music ends.*

BARRETT (*withdrawing*). I'm so sorry to disturb you, sir.

He closes the door. SUSAN *lies still.* TONY *stands.*

TONY. I'm sorry.

SUSAN. Why didn't he knock?

TONY. He made a mistake.

Pause.

SUSAN. Mistake! Well for God's sake, restrict him to quarters.

Pause.

Couldn't he live out?

TONY. Out? No he couldn't.

SUSAN. Well he doesn't have to be here after he's washed up the dinner things, does he?

He looks at her blankly.

TONY. He's got to lock up!

Pause.

SUSAN. Well I think I should go anyway.

TONY. Why?

SUSAN. I'm just going.

TONY. This is ridiculous.

She goes to the door, hesitates.

SUSAN. Come home and stay with me.

TONY. Oh look, . . . stay here.

She goes out.

Interior. Hall. Night.
SUSAN *collects her coat,* TONY *helps her on with it.*
BARRETT *appears, opens front door for her. She looks at him.*

SUSAN. A little late for you, Barrett, isn't it? About time you were tucked up in bed.

TONY *gestures to* BARRETT, *who goes.*

TONY. I'll drive you back.

SUSAN. No.

TONY. I'll walk along with you.

SUSAN (*gently*). No.

She takes his face with her hands, kisses him, goes.
TONY *stands, then goes into drawing-room.*

Interior. Drawing-room. Night.
BARRETT *enters.*

BARRETT. I do apologize for the intrusion, sir. I had no idea . . .

TONY. Don't do it again!

BARRETT. I did knock, sir.

TONY. Oh get to bed . . .

TONY *puts his hand to his head*

TONY. Have you got an aspirin?

BARRETT. Yes, sir. I expect you caught a bit of a chill the other day in the rain, sir.

Interior. TONY's *bedroom. Day.*
TONY *in bed.* SUSAN *drawing curtains, opens windows.*

SUSAN. You need more air.

TONY. Oh I don't know.

SUSAN. No, you don't.

She turns, goes to door, goes out.

Interior. Landing. Day.
BARRETT *is there as* SUSAN *comes out and takes vase of flowers from table, then returns to bedroom.*

Interior. Bedroom. Day.
SUSAN *comes back with a vase of flowers, places them.*

TONY. Oh God! I'm so sorry. I completely forgot. They're beautiful. Thanks very much.

SUSAN. Every time you open a door in this house that man's outside. He's a Peeping Tom.

TONY. He's a vampire too on his Sundays off.

SUSAN. Why didn't you have them in your room?

TONY. Well as a matter of fact he was saying that they're bad in a sick room at night . . .

A knock on the door.

. . . come in.

BARRETT *comes in.*

BARRETT. Your medicine, sir. And the post.

TONY. Oh thank you.

BARRETT *gives* TONY *the capsules and a glass of water.* TONY *takes them.*
BARRETT *leaves the mail on the bedside table. An uneasy silence.*

SUSAN. What did the Doctor say yesterday?

TONY. Oh nothing much. Virus.

BARRETT *picks up the vase to move it to another position in the room.*

SUSAN. Put that down!

Pause.

TONY. Oh put it down, Barrett.

BARRETT (*doing so*). I beg your pardon, sir.

BARRETT goes.

TONY. I do wish you'd stop yapping at Barrett all the time. It'll be a bastard if he leaves.

SUSAN. What the hell would that matter?

TONY. What would it matter? Well, you try and find another like him.

SUSAN. I'm sorry I was rude to your servant.

TONY. Look, he may be a servant but he's still a human being!

She turns, leaves the room.

Interior. Hall. Day.
BARRETT, beating SUSAN to the front door, opens it for her.

BARRETT. I'm afraid it's not very encouraging miss . . . the weather forecast.

She looks at him for a moment steadily, and then goes down the steps. BARRETT closes the door behind her.

Exterior. TONY's house. Knightsbridge Square. Day.
SUSAN stops at the base of the steps. Suddenly looking lost. A wind is blowing through the square.

Exterior. Knightsbridge Square. Early evening.
The wind has now grown in force. The streets are wet.

Interior. Public phone box. Knightsbridge Square. Early evening.
BARRETT stands in the phone box.

BARRETT. Yes. Bolton 62545.

He waits. A group of girls collects outside the box, talking, giggling. The skirt of one of the girls blows up.

BARRETT *observes this blankly. Another girl remarks on his gaze. The girls laugh. The operator tells him to go ahead.*

VERA'S VOICE. Hallo.

BARRETT. Vera?

VERA'S VOICE. Yes.

BARRETT. Are you ready?

VERA'S VOICE. Yes, I'm ready . . .

BARRETT. All right then, tomorrow.

VERA'S VOICE. All right. I've bought something new.

BARRETT. Mm?

BARRETT's *attention goes again to the group of girls. The same girl is trying to keep her skirt down in the wind.*

VERA'S VOICE. . . . I'm wearing it now.

BARRETT. Oh.

VERA'S VOICE. I'll show it to you if you're being a good boy.

BARRETT. I am. Are you being a good girl?

VERA'S VOICE. What?

He grits his teeth.

BARRETT. I said are you being a good girl?

VERA'S VOICE. I am.

BARRETT. I'll be at the station.
You got my last letter, didn't you?

VERA'S VOICE. Oh yes, I got that all right.

BARRETT. All right then. At the station. Tara.

VERA'S VOICE. Bye.

BARRETT *goes out of box. The girl squeezes past him.* BARRETT *jabs her away.*

BARRETT. Get out of it, you filthy bitch.

Interior. Dining-room. TONY's *house. Night.*
BARRETT *has made certain changes in this room too, as throughout the house.*
TONY *is at the table.* BARRETT *standing by.*

TONY. You've mulled some delicious claret, Barrett.

(*He laughs.*) I say, that's rather good, isn't it? Claretty Barrett.

BARRETT. In the army they used to call me Basher Barrett, sir.

TONY. Oh really? Why?

BARRETT. I was a very good driller.

TONY. Ah! (*Pause.*) I like the changes you've been making in the house. You've been enjoying yourself, haven't you?...

BARRETT *clears a little.*

BARRETT. I have, sir . . . thank you very much, sir. Oh by the way, sir, I took the liberty of removing those er chintz frills of Miss Stewart's off the dressing table. Not very practical. (TONY *grunts.*) Haven't seen very much of Miss Stewart recently have we sir?

TONY. Mmmmn? No.

BARRETT. My sister's arriving tomorrow sir, as you agreed.

TONY. Oh yes. Fine.

BARRETT. She's very happy about the arrangement, if you are.

TONY. Well, we might keep her, if she's any good.

Euston Station. Day.
BARRETT *standing on platform. A train draws in.*

Cocktail bar in Soho French restaurant. Day.
TONY *is standing at bar. A man and girl talking.*

GIRL. He's a wonderful wit.

MAN. Terribly funny.

GIRL. Terribly.

MAN. Cheers.

GIRL. Cheers. I'm dying to see him again. I haven't seen him for ages.

MAN. You won't for some time.

GIRL. Oh. Why?

MAN. He's in prison.

SUSAN *enters the restaurant.*

TONY. Hello

SUSAN. Hello.

HEAD WAITER. Good morning, Miss Stewart
SUSAN. Good morning.
HEAD WAITER. Good morning, sir.
TONY. Good morning.
HEAD WAITER. Very nice to see you here again.
SUSAN. Thank you.

They sit. HEAD WAITER *hands them menus.*

HEAD WAITER. I can recommend the Roast Duck.
TONY. What are you having?
SUSAN. Are you better?
TONY. Yes thanks.

They look at each other.

SUSAN. I've brought you a present.

She hands him a package.

TONY. What for?
SUSAN. Because I wanted to.

Euston Platform. Day.
VERA *running down platform towards* BARRETT.

Interior. Soho restaurant. Day.
TONY *and* SUSAN *eating. The restaurant is packed. Hors d'oeuvres. A Bishop and a Curate enter the restaurant.*
HEAD WAITER. Good morning, Bishop.
BISHOP. Good morning.

Euston Station. Platform. Day.
From high, see VERA *and* BARRETT *walk down platform, not speaking. He carries her bag.*

Interior. Soho restaurant. Day.
TONY *and* SUSAN *eating main course, with wine.*

Silence. Camera passes them to middle-aged woman and young woman sitting at table.

OLDER WOMAN. What did she say to you?

YOUNGER
    WOMAN. Nothing.

OLDER WOMAN. Oh yes she did. She said something to you.

YOUNGER
    WOMAN. She didn't. She didn't really.

OLDER WOMAN. She did. I saw her mouth move. She whispered something to you, didn't she? What was it? What did she whisper to you?

YOUNGER
    WOMAN. She didn't whisper anything to me. She didn't whisper anything!

SUSAN. Why don't we go away . . . for a few days . . . mm?

TONY. Where?

SUSAN. Anywhere.

TONY. Agatha and Willy Mountset have invited us down actually.

SUSAN. Well why don't we go there?

TONY. Yes, we could I suppose.

Exterior. London street. Interior. Taxi. Day.
Inside the taxi VERA *and* BARRETT *are sitting, not touching.* VERA *is looking out of the window.*

Interior. Soho restaurant. Day.
TONY *and* SUSAN *with coffee. A constrained silence between them.* BISHOP *and* CURATE *drinking.*

CURATE. I hear Father O'Flaherty won't be at the Cork Convocation.

BISHOP. Flaherty? For the love of God don't be a child. Sure the man wouldn't miss a trip like that, you can bet your last pound on that.

CURATE. Didn't they have to carry him out last time?

BISHOP. Ah for God's sake who didn't they have to carry out?

Cut to TONY *and* SUSAN, GIRL *and* MAN *in background.*

SUSAN. I just don't like him.

TONY. You don't know him. (*Pause.*) I mean surely you can take my word for the fact.

SUSAN. Don't trust him.

TONY. Why?

SUSAN. I don't know.

GIRL. It's the snow. It's the snow I like.

TONY. He looks like a fish with red lips I admit. But apart from that, what's the matter with him? You're making him so bloody important. I mean it seems to me you've got the whole thing absurdly out of proportion.

SUSAN. Yes, perhaps.

They pick up glasses.
BISHOP *and* CURATE *get up.*

BISHOP. And where are you creeping off to now, my son . . . ah?

CURATE. Nowhere Your Grace, nowhere . . . Nowhere at all.

BISHOP. Is that a fact?

SUSAN. Why don't you just tell him to go?

TONY. You must be mad. (*Pause.*) You just don't care about my . . . and what it amounts to is it's my judgement you're criticizing. It's not only ridiculous it's bloody hurtful.

GIRL (*at other table*). They were gorgeous – absolutely gorgeous.

MAN. Were they really?

TONY. I'm sorry. I'm a fool.

SUSAN. You are.

TONY. Well . . . I mean . . .

GIRL. Divine, but I simply couldn't get them on.

MAN. Pity!

Pause. SUSAN *touches* TONY'*s hand.*

SUSAN. Look . . . I'm sorry.

TONY. Well . . . well I wouldn't . . .

He touches her hand, frowning, unsure.

Interior. TONY's *house. First landing. Day.*
BARRETT *showing* VERA *up the stairs. On the first landing she looks into* TONY's *bedroom and at* BARRETT. *He guides her away and up further flight to her room.*

Interior. TONY's *house. Top landing and small room. Day.*
BARRETT *showing* VERA *to her bedroom. She looks round the room and then at him. He regards her, expressionless.*

Interior. Hall. Day.
TONY *is by front door.*

TONY. Barrett!

He goes into drawing-room.

Interior. Drawing-room. Day.
TONY *enters.*

TONY. Barrett!

He unwraps package and takes out a short black silk dressing gown. He hears BARRETT *and throws it on the sofa.*

BARRETT. Did you call, sir?
TONY. Yes. Damn awful lunch. Where were you? Get me a brandy.
BARRETT. Yes sir.

BARRETT *pours brandy and notices gown.*

It's very handsome, sir.

TONY *drinks.*

Oh . . . might I introduce my sister to you, sir? She's arrived . . . she's very excited at the prospect of being with us.

TONY. Oh is she?

BARRETT *turns to door.*

BARRETT. Vera.

Interior. Kitchen. Day.
Boiling water into teapot from kettle. Camera pulls
back to show BARRETT *checking the tea tray. He*
passes it into VERA'*s hands. She exits.*

Interior. Drawing-room. Day.
TONY *lying in an armchair. His feet rest on a foot*
stool. A side table by his chair. VERA *comes in, places*
tea tray on side table with great care, bending over
TONY *to do so.*

Interior. Drawing-room. Twilight.
TONY *still lying, dozing, a book on the floor, the tea*
tray empty. VERA *and* BARRETT *enter with flowers.*
They arrange the flowers on a table by the window.
TONY *watches through half-open eyes. He sees*
VERA'*s face and throat through the flowers, her body,*
in her short black maid's uniform, moving under the
table, her legs.

Interior. Lord and Lady Mountset's country house.
Late afternoon.
LORD *and* LADY MOUNTSET, TONY *and* SUSAN.

LADY
MOUNTSET. Well I'm absolutely certain you'll be fascinated by
Brazil.

LORD
MOUNTSET. Oh yes.

LADY
MOUNTSET. I was in the Argentine of course, briefly, as a girl.
. . . I was certainly fascinated by the Argentine.

TONY. It should be very interesting.

LADY
MOUNTSET. Fascinating, Tony darling.

LORD
MOUNTSET. How many cities are you going to build?

SUSAN. Three.

TONY. Yes, it's – quite a big development.

LORD
MOUNTSET. In the jungle?

TONY. Not exactly in the jungle, no sir. On the plain.

SUSAN. Oh but some of the jungle will have to be cleared, won't it?

TONY. Some of the jungle, yes. A little bit.

LADY
MOUNTSET. That's where the Ponchos are, of course, on the plains.

SUSAN. Ponchos?

LORD
MOUNTSET. South American cowboys.

SUSAN. Are they called Ponchos?

LORD
MOUNTSET. They were in my day.

SUSAN. Aren't they those things they wear? You know, with the slit in the middle for the head to go through?

LORD
MOUNTSET. What do you mean?

SUSAN. Well, you know . . . hanging down in front and behind . . . the cowboy.

LADY
MOUNTSET. They're called cloaks, dear.

Interior. First landing. Morning.
Very close shot of TONY's *bedroom door.* VERA's *hand comes into shot and knocks on it.*

TONY'S VOICE. Come in.

Interior. TONY's *bedroom. Morning.*
TONY *in bed, no pyjamas.* VERA *comes in with break-fast, sets it down.*

VERA. Good morning sir.
TONY. Morning . . . Where's Barrett?
VERA. He's gone out shopping sir.

She opens the curtains and arranges them.

Anything else, sir?
TONY. No thank you.

She picks up about the room. TONY *watches. She goes.*

Interior. Kitchen. Day.
BARRETT *comes in through the kitchen door from the garden.* VERA *enters from hall. They look at each other. She goes to the sideboard and pours tea, crosses to the table and sits on it. Her skirt is above her knees. As* BARRETT *approaches she begins to grin. Her grin fades to an expression of intense antici-pation. As he draws closer to her her head is suddenly flung back in a soundless sexual laugh, mouth open.*

Interior. TONY's *bedroom. Day.*
Close shot of silent valet. BARRETT's *hand taking jacket off it, helping* TONY *into it.*
Pause.
TONY. For God's sake look at this. That's not much good, Barrett!
BARRETT. I beg your pardon, sir.

BARRETT *brushes the jacket gently.*

TONY. Pull your socks up now. Come on, come on, come on, give it a good brush, you won't hurt me.
BARRETT. Perhaps you'd like to take the jacket off, sir?
TONY. No, damn it. Do it on. I haven't got time to mess about.

BARRETT *brushes vigorously.*

BARRETT. Would you turn round sir.

TONY. No. All right, all right. (*Sulkily.*) All right, it'll have to do.

He goes to the mirror.

BARRETT. We heard this morning that our mother's ill up in Manchester, sir. Apparently she's been asking for us. It might be dangerous. Would you mind if we took the night off and came back tomorrow late?

TONY. Both of you?

BARRETT. Well it is touch and go, sir.

TONY. Well that's bloody inconvenient.

BARRETT. I appreciate that, sir, I do appreciate that. But we could leave you a cold buffet and salad.

TONY. I wanted something hot! Couldn't you make it tomorrow?

BARRETT. I suppose we could, sir.

TONY. Make it tomorrow. It'll give us time to get organized.

BARRETT. Right, sir.

TONY. Well I'm off.

BARRETT. Oh there's one other thing I'd like a brief word with you, sir, about, before you go.

TONY. Well what is it?—Where's my Cologne?

BARRETT. It's about Vera.

TONY. What about her?

BARRETT. Well it's her skirts, sir. They rather worry me.

TONY. Her skirts? What's the matter with them?

BARRETT. Well, might I suggest that they're a little short, sir?

Silence.

TONY. A little short?

BARRETT. I should say so.

Pause.

TONY. Well what the hell do you want me to do about it? She's your sister, tell her yourself. Where's my Cologne? . . .

He crosses through dressing room, to bathroom door.

VERA'S VOICE. Don't come in. I'm naked! Who is it?

TONY *stops still. The door remains ajar.*

VERA'S VOICE. Oh, I am sorry, I forgot to lock the door.

TONY. I want my Cologne.

VERA. Your what?

TONY. The bottle . . .

VERA. It's all right, I've got a towel on now.

TONY *grasps the door handle and holds the door firmly towards him.*

TONY. I just want my Cologne.

He waits, his face set.

VERA. What, the one with your initials on?

TONY. Yes.

The door is pulled. TONY *resists the pull, holds the door tight, slightly ajar. Her arm comes through with the Cologne.*

VERA. I'm sorry sir, I thought everyone was out.

For a moment he watches her hand move, searching for him. He then takes the bottle, goes back into his room and dabs Cologne on his handkerchief.

TONY. D'you know Vera's in my bathroom?

BARRETT. I beg your pardon, sir?

TONY. She's having a bath in my bathroom. Well, I mean to say . . . I mean . . . after all . . . you've got one of your own upstairs.

He gives BARRETT *the Cologne.*

Have a word with her.

TONY *exits.* BARRETT *crosses to bathroom and enters.*

Interior. Bathroom. Day.

BARRETT *and* VERA. VERA *in towel. He holds the bottle of Cologne.*

BARRETT. Who told you to take a bath in his bathroom? Who said you could use his bathroom? A gentleman doesn't want a naked girl bouncing about all over his bathroom.

VERA. You told me to, didn't you?

BARRETT. Me? Why would I tell you a thing like that?

He closes the door.

I'll tell you what I'm going to do now.

VERA. What?

BARRETT. I'm going to have a bath in his bathroom.

VERA *turns the tap.*

VERA. You're terrible.

He gives her the Cologne.

BARRETT. And I want that . . . all over me.

He takes off his jacket. She watches him. The water boils into the bath.

Interior. Bedroom. Day.
The square is seen through the window. BARRETT *and* VERA *walking, with bags.* TONY *comes into fore-ground, watches, turns, heavy. Telephone rings.*

TONY. Hallo.

SUSAN'S VOICE. It's me.

TONY. Oh hello.

SUSAN'S VOICE. I've been worried about you.

TONY. Er – can I ring you back?

SUSAN'S VOICE. Well yes – but when?

TONY. Are you at the office?

SUSAN'S VOICE. Yes, but I'm just going out. Are you in tonight?

TONY. Er . . . Yes. Ring me then, would you?

SUSAN'S VOICE. All right, good-bye.

TONY. Bye . . . bye.

Interior. Chelsea coffee bar. Night.
It is crowded. Guitarist. TONY *at table signalling to waitress. She eventually comes to his table and*

*clears some dirty crockery. As she bends over table
she momentarily resembles* VERA. TONY *vaguely
holds menu.*

WAITRESS. Back in a moment, sir.

*She goes. He is left. She comes back towards him but
is waylaid by another table. He starts tapping knife,
suddenly rises, goes to the door. The cashier looks at
him.*

CASHIER. Yes, sir. Can I help you?
TONY. No I haven't had anything.

He goes out.

*Exterior. Brompton Road. Night.
Snow. Late at night. Distant storm approaching.*
TONY *walking along the road, alone.*

Exterior. TONY's *house. Knightsbridge Square. Night.
Snow.* TONY *walking to house. He goes slowly up the
steps.*

Interior. Hall. TONY's *house. Night.*
TONY *switches on light, throws coat onto hall stand,
stands irresolute. He looks at mail, throws it down
unopened, goes to the kitchen.*

Interior. Kitchen. TONY's *house. Night.*
TONY *comes in, turns on the light, pours a glass of
water, puts ice in it, sips it. He puts glass down on the
sink, sits down, picks up paper, stares at it. He looks
for glass, puts down paper, stands, collects glass,
drinks, standing. Suddenly he turns round sharply.*
VERA *is at the door.*

VERA. Oh! . . . I wondered who it was.
TONY. What are you . . . what are you doing here?

VERA. I was just going to bed and – I thought I heard a noise.

TONY. But you went to Manchester.

VERA. I didn't feel too well at the station, so he sent me back in a taxi.

Silence. The tap is dripping.

TONY. Sent you back?

VERA. Yes . . .

Tap dripping.

TONY. How do you feel now?

VERA. I feel a bit better.

He stares at her. She smiles.

TONY. Shall I get you a glass of water?

VERA. I'm glad it was you. I thought it might have been him coming back.

TONY. Has he gone?

VERA. Oh yes – yes he went. I'm glad I'm not alone. I didn't fancy being alone by myself in this house.

Tap dripping. TONY *turns the tap off, turns. Silence.*

VERA. Can I get you anything, sir?

TONY. No . . . no . . .

Phone rings. They look at it. TONY *does not move. It stops.*
VERA *perches on the table*

VERA. . . . Oh . . . isn't it hot in here . . . Isn't it? . . .

The saucepan and crockery glisten on the shelves.

So hot.

The kitchen glistens, the gas stove, the pans. VERA'*s body inclines backward on the table, her skirt half-way up her thighs.*

TONY. Your skirt's too short.

VERA (*looking down at her legs*). My what? That's how all the girls are wearing them. Well that's how they all wear them . . . Why? do you think it's too short?

He comes close to the table. She gestures to his face.

You hot?

A sudden savage embrace.

Oh that's nice that's nice oh that's nice.

Two figures seen distorted in shining saucepans.

Interior. Hall. Evening.
BARRETT *enters, examines mail, walks to kitchen.*

Interior. Kitchen.
BARRETT *studies two plates on table, chicken bones on them.* TONY *appears in the kitchen door.*

TONY. Oh, hello Barrett, how's your Mother?
BARRETT. On the mend, sir.
TONY. Oh, good. Good. Little Vera wasn't very well then?

BARRETT *takes plates to the sink.*

BARRETT. Well no. She looked so poorly at the railway station, sir, I thought it wasn't wise to let her travel. I hope she hasn't been any inconvenience to you.
TONY. Oh not at all. No, she hasn't at all.
BARRETT. Did she manage to do anything for you, sir?

TONY *looks at him sharply.*

TONY. I beg your pardon.
BARRETT. I hope she was well enough to see to your meals.
TONY. Oh yes, yes, we . . . I had lunch.
BARRETT. I notice she didn't do the washing up.
TONY. Still under the weather, I suppose.
BARRETT. Under the what, sir?
TONY. The weather.
BARRETT. Oh yes.
TONY. Oh Barrett, you wouldn't like to go to the off-licence for me would you, for a quart of beer? I've got rather a thirst.

BARRETT. There's plenty of beer, sir.

TONY. Yes I know that, but I want some plain brown ale.

BARRETT. Certainly, sir.

> BARRETT *exits.*

> *Interior. Hall. Evening.*
> BARRETT *goes out front door.* TONY *appears immediately and calls.*

TONY. Vera!

VERA. Yes sir?

TONY. Come down a minute.

VERA. I'm coming. Where are you?

TONY. Down here. He's back.

> *He steps into library door. She comes down the stairs. As she passes him, he grasps her from behind. She screams, wheels round, giggling.*

VERA. Oh you . . . what are you doing?

> *He pulls her into the library.*

> *Interior. Library alcove.*
> *He seats* VERA *in the leather chair.*

VERA. I've got to wash up.

TONY. I've sent him to the pub, he'll be back in a minute.

VERA. Who cares about him?

TONY. Well, he's your brother.

VERA. What are you doing? (*Giggles.*)

> *Exterior. Knightsbridge Square. Evening.*
> BARRETT *approaching* TONY's *house steadily.*

> *Exterior. Library. Evening.*
> VERA *and* TONY *in embrace.*

> *Exterior.* TONY's *house.*
> BARRETT *up the front steps, opens the door.*

Interior. Library. Evening.
TONY *and* VERA *half lying on the table.* TONY *hears the door.*

TONY. Come down at twelve o'clock.

He goes quickly through the library door into the garden.

Interior. Hall. Evening.
VERA *meets* BARRETT *at foot of stairs. She looks at him.*

VERA. I'm going to bed, I'm tired.

He watches her go upstairs and goes into drawing-room.

Interior. Kitchen. Night.
BARRETT *pouring a glass of brown ale.* TONY *comes in through kitchen door from garden.*

TONY. Oh hullo Barrett. Just getting a bit of air in the garden.

BARRETT. Rather cold, sir.

TONY. Got the beer? Oh good.

BARRETT. Anything else you want, sir?

TONY. No thanks, I'll be going out soon but I'll be back before . . . midnight. There'll be no need for you to wait up for me. I'll lock up myself.

BARRETT. Right, sir.

TONY *picks up glass of ale, sips, grimaces.*

Interior. Drawing-room. Night.
Later. Near midnight. TONY *drinking whisky. He jumps up, looks at watch, goes out.*

Interior. Hall. Night.
TONY *comes out of the drawing-room and goes up the stairs.*

Interior. First landing. Night.
TONY comes up from the hall and continues up the stairs to the top landing.

Interior. Top Landing. Night.
It is dark. TONY comes up stairs, looks warily at BARRETT's door, then taps very lightly on VERA's door. After a few seconds her voice is heard through the keyhole.

VERA. All right, I'm coming. Go down.

TONY goes downstairs.
There is a pause and the light goes on in VERA's room. She opens the door carefully and looks out.

Interior. VERA's room. Night.
A low angled shot from the stairs. As VERA opens the door further to come out, BARRETT can be seen in her bed reaching for a newspaper which he picks up and reads. She exits.

Interior. Drawing-room. Night.
TONY pulls VERA to him in the half darkness.

TONY. Are you cold?

VERA. No.

TONY. What about him? Is he asleep?

VERA. His room's dark.

He stares at her. He lowers her into the leather chair, swings the chair so that she faces him. Her legs stretch out across the arms of the chair.

Interior. First landing. Day.
VERA knocks on TONY's door.

TONY. Come in.

VERA. Can I have your tray, sir?

She goes in. Camera stays on closed door.

Interior. Hall. Day.
BARRETT *comes from kitchen to alcove under the stairs and hides there.*

Interior. First landing. Day.
VERA *slips out of* TONY's *door, flushed, and goes downstairs carrying the tray.*

Interior. Hall. Day.
VERA *comes downstairs, puts tray down on hall table and looks at herself in mirror. Suddenly* BARRETT's *hands reach for her. He pulls her back out of sight. A sharp gasp from her, a grating 'Aaaaahhh' from him. A phone can be heard ringing off screen. Stay on empty hall.*

Interior. TONY's *bedroom. Day.*
TONY *still in bed. He is on the telephone.*

TONY. Hallo.
SUSAN's VOICE. Hallo.
TONY. Oh hullo Susan.
SUSAN's VOICE. Did you get my note? I expect you've been rather busy?
TONY. Yes. I have been rather busy, actually, with one thing and another.
SUSAN's VOICE. Well what time will you call then?
TONY. Oh about two-thirty. Should give us time enough to get down there. I'm having lunch with my father's solicitor.
SUSAN's VOICE. All right. Well see you then.
TONY. Right. Bye.
SUSAN. Bye.

Interior. Hall. Day.
TONY *runs up from below and opens the door of* VERA's *bedroom.*

Interior. VERA'*s bedroom. Day.*
VERA *is in bed. She is pale, limp, trembling, exhausted.*
TONY *goes in.*

TONY. What's the matter?

VERA *looks a child, trembling continually.*

TONY. What's the matter. What is it?
VERA. I'm not well.

He sits on the bed.

TONY. What is it?

No answer. He touches her hand.

He's gone out . . . I . . .

She looks at him with a tense distrustful smile. She speaks suddenly and harshly, with a bitter reined hysteria.

VERA. Come on then.

Interior. Hall. Day.
BARRETT *opens front door to* SUSAN. *She carries flowers.*

BARRETT. I'm afraid the master's not at home.
SUSAN. I know. Collect my things from the taxi please.

BARRETT *goes out of the house to collect parcel from taxi.* SUSAN *moves into the drawing-room.*

Interior. Drawing-room.
SUSAN *picks up a vase.* BARRETT *comes in.*

SUSAN. Fill this with water. Where's the parcel?
BARRETT. It's in the hall, Miss.
SUSAN. Bring it to me.

BARRETT *collects the parcel and brings it in. He goes out with vase. Re-enters with it.* SUSAN *arranges flowers in the vase.*

SUSAN. How do you like them, Barrett?

BARRETT. I'm not certain that the flowers wouldn't be better in a different jar, Miss.

SUSAN. I thought you'd be uncertain, Barrett. (*She opens the parcel and throws a number of small cushions from it on to the sofa.*) What do you think of them?

BARRETT. I beg your pardon?

SUSAN. What do you think of the cushions?

BARRETT. It's difficult to say what I think of them, Miss.

SUSAN. Shall I tell you the truth, Barrett?

BARRETT. Yes, Miss.

SUSAN. The truth is, I don't care what you think.

Pause

I want some lunch. A salad will do. Use the tarragon I bought on Wednesday.

BARRETT. Yes, Miss.

She takes a cigarette.

SUSAN. Light . . . Put that coat down and give me a light.

BARRETT *lights her cigarette. Moves to the door.*

SUSAN. Barrett! Come here.

He goes to her.

Do you use a deodorant?

He stares at her.
Tell me. Do you think you go well with the colour scheme?

BARRETT. I think the Master's satisfied.

SUSAN. What do you want from this house?

BARRETT. Want?

SUSAN. Yes, want.

BARRETT. I'm the servant, Miss.

SUSAN. Get my lunch.

Exterior. LORD MOUNTSET'S *estate. Day.*
Gracious turreted house. Lawns and arbours. Undulating fields sweep down to lake. Poplars. Two figures far down by the lake. Keep on them for some seconds in the distance. They are throwing snowballs.

Exterior. The lake. Day.
TONY *and* SUSAN *running. They stop and kiss.*

SUSAN. Why don't you come up to my room? There's a
wonderful view from there. Or what about your
room? What's it like from yours?

TONY. It's not very good from mine.

SUSAN *laughs.*

TONY. The best view . . . is from our room . . . at the
house. What about leaving tonight?

SUSAN. Wouldn't that be a little rude?

TONY. No . . . no . . . they won't mind.

Interior. TONY's *car. Evening.*
TONY *driving.* SUSAN *huddled close to him.*

Exterior. The square. Night.
*The car coming into the square, drawing up to the
house. It slows.*

Interior. Car. Night.

TONY. There's a light on in my room. Quarter to twelve.
Who the hell's in my room?

Interior. Hall. TONY's *house. Night.*
The dark hall. TONY *opens the front door softly. He
walks carefully to the stairs, treads halfway up and
halts.* SUSAN *remains at the bottom.*
A light comes through his bedroom door, which is ajar.
Voices:

BARRETT. Give us one over.

VERA. You've only just had one.

BARRETT. Well I want another one.

Pause.

VERA. All this bloody smoking, it drives you mad.

BARRETT. You're driving me mad.

Pause.

VERA. Come on . . . oh come on for Christ's sake, put it down.

BARRETT. I've only had one puff.

VERA. Oh come on put it down.

BARRETT. I'm worn out. What's the matter with you?

VERA. I know someone who wouldn't say no.

BARRETT. Him? He'd be on the floor.

Bedcreak. Rustle.

Let me finish this fag. You're like a bloody machine.

VERA. I know I am but I can't help it.

TONY *rests his head against the wall.*

SUSAN. It's your servants.

There is a sudden silence in the house. BARRETT's *voice.*

BARRETT. There's someone there.

VERA. No, there isn't.

BARRETT. Did you lock up?

VERA. Of course I did.

BARRETT. What about the bolt?

VERA. Oh no . . . well I didn't bolt.

BARRETT. You bloody little idiot!

A silence. TONY *and* SUSAN *remain still.* BARRETT's *naked shadow appears at the top of the stairs.*
TONY *turns and looks up. A long silent stare between them.*
Suddenly, harshly, raucously, VERA's *voice.*

VERA. There's no one there. I told you. Oh come on, Hugo. You'll catch your death of cold out there. I'm waiting for you. Come and look at me, I'm all here waiting for you! Come on, what's the matter with you? I'm all rosy lying here. I'm rosyyyyy! What the bloody hell are you doing?

BARRETT *turns and goes back.*

Interior. Drawing-room. Night.
TONY *enters the dark room, covers his face.* SUSAN
follows, switching on lights.

SUSAN. What are you going to do?

He does not answer.

SUSAN. This is your house.

Silence.

SUSAN. They're in your room, in your bed.

Pause.

Did you know this was going on?

Pause.

TONY *abruptly shivers, clenches his fist and goes to the
door.*

TONY. Barrett! Barrett! Come down here.

He comes back. A tense silence.

I think I should see him alone.
SUSAN. Why?

BARRETT *appears at the foot of the stairs and stops
at the drawing-room door.*

TONY. Come here.

He steps into the room.

I want an explanation.
BARRETT. Might I speak to you alone, sir?
TONY. Do you realize you've committed a criminal
offence?
BARRETT. Criminal, sir?
TONY. She's your sister, you bastard!

BARRETT *looks at him.*

BARRETT. She's not my sister, sir. (*Pause.*) And if I might say
so we're both rather in the same boat.

Silence. BARRETT *looks at* SUSAN.

He knows precisely what I mean . . .

She stares at TONY.

BARRETT. . . . In any case, apart from the error of being in
your room I'm perfectly within my rights. Vera's
my fiancée.

TONY. What!? (*dully*).

BARRETT *goes to door*.

BARRETT. Vera.

They wait. She comes down to door.

BARRETT. Owing to this unfortunate incident, Vera, we shall
have to tell our little secret to Mister Tony. Come
on . . . don't be shy. Go and tell him, go on.

VERA. Hugo and I are going to be married.
Well, you've done all right, what are you worrying
about? You can't have it on a plate for ever, can
you? Oh come on Hugo!

BARRETT *inclines his head slightly and they both go*.

TONY. Get out! Both of you!

SUSAN *is sitting*. TONY *sits on the arm of a chair.
Sounds of drawers being pulled out, cases banging,
from upstairs*. TONY *rises and pours a drink, drinks
it, pours another. They do not look at each other. He
stands, goes to record player, puts on a record*. 'All
gone.'

GIRL SINGING
. . . my mouth
How can I bear (*Door slams*.)
The ghost of you here
Can't love without you . . .
. . . must love without you
Now while I love you alone
Now while I love you alone
Now while I love you
Can't love without you
Must love without you—alone

Now while I love you
Can't love without you
Can't love without you alone.

Silence between them. Sounds of BARRETT *and*
VERA *descending stairs. The front door slams.* TONY
turns and looks at SUSAN. *They look at each other.*
Eventually TONY *in a half-appeal, half-demand,*
whispers:

TONY. Come to bed.

She slowly stands. He half moves to her. She turns,
goes out of the door and out of the house.
He stands, alone. Switches off record. Looks at door,
slowly moves out of room.

Interior. Stairs. Night.
TONY *slowly ascending stairs.*

Interior. VERA'*s bedroom. Night.*
TONY *enters room, looks at disordered bed. He goes to*
it, lies flat out on it.

Interior. Hall. Day.
TONY *is alone in the house. He treads unsteadily down*
the stairs and goes into kitchen.

Interior. Kitchen. Day.
The kitchen is very untidy. He rummages amid the un-
washed plates for a can of fruit juice. It is empty. He
throws it away. He fumbles in a corner for a bottle of
squash. It has only dregs in it. He unscrews the top and
puts it to his nose, grimaces, looks into the bottle. The
orange flakes appear atrophied in the stagnant juice.
He screws the top and lifts up the lid of the waste bin.
The bin is full to bursting with rubbish, its top covered

with fish-bones. He tries to lodge the bottle between
two piles of crockery on the draining board, the bottle
slips and falls with a bang. He kicks it viciously.

Exterior. London street. Night.
TONY, quite aimless, walking spasmodically. He is
drooped. He stops to watch the buses and taxis go by.
His face in the passing lights is haggard, blank.

Interior. Public phone box. Night.
TONY dialling number. He listens.

SUSAN'S VOICE. Hello. Who's that? Tony? Hello who is it? Hello.

He replaces the receiver.

Interior. Drawing-room. Night.
TONY in room, which is also in some disarray. He is
unshaven, drinking a large whisky. He goes to record
player and with slightly trembling hands puts a record
on the turn-table. He lifts the head and attempts to
place it in the groove. Three times he fails, the needle
sheering off the side of the record. Suddenly his
trembling hand jerks the head which scrapes in a
grating scratch across the record. He stands hunched.

Interior. First pub. Evening.
TONY wanders into the saloon bar of a pub which is
half empty. He goes to the bar, orders whisky, sits next
to a man. Beyond the man is a partition that separates
the saloon bar from the private bar. Both bars are
visible in full mirror behind the barman. BARRETT is
sitting up at the private bar just beyond the partition.
TONY has not seen him. He drinks half his whisky in a
gulp and is then conscious of being watched. He looks
into the mirror, sees BARRETT. He looks away. Then
half back, then away again. For some minutes there is

a quiet in the pub, the only sounds being the bell on the cash register and the spasmodic sound of conversation. At the bar, BARRETT *and* TONY, *with the third man between them, look into their glasses intently, glance up at the bottles on the shelves. Neither of them moves. The third man, an oldish man, stands gloomily. The third man suddenly speaks to no one in particular.*

MAN. I had a bit of bad luck today.

There is no response. The BARMAN *appears, polishing some glasses, looks vaguely for any further orders, withdraws.*
I really had a bit of bad luck.

Silence.

It'll take me a good few days to get over it, I can tell you.

Pause. The man turns to TONY *as if* TONY *had spoken.*

Eh?

TONY *is blank. The man finishes his drink and turns to go.*

You're right, there.

He goes. Silence. BARRETT *and* TONY *look at each other.* TONY *non-committal.* BARRETT *seems shabbier, uneasy, his breath is laboured.*

BARRETT. Might I buy you a drink?

TONY *does not answer.* BARRETT *signals nervously to the* BARMAN, *points to* TONY's *glass.*

BARRETT. Scotch. Large scotch.

The drink arrives and he pays for it. TONY *sips it immediately, with no gesture.* BARRETT *begins to speak, in a low voice, very quickly, stuttering, compulsive.*

BARRETT. I wanted to come and call round on you . . . but
. . . I tell you what though . . . I was led up the
garden path. I couldn't be more sorry, honest. I
was besotted by her long before I came to you. I
was simply besotted by her. I thought she was keen
on me too – we were saving up money to get
married . . . her father was a brute. You see I
. . . I couldn't bear to see her . . . suffering –
but I had to pay him like – you know, to pay him to
get his consent to take her away. I had to find her a
home somewhere that – that's why I told you she
was my sister – I thought she was devoted to me . . .
anyway – you see I . . . I didn't know a thing
about what was going on between you two until
that night. That night I got it out of her . . . I
twigged she was just a scrubber . . . She never in-
tended to marry me, and d'you know what she's
done now? Gone off with my money . . . she's
living with a bookie in Wandsworth – listen, give
me – give me another chance, sir . . . I was so
happy there with you . . . it was like bliss . . .
we can turn over the page . . . I'm with an old
lady now in Paultons Square – ringing the bell all
day long – up and down those stairs – all day long –
I'm skin and bone . . . I deceived you – I played
you false – I admit that – but she was to blame – it
was her fault. She done us both . . . if you can find
it in your heart sir . . . give me another chance.

He stops, looking down at his glass, biting his nails.
TONY *is still, expressionless.*

Exterior. Square. Winter.
Some weeks have passed. A wind blows through the
square.

Interior. Hall. TONY's *house. Day.*
The house is changed. It is airless, dark, oppressive.
Curtains and blinds are almost constantly drawn.

There are no longer any flowers. The log fire has been replaced by illuminated gas logs. The sleek television in the bedroom has been replaced by a heavy Console, now in the drawing-room. Cheap sex magazines replace the expensive monthlies. There is an overlay of BARRETT *everywhere. Photos of footballers cellotaped to mirrors. Pornographic calendars. Nudes stuck in oil paintings. The furniture has subtly changed, the rooms no longer possess composition. Elegant pornographic books have been yanked from* TONY's *bookshelves and are strewn about. The bookshelves are left disordered and heavy with dust.* BARRETT's *brown paper obscene books are piled about, and cellophaned piles of photos. The ashtrays are crammed full, glasses half empty and empty beer bottles are on the liquor trolley.* BARRETT *is now dressed in a rough sweater, corduroy trousers and heavy boots.*

Interior. Drawing-room. Day.
TONY *is sitting at a table, doing a crossword puzzle. He is in his pyjama jacket.* BARRETT *enters, dressed in sweater and tight trousers.*

BARRETT. You still sitting there?

TONY. What's this? 'It's waxed so will soon wane', five letters.

BARRETT. I haven't got time for all that.

TONY. Well you ask me soon enough when you want some help.

BARRETT. Look at all this muck and slime. It makes you feel sick.

TONY. Well do something about it. You're supposed to be the bloody servant!

BARRETT. You expect me to cope with all this muck and filth everywhere, all your leavings all over the place, without a maid, do you? I need a maid to give me a helping hand. I'm not used to working in such squalor. Look what I've got on my hands, you! As soon as I get the Hoover going you're straight up it. You're in everybody's way.

TONY. Oh why don't you leave me alone?

TONY gulps some beer. BARRETT *lights a cigarette, and pensively flips the pages of a leather-bound book.*

. . . What's this? 'It's waxed so will wane soon?' Five letters.

BARRETT. Look, why don't you get yourself a job instead of moping around here all day? Here I am scraping and skimping trying to make ends meet . . . getting worse and worse . . . and you're no bloody help . . . d'you know that butter's gone up twopence a pound?

TONY. As a matter of fact I'll be meeting a man very shortly.

BARRETT. What man? The man from Brazil? What's he going to do for you? Come down by helicopter on the roof? Eh?

TONY. Oh why don't you shut up!

Interior. Hall. Day.
TONY *storms out of the drawing-room.*

TONY. Barrett!

He goes up the stairs.

Barrett!

Interior. BARRETT's *bedroom. Day.*
BARRETT *is in bed.* TONY *enters and pulls the clothes off him.*

BARRETT. What's the matter with you?

TONY. Get out of it!

BARRETT. What you doing?

TONY. There's tea dregs on the carpet.

BARRETT. Where?

TONY. In the drawing room.

BARRETT. Well I didn't put them there.

TONY holds a damp rag to BARRETT's *face.*

TONY. Now here you are. Use it.

BARRETT. Don't do that to me.

TONY. Clear it up!

BARRETT. Not my fault – them tea dregs.

TONY. You filthy bastard!

BARRETT. Right. I'm leaving!

BARRETT *gets out of bed. Their voices clash and rise.*

TONY. That's exactly what I want.

BARRETT. You talk to me like that . . .

TONY. Now leave my house alone . . .

BARRETT. . . . after all I've done for you.

TONY. . . . Get down and clear it up.

BARRETT *goes out.*

Interior. Stairs and landing. Day.
BARRETT *comes briskly down the stairs, followed by* TONY.

BARRETT. I won't stand for any more of this.

TONY. Take your pigsty somewhere else.

BARRETT. It's not my pigsty, it's yours.

TONY. You creep!

BARRETT. Nobody talks to me like that!

TONY. D'you know what you are? I'll tell you.

BARRETT. I know all about your sort.

TONY. You're a peasant.

BARRETT. I'll tell you what I am, I'll tell you what I am. I'm a gentleman's gentleman. And you're no bloody gentleman!

TONY. You think I'm past it? I haven't had a drink all morning. I'm through with it. I'll knock your head off.

BARRETT. Violence will get you nowhere.

TONY. If you don't get down and wipe those tea dregs up I'll stick your nose in them.

BARRETT (*laughing*). You're funny.

Interior. Dining-room. Day.

Morning. TONY *and* BARRETT *in the dining-room.*
BARRETT *is smoking, sitting, doing a crossword puzzle.* TONY *is looking out into the garden. Long silence.*
Children's voices outside.

TONY. I wouldn't mind going out for a walk.
It must be quite nice out.

He remains still.
BARRETT *continues his crossword.*
Silence.

Interior. Hall. Stairs and landings. Evening.
TONY *is at the top of the stairs,* BARRETT *at the foot. They are playing a game of ball, in which, according to their own rules, the ball must be bounced off the wall or on the stairs past the opponent. A point is scored for each pass. Twenty-one is game.*
A longish rally is in progress. Both breathe hard, concentrating intently. Finally, BARRETT *skids the ball past* TONY.

BARRETT. Watch it!
TONY. No, out of play – out of play!
BARRETT. Right – got you!
TONY. Bit wild! (*Laughs.*)
BARRETT. Nearly got you then . . .
Hah! . . . thirteen ten . . . ?
. . . counting . . . ?
TONY. Well I can't do it any more. I have to bend all the time.
BARRETT. What about me? I'm in the inferior position. I'm playing uphill.
TONY. I need a drink.
BARRETT. That's the point of the game, the bending. You're getting as fat as a pig. You need the exercise.
TONY. Right. Service! *He smashes the ball past* BARRETT.
Fourteen twelve!
BARRETT. That wasn't fair, I wasn't ready.
TONY. I said service, didn't I?

BARRETT (*picking up the ball*). I'm not having that point counted.

TONY. What do you mean? That's a perfectly fair point. What about the other night? You did about six of them like that.

BARRETT. There's no need to take advantage of the fact that you're in the best position.

TONY. My dear . . .

BARRETT. . . . you ought to be able to play the game according to the rules.

TONY. My dear Barrett, you're just a little upset because you're losing the game.

BARRETT. Oh! . . . take your ball!

He throws the ball hard at TONY, *who catches it.*

TONY. Take it yourself!

TONY *throws the ball back viciously. It hits* BARRETT *on the nose.*

BARRETT. Aaahhh!

He clutches his nose. TONY *runs down.*

TONY. Well, what's the matter?

BARRETT. I'm going.

TONY. It couldn't have hurt.

BARRETT. Get out of it. I'm off. I'm not staying in a place where they just chuck balls in your face!

TONY. Oh don't be silly! Come on, let's have a drop of brandy. I'll tell you what we'll do, we'll call that game a draw. Now here you are. Isn't that fair?

BARRETT. Stuff your brandy.

TONY. Don't talk to me like that!

BARRETT. Stuff you and your brandy! Get back to your coal-heap and leave me alone for Christ's sake.

TONY. Now look, Barrett, don't you forget your place. You're nothing but a servant in this house!

BARRETT. Servant? I'm nobody's servant. Who furnished the whole place for you? Who painted it for you? Who does the cooking? Who washes your pants? Who cleans out the bath after you? I do! I run the whole bloody place – and what do I get out of it? Nothing!

TONY. Now listen, Barrett –

BARRETT. I know all about you, sonny . . .

TONY. Now look . . . Listen, I am grateful, honestly . . . Don't be daft. You know I am. I don't know what I'd do without you.

BARRETT. Well go and pour me a glass of brandy.

TONY. Well that's what I suggested in the first place.

BARRETT. Well don't just stand there! Go and do it!

TONY *runs into the drawing-room and pours* BARRETT *a large brandy.* BARRETT *watches him from the hall.*

Interior. Drawing-room. Evening.
The same evening. TONY *and* BARRETT *eating dinner. Black candles. Black ceiling.*

TONY. Fabulous.

BARRETT. Not bad.

TONY. It's fabulous.

BARRETT. Bit salty.

TONY. No, no. It's marvellous.

Silence. They eat.

I don't know how you do it.

BARRETT. It's nice to know it's appreciated. It makes all the difference.

TONY. Well, I do appreciate it.

Pause.

BARRETT. You know sometimes I get the feeling that we're old pals.

TONY. That's funny.

BARRETT. Why?

TONY. I get the same feeling myself.

Pause.

BARRETT. I've only had that same feeling once before.

TONY. When was that?

BARRETT. Once in the army.

TONY. That's funny. I had the same feeling myself there, too. Once.

Interior. Hall. Stairs and landing. Night.
BARRETT stands inside the drawing-room door. His
hands are over his eyes. He is counting aloud.

BARRETT. Forty-seven, forty-eight, forty-nine, fifty.

He takes his hands from his eyes and goes into the hall.
Here, he stands and talks aloud, to a listener.

I've got a tiny feeling that you're not downstairs at
all. I think you're up there, aren't you? Now I'm
on my way up to get you.

He races up the stairs. At the top he speaks:

Where's your little lair this time?
Puss, puss, puss, puss, pussy, puss, puss, puss,
puss, puss, puss.

He opens his own bedroom door violently and looks in,
comes out. He does the same in VERA's room, and then
runs downstairs to TONY's room at a very great pace
and pulls the door open.

Interior. TONY's bedroom. Night.
BARRETT enters, creeps about, looking.

BARRETT. I'm getting warm! You're hiding but you'll be
caught. You've got a guilty secret, you've got a
guilty secret, but you'll be caught. I'm coming to
get you, I'm creeping up on you!

Interior. Bathroom. Night.
TONY is jammed in the corner behind the door. (The
bathroom is in complete disorder.) His eyes are staring
with excitement. BARRETT's voice comes nearer.

BARRETT. I'm getting warm, I can smell a rat, I can smell a
rat . . .

TONY shivers. The door bursts open. BARRETT
charges in and confronts him. BARRETT utters a
terrifying maniacal bellow. TONY faints.

Interior. Hall and front door. Night.

BARRETT *comes down the hall, opens the door.* VERA.

BARRETT. What do you want?

VERA. I want to speak to him.

BARRETT. Clear off out of it.

VERA. I want to speak to him.

BARRETT. Out of it. Quick.

TONY appears in the hall. She darts in. BARRETT *puts out a foot. She falls.*

Come on out! Come on.

VERA *(rising to* TONY). Look I want . . . please . . .

TONY. I'll speak to her, leave her.

He goes into the drawing-room. She follows.

VERA. Eh . . . now listen here . . . look . . . I'm not making a go of it, see? . . . I'm ill.

She looks as though she might fall. TONY *does not offer her a chair.*

I come to you.

He looks at her, says nothing.

I'm broke . . . I'm ill, you see, that's what it is . . .

Silence.

So I come to you, you see.

Silence.

TONY. Go to your bookmaker.

VERA. What?

TONY. Go to your bookie.

VERA. What bookie?

TONY. The one you ran off with.

VERA. Run off? Who ran off? What's he told you, eh? He chucked me out, soon as we left here. He chucked me out. He's finished me. Listen, I got to go to hospital, they're taking me in . . . give me a few quid . . . just . . . go on . . . just . . .

TONY. What about what you did to me?

VERA. It was him. He made me. I loved you though. I still love you.

She goes into TONY'*s arms. He holds her, uncertain.* BARRETT *comes in, looks.*

BARRETT. Tch, tch, tch. Playing games with little Sis again, are you? That won't get you anywhere, Tone.

TONY *hesitantly lets her go, blinks, goes out.*

Interior. Hall. Night.
BARRETT *escorting* VERA *from room into hall to door.* TONY *is standing at the back of the hall.*

BARRETT. Come on, little sister, out of it.

VERA (*to* TONY). It was him. He done it.

She breaks away. BARRETT *grabs her and pulls her to the door.*

BARRETT. Come here, stinking the place out.

TONY *goes back into drawing room.*

VERA (*calling after him*). I love you!

BARRETT. Get back to your ponce. Move out of it.

He pushes her out of the door.

Interior. Drawing-room. Night.
TONY *is pouring whisky.* BARRETT *comes in.* TONY *looks at him.*

TONY. Slut.

Interior. Drawing-room. Evening.
BARRETT *handing* TONY *a bottle with no label.*

BARRETT. I've got something special for you, from a little man in Jermyn Street.

TONY *looks at bottle.*

TONY. Not for me.

BARRETT pours a glass.

BARRETT. Oh come on. Have a little sip, see what it tastes like.
TONY. I told you, I'm not drinking.
BARRETT. Just have a little sip, that's all, just a sip.

TONY looks sulkily at the glass, picks it up and sips.

TONY. Mmmmmm. Ooh, it's marvellous.
BARRETT. There you are, you see. I can still think of things that'll please you, can't I? You won't get any better than me you know. What do you want? An old hag running round the house, getting you up in the morning, at the crack of dawn, telling you what to do? My only ambition is to serve you, you know that don't you?
TONY. I'm sorry. I've been a bit edgy lately.
BARRETT. Oh well I mean, I admit, I make mistakes, but, well after all I'm only human aren't I? You wouldn't like me if I wasn't human, would you?
TONY. The place could be cleaner, that's all.
BARRETT. I know, I know it could be a bit cleaner. That's what I've been going on about for days.
TONY (*with sudden intensity*). Listen . . .
The intensity fades. He loses track of his thought.

Listen . . .

With great concentration he forces the words out.

Perhaps we could . . . both . . . make . . . an extra effort.

He looks up suddenly at BARRETT, the expression on his face one of entreaty. BARRETT smiles.

BARRETT. You're right there, Tone, you're dead right. That's what we ought to do.

TONY's face is at once confused, irritated. He suddenly begins to rake his hair violently, scratching his skull with his fist, his elbow raised, his posture resembling that of a chimpanzee.

Interior. Bedroom. Night.
Portable record player. TONY *listening, with glass.*
Chime of front door bell. BARRETT *enters.*

BARRETT. Hey! Your other one's here.

TONY. What?

BARRETT. Your old flame. One yesterday, one tonight. You are popular aren't you. She's waiting.

TONY. Did you tell her we were expecting visitors?

BARRETT. I did. But I also took the liberty of showing her into the drawing-room. After all – she is a lady, isn't she?

TONY *goes down.*

Interior. Drawing-room. Night.
SUSAN *is gazing at the changes of the room.* TONY *comes in, slams the door.*

TONY. Hello.

He stands smiling, slightly swaying.

SUSAN. Vera's been to see me. She says you owe her some money.

TONY *bends forward in a fit of soundless laughter. She watches him.*

SUSAN. I think you owe her some kind of compensation.

TONY. She's a liar, they're all liars. You didn't come here because of Vera. It's all gone. Leave it alone.

He goes closer to her.

You don't want to . . . come here . . .

SUSAN (*dully*). I love you.

The front door is heard opening. Girls' voices. BARRETT's *voice. Giggling, going down the passage.*

SUSAN. Who's that?

The record in the bedroom is turned louder.

TONY. Friends.

A WOMAN'S VOICE *is heard.*

VOICE. Where's Tony?

SUSAN. Don't you . . . like me at all?

TONY (*non-committal*). Yes . . .

WOMAN'S VOICE. Where's that Tony?

SUSAN. Well what's wrong with me then?

BARRETT'S

VOICE. Hey come on, we're waiting for you.

TONY. Nothing's wrong with you. (*Laughs.*) Come and join the party.

He takes her by the hand. She does not resist.

Interior. Bedroom. Night.
BARRETT *and four women including* VERA *are in the room.*

RECORD. Give me my death
Close my mouth
Give me my breath
Close my mouth etc.

TONY. Where's my drink?

BARRETT. It's here. (*To* SUSAN). Do you want one, love, eh?

SUSAN *stands still inside the door.* TONY *gulps his drink.*

GIRL SINGING
Now while I love you alone . . .
Now while I love you alone.

A girl pulls TONY *gently away.*

TONY. What are you doing?

She takes him in a corner and whispers to him. Another girl joins them. They bend over him, whispering. He staggers away. A woman in a large black hat pulls him down on the bed and kisses him.

BARRETT (*to* SUSAN). Do you know where we're going in the morning?

Pause.

We're going to Brazil in the morning. (*He grins.*)
Aren't we Tone? (*To* SUSAN.) Have a fag.

TONY *lies on the bed staring glazed at* SUSAN. SUSAN
moves to BARRETT *and kisses him. He laughs and
holds her. She looks at* TONY. *His mouth is open, he
moves from the bed. One of the girls touches him.
He shivers, stumbles, falls and collapsing, brings
tablecloth, glasses, bottles down with him.*

BARRETT. Tch, tch, tch.

TONY *sits a second, glass-eyed. The record player
still plays. He suddenly reaches up to the shelf and
sweeps it on the floor. There is a smash and grate of
record and pick-up head.*

TONY (*in a sudden dazed childish horror, in a monotone*).
Get out, get out. Get 'em all out.

His hand swinging knocks a bottle over.

Get out.

BARRETT. Come on then, out. (*He nudges* SUSAN.) You too.
Come on.

The women go to the door. BARRETT *whispers to
them.*

Make it tomorrow night. (*Confidential.*) And bring
John.

*Interior. Hall and stairs. Night.
The women go down and out.* BARRETT *halfway
down stairs, turns.* SUSAN *is still at bedroom door.*
TONY *sits on floor, head drooping. She stares at him,
expressionless.* BARRETT *calls up stairs.*
Eh you! Come on!

He emits a piercing whistle. No response.

OY!

*She turns, walks slowly downstairs. She stops and
looks at him, and then hits him with all her might,*

with closed fist, across the face. He staggers, his fists clench. He looks at her. She is still. Slowly he recovers his composure. He turns, goes to the front door, holds it wide open. With a smile, he inclines his head towards her. She leaves the house.

Exterior. House. Night.
SUSAN *walks across the dark square. She looks back at the house, turns, walks on. The camera holds on the house and closes slowly in toward the door.*

Interior. Hall. Night.
BARRETT *locks door and bolts it. He walks slowly up the stairs.*

Interior. Landing. Night.
TONY *crawls onto the landing and sits in a corner.*

Interior. Stairs. Night.
Close up of BARRETT's *hand trailing the banister, as he climbs the stairs.*

The Pumpkin Eater

The Pumpkin Eater was first presented by Columbia Pictures Corporation on 15th July 1964 with the following cast:

JO	Anne Bancroft
JAKE	Peter Finch
GILES	Richard Johnson
DINAH	Francis White
	Kate Nicholls
FERGUS	Fergus McClelland
	Christopher Ellis
SHARON	Sharon Maxwell
	Mimosa Annis
MARK	Kash Dewar
ELIZABETH	Elizabeth Dear
	Sarah Nicholls
PETE	Gregory Phillips
	Rupert Osborn
JACK	Michael Ridgeway
	Martin Norton
MR ARMITAGE	Alan Webb
MR JAMES	Cedric Hardwicke
PHILPOT	Maggie Smith
YOUNGEST CHILD	Mark Crader
NANNY	Faith Kent
DOCTOR	Cyril Luckham
INGRAM	Eric Porter
WOMAN IN HAIRDRESSERS	Yootha Joyce
CONWAY	James Mason
MAN AT PARTY	Gerald Sim
BETH	Janine Gray
MRS JAMES	Rosalind Atkinson
UNDERTAKER	John Junkin
SURGEON	Anthony Nicholls
WAITRESS AT ZOO	Leslie Nunnerley
THE KING OF ISRAEL	Frank Singuineau
PARSON	John Franklin Robbins

Directed by Jack Clayton

The Pumpkin Eater

*Exterior. Large house in St John's Wood, London.
Summer day.*   *PRESENT DAY
Bonnet of a Jaguar foreground.* JO *is standing at the
window, looking out. Reflected in the window pane
demolition of buildings, tall skeletons of new constructions.*

Interior. Sitting-room.
JO *at window, looking out.*
Another angle : JO.
She turns, stares at the room.

Interior. Sitting-room.
*We see the room. It is large, expensively furnished.
Bookshelves, a piano, pictures, numerous thick rugs,
etc. On a small table, tea for one is laid.*
Another angle.
JO *goes to table, pours tea into the cup.*
Close on JO's *hands.*
*She holds the cup tightly in its saucer, does not pick
it up.*

Interior. Hall.
JO *comes quickly out of living room. As she turns into
hall, letters thud on to carpet through the letter box.*
Another angle : JO.
*She looks at them for a moment, makes no attempt
to pick them up.*
Another angle : JO.
*Footsteps above. She looks up. Through bannisters
along first landing, a man's legs walking quickly.*

Another angle : JO.
*She stands still. Water heard rushing into a basin
from above.*

Exterior. Garage of St John's Wood. House. Day.
PRESENT DAY
*Brilliant sunlight, heat haze. Pool of petrol. The
Jaguar, the Floride, the child's scooter.* JO *bends to
pick up scooter.*
*The shining Jaguar, from her eye level as she bends.
Sunlight.* JO's *face.*
Sun on wheelcaps.
JO.
She straightens, scooter half held.
Another angle.
*Her hands drop scooter. She moves swiftly towards
garage.*

Exterior. Side door of house. Day.
JAKE *appears at side door. Stands looking left and
right.* JO *is not there. He gets into the Jaguar.*

Interior. Jaguar. Day.
JAKE *sits, adjusts his tie in the mirror, lights a
cigarette, starts motor. Suddenly catches sight of* JO
in the mirror.
The mirror. Reflecting interior garage.
JO *in the corner of the dark garage. Still, amid junk.*
Another angle, Jaguar.
JAKE *gets out of car and crosses to garage.*

Interior. Garage. Day.
JAKE. What are you doing? (JO *looks at him.*) What are
you doing?
JO. Nothing.

JAKE *crosses to her, touches her arm.*

JAKE. I thought you were going shopping.

Silence.

It's late. I've got to go. (*Pause.*) How are you feeling?

Pause.

JO. All right.

Pause.

JAKE. Look, I've got to go out to dinner . . . I'm sorry.
JO. All right.

JAKE *kisses her tenderly, speaks with a smile.*

JAKE. Do you think you're going to get over this period in your life, because I find it very depressing.

He turns away, moves back to Jaguar, gets in and drives off.
Another angle : JO
watching car disappearing. She walks down path to front gate and into street. The car has disappeared. She turns, looks at the house.

Interior. Barn. Day. TEN YEARS EARLIER
A large room, sub-divided by numerous home-made partitions. It is sparsely furnished but crowded with children. JO is at a table making pastry. Some of the children are playing on the floor with train sets and home-made constructions of roads and stations. The smallest girl apart, examining a doll's house.
Another angle towards door.
It opens. GILES and JAKE enter. A child (DINAH) rushes up to them.

CHILD ONE. Daddy – I was going to be the signal-box man and now look!

GILES. All right. (*To* JO.) Darling, this is Jake. (*To* CHILDREN.) What is it?

JO (*to* JAKE). Hullo.

CHILD TWO. Dinah's got no right to open the gates until the express has been through.

JAKE (*to* JO). Glad to meet you.
CHILD THREE. You can't stop a non-stop express.

> JO *and* JAKE *shaking hands. Her hands covered with flour.*
> JAKE *playing bricks with children.*

JAKE. What's this bit going to be?
CHILD TWO. The ladies' lavatory.
JAKE. Where's the ticket office?

> *Another angle :* JO *and* ELIZABETH.

ELIZABETH. Who's that?
JO. A friend of Daddy's.
CHILD TWO. These are oil pipes. They take the oil.

> *Another angle :* JAKE *looking at* JO *over bricks, as –*

CHILD THREE. We don't want any oil. There are no diesels on this line.

> *Another angle :* GILES *coming from makeshift kitchen with tray of tea.*

JAKE. Where's the control tower?
CHILD TWO. This isn't an airport, it's a station.
JAKE. You could have a helicopter.

> *Another angle : the two oldest boys chasing each other.*

CHILD TWO. That's my diesel!
CHILD THREE. It's broken down.
CHILD TWO. Give it to me!
JO. Pete!

> *Child* (JACK) *climbs over partition.*

GILES. Jack!

> *Another angle : the partition.*
> *As child* (PETE) *clambers after* JACK. *It collapses.*
> *Another angle :* GILES *at partition with hammer and nails.*

CHILD TWO. He had my diesel!

GILES. This is about the sixth time.

Another angle. JO *moving away to light cigarette.*
Close-up. JAKE *looking at her.*
Close-up. JO.
Back to GILES *holding up three planks of partition,*
examining them. One plank falls.
Plank falling.

Large close-up.
JAKE *kissing* JO's *ear.*
(*No background noise.*)

Interior. Study in JAKE's *father's house. Evening.*
APPROX. TEN YEARS EARLIER
JAKE's *father* (MR ARMITAGE). *He,* JO, *and* JAKE
sit, with drinks, eating cheese straws.

MR ARMITAGE. But why on earth do you want to marry Jake?

Short pause. JO *giggles.*

JAKE. Why not?
MR ARMITAGE. It's incomprehensible.
JAKE. What is?
MR ARMITAGE. He'll be an impossible husband.
JAKE. Oh now, wait a minute –
MR ARMITAGE. I assure you. I mean, he's got no money. He's
bone lazy. He drinks too much. He's quite useless.
JAKE. Oh thanks.
MR ARMITAGE. What do the children say?
JAKE. We haven't exactly discussed it with them.
JO. They . . . don't mind.
MR ARMITAGE (*to* JAKE). Do you like children?
JAKE. Of course I like them. Of course I do.
MR ARMITAGE. Have you actually known any?

Interior. Living-room. JO's *father's house. Day.*
SAME PERIOD
JO's *father* (MR JAMES). JO *and* JAKE.

MR JAMES. Do you realize what you're saddling yourself with?

JAKE. Er . . . Yes . . . yes . . .

MR JAMES. A zoo. A children's zoo. And their keeper. Are you reconciled to having to keep the zoo and its keeper?

JAKE. Yes . . . of course . . . I mean . . .

MR JAMES. Are you fit?

JAKE. Well . . .

MR JAMES. I take it you know something of my daughter's record?

JO. My what?

JAKE *laughs.*

JAKE. Yes, I know. (*Pause.*) I want to marry her.

MR JAMES. You're a fool. Still, the least I can do is to give you some kind of a start, I suppose. You think that's fair?

JAKE. Fair?

MR JAMES. I think you're a fool, but I'll give you a start. A start. Do you think that's fair?

JAKE. Oh yes, that's fair . . . quite . . . very fair.

MR JAMES. Right. Well, first of all we've got to shed the load. There's too many children.

JO. What do you mean?

MR JAMES. I suggest we send the eldest two to boarding school. That will be two off your hands.

JO. No! That's ridiculous.

MR JAMES. Now listen, this is Jake's business, not yours. It's the burden on him that's ridiculous.

JO. But I don't want them to go away to school.

MR JAMES. Look, be sensible. They'd love it.

JO. They wouldn't love it.

MR JAMES. I'd love it. Jake'd love it. And they can come to stay with us in the holidays.

JO. Why don't we just give them away?

JAKE. It's only the first two. I mean, there are others.

MR JAMES. Now listen. I'm not going to have you trailing home with half a dozen more children in five years' time and another messed up marriage on your hands. You're not going to be allowed to crush this poor boy before he starts. He's going to have to work like a slave as it is.

JO. But we can't afford to send them to school.

MR JAMES. I'm paying.

JAKE. Oh . . . thanks. Thanks very much.

MR JAMES. And I've managed to buy you a fairly good lease on a house in London. Quite reasonable. It's an old one but it should suit you – it'll pretty well clean me out, but you might as well have the money now as when I'm dead.

Interior. Kitchen – St John's Wood. House. Day.
                              PRESENT DAY
Close on tray. With tea being set on draining board, with a sharp sound.
Another angle : JO *stands, does not touch crockery.*
Another angle : at window.
Glimpses of demolition through window.
Another angle : JO.
She turns away, clutching her arms, walks vaguely about the kitchen, her heels clicking on the tiled floor. An immaculate, gleaming modern kitchen, spotless, nothing out of place.
Another angle : JO.
As she moves, we see : new dishwasher, new refrigerator, new washing machine and spin dryer, new electric oven, racks of gleaming crockery, photograph on teak wood wall, a large photo pinned from a magazine of MR JAKE ARMITAGE, MRS ARMITAGE *and their* CHILDREN.
JO.
She glances at it.
Another angle : She continues walking, her fingers tracing on the work top.

Exterior. House in St John's Wood. Day.
          APPROX. TEN YEARS EARLIER
The house is considerably more shabby, both inside and out, than in the present day sequences.
A furniture van is parked outside. Men are carrying

furniture from it into the house. Objects, furniture, heaped and strewn about outside, through the ground floor, up stairs. We see certain recognizable objects from the barn. In foreground, a child's bike and scooter.

The Morris Minor turns the corner and draws up. CHILDREN *fall out, followed by* JAKE *and* JO. *Again, we hear no sound until:*

CHILD. They've got here before us!

The children rush up the path.

Interior. Hall.
Through open door, we can see the empty kitchen. JO *is confronted with a piece of furniture.*

JO (*to* REMOVAL MEN). Mmm . . . upstairs. The first floor front . . . left . . .

Children rush up and down stairs.

Don't get in the way.

She stands in the chaos. JAKE *appears, kisses her.*

Interior. Landing (that night).
Silence. Nightlight through windows. Open doors. Their voices heard. There is certain junk (odd pieces) on landing, rolls of carpeting.

JO. My first marriage. You're my first husband.
JAKE. You've been married three times.
JO. No. You're the first.
JAKE. Are the children asleep?
JO. Yes.
JAKE. I'll close the door.

JAKE *moves to door and closes it.*

JO. I want to go away with you . . . and come back with you . . . and live with you.
JAKE. You will.

JO. You'll never go from me . . . we'll have the same life. Do you want anything else?

JAKE. No. I don't want anything else.

Interior. Bathroom. Evening.
APPROX. EIGHT YEARS EARLIER
Bathroom, small, crowded and full of steam. DINAH *in bath,* JO *washing her ears and neck.* JAKE *is drying a smaller* BOY *with a large towel.*

BOY (*to* JAKE). Can I tell you a story?

DINAH (*to* JO). Do you like living in this house?

JO. Why? Don't you?

DINAH. Yes.

BOY. A story about a killer whale.

JO *leaves* DINAH *to wash herself and takes the boy's pyjamas from towel rail.*

DINAH. How long are we going to live here?

JAKE. We're moving in the morning.

DINAH. We're not! Where?

JAKE. Building a big house on top of that hill.

DINAH. What hill?

JO *reaches for the* BOY *with his pyjamas.*

JAKE. I haven't done his feet. Lift your foot.

BOY *lifts his foot.* JAKE *dries it.*

BOY. It's about this whale . . .

DINAH. What hill?

JO. By the barn.

DINAH. What, in the morning?

JAKE. Well, we'll have lunch first.

JO (*to* JAKE). Hurry up.

BOY. It's a story about two whales and a shark.

DINAH. What sort of house?

JAKE. With eight bathrooms. All for me.

Interior. Sitting-room. Morning.

APPROX. SEVEN YEARS EARLIER
JO *is putting a sweater on a small boy, who is strug-*
gling in her arms, trying to join the other children
whom we can see beyond JO, *playing in the garden.*
JO *is pregnant.*
JAKE'S VOICE (*calling*). Where's the opener?
JO (*calling back*). Just a minute –

Interior. Kitchen. Morning.
It is filled with steam. We hear sounds of children.
JAKE *is holding two cans of beer and searching for the*
opener. He regards the steaming pans on the gas stove,
looks into the oven at the joint, closes oven door, his
face blank.

Interior. Sitting-room.
JAKE *enters. He stops centre of room and reacts for a*
second to the children thudding about upstairs, and
their shouts from the garden. He comes to table, finds
opener.
JO *finishes inserting the* SMALL BOY *into his sweater,*
sets him down. He rushes out to the garden.
JAKE, *with a grimace, opens can. It spurts over the*
wall, where we can already see the stains from pre-
vious moments of this kind.
JAKE. Want one?
JO. Yes, I'll have one.

He hands her opened can. She takes it. JAKE *opens*
second can. It also spurts over wall.

JAKE. Aaaahh!
JO. It's all right, it'll wipe off.
JAKE (*looking at can*). It's ridiculous.

JAKE *sits at table on which are sheets of writing paper.*
He looks at them and throughout the ensuing dialogue
vaguely scratches out words with his pen.
Shouts and thuds from garden and upstairs. JO *drinks*
from can.

JO. Let's go out today.

JAKE. Umm? Where?

JO. I don't know. Take them out.

JAKE. All of them?

TWO CHILDREN rush in from garden, through the room and upstairs. JAKE looks at JO, chuckles shortly, dryly.

JO. I'll take them out, if you like, this afternoon. You can have a rest.

JAKE. No, no, don't be silly.

JO (*touching him*). No, really, I will. I will.

JAKE. No, no, I wouldn't dream of it. After all, it's Saturday, we can go out.

Loud crash from above.

What are they *doing* up there?

Pause.

JO. Do you want turnips or swedes?

JAKE. Turnips or swedes?

JO. Yes. Or both if you like.

He looks at her blankly.

JAKE (*with sudden concentration*). Turnips or swedes. Wait a minute. Just a minute. Let me think about it.

Interior. Kitchen. Day.
APPROX. FIVE YEARS EARLIER
A young woman (PHILPOT) is sitting on the old-fashioned sink cleaning saucepan lids with steel wool, slowly, as she speaks towards the open doorway into the hall, where JO is visible in the foreground using an old Hoover.

PHILPOT (*above Hoover noise*). Wives don't usually like me. I like them. That's the funny thing. But I seem to worry them somehow. I don't know. They get so ratty, people's wives. The funny thing is that I like them better than their husbands, do you think that's funny or not? Perhaps I'm not normal. I'm quite normal really, I'm sure I am.

JO *has finished Hoovering and switched off. She enters kitchen as:*

But perhaps it's just that I'm *ab*normal. I can't see how I can be, can you? I mean . . . I've been told that I'm frigid, but I don't see how you can tell, I mean – honestly, how can you tell?

JO. I shouldn't think you are. Just a minute.

JO *moves to get hot water.* PHILPOT *sits on old-fashioned icebox.*

You don't look it anyway.

PHILPOT. I think you're marvellous – I really do, I think you're absolutely marvellous. You're so capable. All you do, all the children and everything, the way you cope. Of course, Jake's the most fabulous husband and father. He's *the* most fabulous –

JO *touches* PHILPOT's *leg.*

JO. Can I get in the . . .

PHILPOT *moves her legs.* JO *opens icebox.*

PHILPOT. – *the* most fabulous father. How many are his?
JO. Er . . . one . . .
PHILPOT. One. One is his. And the others aren't his?
JO. No, they're not.
PHILPOT. But he's a wonderful father to them all, isn't he?

Exterior. Hampstead Heath five years earlier. Day. A damp, drizzly day. JO *and the* CHILDREN. *Hill. Running.*

CHILD ONE. Why does Philpot have to stay with us?
JO. She's been turned out of her flat.

CHILD TWO. But why does she have to stay with us? We've got enough people.

JO. She's looking for another one.

CHILD TWO. I've never seen her look.

CHILD ONE. Who is she?

JO. She's a friend of a friend of Daddy's.

CHILD ONE. Why does she have to sleep in my bed? Why can't I sleep in my bed?

They run downhill. In the background, we see girls playing netball. DINAH *stands alone. They go to her.*

DINAH. I've got a pain.

MISTRESS (*calling*). Dinah!

DINAH *goes towards game. Game continues. Damp, muddy.* JO *and* CHILDREN *watch game vaguely from the rise.*

CHILD ONE. Why doesn't Philpot go home?

JO. She hasn't got a home.

CHILD THREE. She smells of fish.

CHILD TWO. She doesn't. She smells of onions.

CHILD THREE. Fish.

CHILD ONE. She had a spot on her chin yesterday, but this morning she'd squeezed it.

CHILD THREE. She stinks of fish.

JO. She doesn't stink at all. Now stop it.

CHILD TWO. What's the difference . . .

JO. Anyway, it's just perfume.

CHILD THREE. What is?

JO. Anyway, I like her.

CHILD ONE. Dad had to catch her yesterday when she fainted. It must have been awful, the smell.

JO. Fainted?

CHILD THREE (*falling*). Do you faint like this? Is this how you faint?

CHILD TWO. She fainted. Dad caught her.

JO (*to* CHILD THREE). Oh for goodness sake get up! You're smothered in mud, look at it.

The limp netball game.

MISTRESS. Come on, keep moving, keep moving. Keep at it.
Keep at it. Come on, pass the ball. Keep moving.
Keep at it.

The GIRLS *move in the drizzle.*

Exterior. Group on hill. Shooting up from game.
Prams moving across upper field. JO *and* CHILDREN
move away.

Interior. PHILPOT'*s bedroom. Morning.*
It is obviously a child's room, although PHILPOT'*s*
belongings are scattered around – clothing, ribbons,
hairpins, a pair of laddered stockings, a shawl . . .
JO *with tray.* PHILPOT *in bed.*

PHILPOT. He's a brilliant writer. It must be wonderful to have
a man working in the house, mustn't it, working at
home, you shouldn't have brought me tea, really, I
should get up, I mustn't have tea in bed, really, it's
bad for me, but honestly it must be so challenging
to write for films, don't you think, it's so challenging, don't you think, the cinema is, wouldn't you
say, but of course his understanding is so extraordinary, his innate . . . the way he draws his
characters . . . swift strokes . . . so swift . . .
and for you of course after all your struggles to
suddenly have success on the doorstep, after all
those husbands you've had and everything, but of
course you're so intelligent and everything and of
course so beautiful, do you help him much with his
work?

JO. Not much.

Pause.

Are you feeling any better?

PHILPOT. Better?

JO. You weren't too well the other day.

PHILPOT. I'm perfect. It's so warm here. *Real.* You know, so
real. I've never felt such a sense of *reality*, as there
is here. Do you know what I mean?

Interior. Kitchen five years earlier. Afternoon.
JO *vaguely washing.* JAKE *making tea.*

JO. Does Philpot faint much?

JAKE. What?

JO. Philpot. Does she do a lot of fainting?

JAKE. How the hell would I know?

Pause.

I mean, why should she faint? What's she got to faint about?

JO. The children said she fainted yesterday.

JAKE. I don't know. Did she?

JO. They said you caught her.

JAKE. Me?

JO. Yes.

JAKE. Why would I catch her?

JO. To stop her . . . banging her head on the . . .

JAKE. What head? What are you talking about?

JO. Did you catch her when she fainted?

JAKE (*a shout*). How do I know?

He bangs the table.

Interior. Kitchen. London house. Day.
                              PRESENT TIME
Water running. Tea tray set for one. JO *turns off tap. Goes out of kitchen into hall.*

Interior. Hall five years earlier. Night.
As the front door closes softly.

Interior. Sitting-room five years earlier. Night.

JO. Where's she gone? (*Pause.*) She's just gone out the front door.

JAKE. Has she?

JO. That's a bit odd, isn't it?

JAKE. What?

JO. I mean, we've just come in, haven't we? Now she's gone out.

JAKE *yawns.*

JAKE. Probably gone for a walk. Why don't you take off your coat?

Pause.

JO. What? (*Pause.*) Why has she gone? (*Pause.*) She's . . . Do you want some coffee?

JAKE. No thanks.

Pause.

JO. What did you think of the film?

JAKE *grimaces.*

What did you think of the bloody film?

JAKE. Nothing! I didn't think anything of it!

JO. Is your film going to be better, the one you're writing, do you think it's going to be better?

He stands.

JAKE. Listen –

JO. Do you like sitting between two women? Does that thrill you? Does it give you a thrill?

JAKE. Yes, it does. It really does. What do you think I should do about it? What shall I do, go and see a psychiatrist about it?

He sits. Pause.

JO. All right, what –

JAKE. Look. Listen –

Pause.

It was nothing, nothing. Don't you understand?

JO. What do you mean, it was nothing?

Pause.

What do you mean, nothing?

JAKE. What do you think I mean?

JO. What did you catch her for?

JAKE. I didn't catch her!

JO. She fainted.

JAKE. What does it matter if I caught her or not? I didn't catch her, it doesn't matter, can't you understand? Who cares?

JO. I care.

JAKE. What about? What's it all about?

JO. I care about you. Who else?

JAKE. Me? You don't care about me. All you care about is that bloody great army of children I'm supposed to work my guts out for. That's all you care about. Where the hell do I come in?

Pause.

I can't even take a bath in peace, I can't . . . I can't even go to bed with you without one of them comes barging in in the middle, but so what, you just . . . I'm sick of living in a bloody nursery. Where the damn hell do I come in?

She giggles.

What are you sniggering about? It's funny when I tell you the truth for once, I suppose.

JO. The truth?

JAKE. That I'm capable of fancying someone else. I'm a perfectly normal man who's capable of fancying someone else.

They look at each other. He goes to table and pours a drink. He sits near her, pulls her on to his lap. She regards his face calmly.

JO. Aaah.

JAKE. She was just here, that's all. I was bored with the script, that's all. It was nothing. Forget it.

JO. Did you sleep with her?

JAKE. Don't be silly.

JO. You didn't?

JAKE. No.

JO. You promise?

JAKE. Yes.

She kisses him.

JO. Do you still want to?

He laughs.

JAKE. Yes.

He laughs again, kisses her.

Interior. PHILPOT's *room. Night.*
JO *pushing all* PHILPOT's *belongings into a shawl.*

Exterior. By dustbins. Night.
JO *piling all stuff by the dustbins. She stands still in the night, becomes cold, turns.*

Interior. Stairway. Night.
JO *ascends stairs, stands still at top. Sound of a child muttering in its sleep.*

Interior. Main bedroom. Night.
Moonlight. JO *enters, moves to bed, stops, looks at* JAKE *asleep. She sits on the dressing table stool watching him, her hands tightly clenched.*
Eventually she gets into bed. JAKE *turns, snores.* JO *retreats to the edge of the bed, away from him, staring at him with eyes open, clutching the pillow between them.*

Series of shots. **PRESENT TIME**
JO *as we follow her. The street backgrounds change. She enters a large department store (Harrods).*

Interior. Harrods. Afternoon.
We follow JO *as she walks through various departments. See:*

Row of gleaming refrigerators.
Row of beds.
Shoppers hustling by. A salesman demonstrating a
very efficient Hoover.
JO *wandering through store.*
Children's clothing, bottles of scent, children's toys,
handkerchiefs.

Interior. Linen department. JO.
She suddenly stops and stands there in the centre of
the floor, crying.
Another angle : shoppers passing, glancing at JO *curi-*
ously.
Another angle : JO *standing quite still, crying sound-*
lessly.
Long shot : JO *standing there, crying. The many*
shoppers, still looking at her, have moved away, leav-
ing her standing isolated and motionless. Eventually
a SALESLADY *approaches, takes her arm and guides*
her away.

Exterior. House in St John's Wood. Late afternoon.
A taxi draws up outside. JO *is helped out by a uni-*
formed NURSE. *The front door of the house opens.*
Certain CHILDREN *in school uniform appear from*
inside the house and stand watching. Silence. The
NURSE *and* JO *walk up the path.*

Interior. Hall.
Silent CHILDREN, *including the* SMALLEST CHILD
with the NANNY. JO *and the* NURSE *enter.* DINAH
comes to them.
DINAH (*to her mother*). I couldn't find Daddy. I called the
studio but he wasn't there. I left a message.

As NURSE, JO *and* DINAH *move upstairs, one* CHILD
pushes another, and a crying row breaks out.

Interior. First floor landing and stairs. Night.
The DOCTOR *is descending the stairs.* JAKE *can be seen waiting in the hall.*

JAKE. Let's go in here, shall we?

DOCTOR. Yes.

They go into the sitting-room. The door is pushed to, but it swings back a little.

Interior. Landing. Night.
We see the door of the sitting-room below, ajar. Light through chink. Hear murmurs. JO's *bedroom door opens.* JO *slips out. Looks down.*

Interior. Stairway. Night.
JO *moves silently, halfway down the stairs, crouches there, listening. Sound of a soda syphon. The voices of* JAKE *and the* DOCTOR *are only occasionally heard clearly. The* DOCTOR *appears to be at the far end of the room. His voice is low, his tone grave.*
JAKE *is clearly walking about, his shadow sometimes appearing through the chink. Only when he is close to the door do we hear his words. These are interspersed with murmured questions and comments from the* DOCTOR.
JO *sits crouched on the stairs, listening.*

JAKE. Would you like a drink?

DOCTOR. Er, no, not for me, thanks.

JAKE. I should have got in touch with you before.
It's been getting worse all the time. Going on for ages. There was a girl friend of hers staying with us for a time, then she left . . . Mmmm . . . yes, it was round that period, but it's been . . . getting worse all the time.

DOCTOR. What exactly?

JAKE. I don't know. I . . . I can't get near her. She, she thinks everybody's . . . against her, keeps finding fault all the time. You know the sort of thing.

DOCTOR. Haven't you any idea why?

JAKE. No. I mean, breaking down in Harrods like that. Harrods of all places!

DOCTOR. Has there been any . . . kind of trouble between you?

JAKE. No.

DOCTOR. There's nothing particular, no specific problem?

JAKE. No. Nothing at all.

DOCTOR. I think perhaps she should see a psychiatrist.

JAKE. Should she?

DOCTOR. It might be a good idea.

JAKE. All right. If she wants to.

DOCTOR. He might want to see you too.

JAKE. Me?

DOCTOR. Yes. After all, you are her husband.

JAKE. I don't really see what I . . . She probably wants to have another child. That's what it is.

DOCTOR. Oh. Well, why doesn't she? She's a perfectly . . . healthy woman.

JAKE. We've got enough! Have you counted them? Well, any sane person would know we've got enough. When is she going to face facts? I mean she's a beautiful woman, she could . . . join in . . . live . . . all she wants to do is to sit in a corner and give birth.

JO *stands, retreats. The door opens. She stands at the top of the stairs.*

Another angle : stairway.
JO *standing at top, by her bedroom door, in the shadows.* JAKE *comes out of sitting-room below with* DOCTOR, *looks up, does not see her. He gets the* DOCTOR's *coat.* JO *steps back into :*

Interior. Main bedroom.
JO *stands in doorway, listening, as :*

DOCTOR'S VOICE. I'll give you a ring about it. Be kind to her.

JAKE'S VOICE. . . . Kind? I'm always kind.

DOCTOR'S VOICE. Good night.

JAKE'S VOICE. Good night.

> *Sound of front door closing.* JO *gets into bed, glances at door expectantly. But* JAKE *does not come up the stairs.*
> *Another angle:* JO *in bed, listening. She hears the whirr of the telephone dial.* JAKE'S VOICE *speaks softly.* JO *looks at bedside telephone, stares, does not pick it up.*
> *Another angle:* JO *in bed eyes open. The ting of the receiver, from downstairs. Silence.*
> *Footsteps.*
> JAKE *comes in.* JO's *eyes are closed.*

JAKE (*sitting on bed*). Asleep?
JO. No.

> *He caresses her.*

JAKE. You'll be all right.
JO. I am.

> *Pause.*

When are they going to finish the house?
JAKE. Soon.

> *Pause. She closes her eyes. He strokes her hair.*

> *Interior. Sitting-room. Evening.*
> JO *and* JAKE *sitting. He is reading a book. She has a magazine on her lap. Silence.*

JAKE. We've finished the script.

> *Pause.*

We're going . . . to Morocco for a couple of weeks.
JO. Mmm-hmm.

> *Pause.*

JAKE. Would you like to come?

> *Pause.*

I mean . . .

JO. Oh, I . . .

Pause.

JAKE. It'd mean living in tents and all that . . . but . . . if you felt like it . . .

JO. Couldn't just . . . sit in a tent . . .

JAKE. You wouldn't have to stay in the tent.

Silence.

JO. Timothy loved the train.

JAKE. What train?

JO. Your birthday present. The one your secretary sent for you.

JAKE. Well, anyway . . . the Doctor . . . we've arranged for a very good man for you to go and see.

Silence.

Why don't you come down to the studio tomorrow?

JO. What for?

JAKE. Meet everyone. They all want to meet you. Watch . . . the work. It might interest you.

JO. I don't want to come to the studio.

Pause.

JAKE. You're not interested . . . in what I do.

Pause.

JO. You never ask me.

JAKE. I've just asked you. I've asked you dozens of times.

JO. You don't want me to come.

JAKE. That's silly.

JO. No. It's not what you want.

Pause.

JAKE. You've never shown the slightest interest . . .

JO. Why are we talking about it?

Pause.

JAKE. You're just not interested in what I do, are you?

JO. You leave me. You're never with me.

JAKE. I have to work! It's my life.

JO. Where's mine? Where's my life?

Pause.

JAKE. With me.

She laughs.

I've worked, haven't I? What's wrong with that? I've had to work, haven't I? What did you expect me to do? The children go to good schools –

JO. Do you love me?

JAKE. I wouldn't be here if I didn't.

JO. You'd always be here if you did.

JAKE. Oh, that's ridiculous.

JO. Always.

Pause.

JAKE. You resent the money, don't you? That's what you resent.

JO. Money? It's nothing to do with the money.

JAKE. Look at that damn kitchen! Look at all this! What about the new house? You wanted it. I've done it for you. But all you want now, I suppose, is just to go back and live in that barn!

JO. It's nothing to do with the kitchen, it's nothing to do with the money – it's nothing to do with any of it!

JAKE. Well, *what*? What is it? What *do* you want? What?

She does not reply. He stands.

JO. You're going out.

JAKE. I have to.

JO. Don't go out now. Why are you going out now?

JAKE. I've got to. You know that. I can't not go.

JO. Stay. Not for long.

JAKE. I'm late. I'm late. It's business, it's not friends, it's business. If it were friends you could come.

JO. What friends? We haven't got any friends. The only friend I ever had was Philpot, but she was more your friend, wasn't she, than mine? But of course you've had lots of friends since Philpot, haven't you? Lots of nice friends. For years.

JAKE. You're quite wrong.

Pause.

JO. I don't want to come to the studio. I don't want to meet your . . . people. Never. Never.

The young NANNY enters.

NANNY. They're ready to say good night to you, Mrs Armitage.

No response.

Mrs Armitage –

JO *lifts her head, smiles. Silence.* JAKE *stands.*

JAKE. Are they . . . out of the bath?
NANNY. Yes.

JAKE *goes out and upstairs with* NANNY. JO *sits still.*

Exterior. St John's Wood. House. Day.
JAKE *is getting into a large car outside house.*
CHAUFFEUR *holding door.* CHILDREN *running, shouting.* JAKE *waving.* JO *standing holding a* CHILD *by its hand.* JAKE *waves, she waves. Car door slams; car drives off.* CHILDREN *run and wave.* JO *waves,* JAKE *waves out of window.*

Interior. Psychiatrist's office. Day.
Darkened, soft lights. JO *sitting in armchair. Psychiatrist,* (INGRAM) *at desk.*
INGRAM. Do you like children, Mrs Armitage?

She giggles.

JO. They don't do you any harm.
INGRAM. You have a remarkable number.

JO. I had them of my own free will.

INGRAM. Of course.

JO. Nobody forced me to have them.

Pause.

INGRAM. Your two eldest boys have been at boarding school for some years.

JO. Some years, yes.

INGRAM. You agreed to their going away.

JO. Yes.

INGRAM. Have you seen them recently?

JO. Not recently.

INGRAM. Do you want to see them?

Pause.

JO. I believe they're doing terribly well.

Pause.

INGRAM. Tell me about your first husband.

JO. Oh . . . I can't remember.

INGRAM. Really? You were married to him for two years.

JO. He was . . . sweet . . . quite sweet . . . Drank a bit, I think . . . second one died, he was killed . . . he was nice . . . third one was a violinist . . . Giles . . . he was nice . . . we lived in this barn . . . with the children . . . hardly went out, really . . . some years, I think . . .

INGRAM. Why did you leave him? What happened?

JO. Happened? Nothing happened. Nothing happened at all.

Interior. Main bedroom. Day.
JO *drinking hot milk.* DINAH *with her.*

DINAH. What about this book? Do you want to read it?

JO. Which one's that?

DINAH. It's the one about Trotsky.

JO. Oh yes.

DINAH. It's pretty marvellous. He was assassinated you know.

JO. Was he?

DINAH. Didn't you *know*? They killed him. They assassinated him.

JO. Who did?

DINAH. God, it's a fantastic story. They sent this man, you see.

JO. I'll read it downstairs.

DINAH. You getting up?

JO. Yes, I feel better now.

DINAH. Don't you cry any more?

JO. No.

DINAH. Why do you cry like that?

JO. I don't. I feel better.

DINAH. Do you miss him? Is that it?

JO. Who?

DINAH. Daddy.

JO *smiles, gets out of bed.*

Anyway . . . you know . . . read that book . . . it'll cheer you up.

JO. Yes, I will.

Interior. Psychiatrist's office. Day.
JO *and* INGRAM.

JO. What has Jake got to do with me? Why do you keep asking me about Jake? I come here and all you ask me about is Jake. Why the hell don't you see Jake? Perhaps it's him you should be seeing, not me. There's nothing to *say* . . . about him.

INGRAM. Do you like him?

JO. No.

INGRAM. Do you love him?

JO. . . . Yes, so what? You don't –

INGRAM. What?

JO. I've forgotten what I was going to say.

Pause.

INGRAM. Do you think Jake is liable to change?

JO. I'm no match for him.

INGRAM. You're no match for him?

JO. No.

INGRAM. What do you mean?

Pause.

Do you think he's liable to change?

JO. No.

INGRAM. What would you say was the difference between Jake and your previous husbands?

JO. They weren't necessary.

Pause.

INGRAM. When you say –

JO. You should have a bowl in front of that gas fire.

INGRAM. A bowl?

JO. Of water – a bowl of water.

INGRAM. Ah, yes.

JO. You need it, for Christ's sake.

INGRAM. Mmm . . .

JO. The trouble is, if you have a bowl of water people throw matchsticks into it, and they float about for days, and become soggy, the water becomes black, and then anyway, it all dries up anyway. So perhaps you're better off without it.

Pause.

INGRAM. Do you find the thought of sex without children obscene, Mrs Armitage?

JO. No.

INGRAM. Really? Are you sure the idea doesn't disgust you? I mean, don't you find the idea messy? Isn't sex something you must sanctify, as it were, by incessant reproduction?

Pause.

JO. I shall have to give that question a little thought.

INGRAM. You would do well to, I think.

Pause.

I won't be seeing you for a couple of weeks. Just chew it over, and take the pills of course.

JO. Couple of weeks?

INGRAM. Oh, I'm sorry, haven't I told you? We're off to Gstaadt on Friday for a spot of skiing. It's my great passion, I'm afraid.

JO. Skiing?

INGRAM. Oh, and cut down on liquids as much as you can. Can we make an appointment for the . . . 19th?

JO. Can't make it. No . . . can't make the 19th.

INGRAM. The 20th?

JO. Can't make it.

INGRAM. Oh come now . . .

JO. What liquids?

INGRAM. Liquids.

JO. Yes, but what liquids? Listen, why are you going to Gstaadt? Why don't you go to Cortina? Why Gstaadt? Where is Gstaadt? Why the hell don't you go to Cortina? Or Kitzbuhel?

Interior. Hairdressing salon. Day.
Rows of chairs, all occupied. Hair dryers. JO *sitting under dryer, looking at a magazine. The* WOMAN *next to her is looking at her. She is middle-aged.*
The WOMAN *leans over.* JO *looks up, sees the large face of the* WOMAN *close to her. The* WOMAN *is smiling, talking, her mouth moves.* JO *lifts her dryer to hear.*

WOMAN. I hope you don't mind, I've just been looking at your photo in one of these magazines, you know, a photo of you all, all your family, all your wonderful children and your wonderful husband, I thought you must be the same person.

JO. Oh . . . yes.

WOMAN. I think you're much lovelier than your photo. I really do. I was . . . I had a . . . Do you mind me speaking to you?

JO. Er . . . no . . .

WOMAN. To tell you the honest truth, my life is an empty place, to tell you the dog's honest truth. Your eyes are more beautiful than in that picture. I bet you didn't always have things so good, that's why you appreciate, don't you? I never dreamed I'd meet you like this and I mean you're so kind, you're so full of sympathy for me. My husband doesn't come near me any more, no, nowhere near me. Don't you think I'm attractive any more? I think I'm still attractive.

JO. Of course you are.

WOMAN. I'm not as attractive as you. But in a different way I am. That's one thing I do know. I had a hysterectomy operation four months ago. Yes, a hysterectomy. You know, they take it all away. But you should see the way men look at me. The way they still look at me. My word of honour. You can tell by that, you see. I'm desirable. I'm not old. I know. But he doesn't seem to care about cheering me up any more . . . Oooh, I'm so thirsty.

Pause.

JO. Would you . . . like a cup of tea?

WOMAN. I'm off liquids.

Pause.

JO. Well, I . . . I am sorry . . .

WOMAN. It's no bloody use being sorry, chum. What are you going to do about it? I've just told you my life is an empty place.

JO. What do you want me to do?

WOMAN. I don't want any favours, for a start. Don't patronize me, for a start.

JO. I'm really not. I'm really not.

WOMAN. 'I'm really not. I'm really not.' God! I thought you'd be different. I thought you'd be a different woman to the one you are, Miss. I thought you'd be a very different woman.

JO. I'm sorry . . .

WOMAN. You're what? I do a weekly wash in a copper boiler!
Oh, you've got such wonderful children, wonderful, wonderful, wonderful, wonderful. You're

wonderful too. You must be a lovely woman. You must be such a lovely woman. I think women are the only ones . . . They're the only ones. I can see your grace and your sweetness just sitting here. What does your husband think of you, eh? Does he find you attractive? Eh, I've been wondering, do you think your husband would find me desirable? Eh?

JO. Look . . . I don't actually feel very . . .

WOMAN. I'd show him some tricks, I'd show him some tricks. Heh! You want to bet? . . . I'd show him a few things I bet you don't know. My love. My little darling. Anyone ever clawed your skin off? You see these claws? Ever had your skin clawed off?

An ASSISTANT *comes to the* WOMAN. *She looks curiously at them both.*

You going to give me two curls there, this time? Over the ears, two curls, one either side, two lovely curls at each side, are you? Are you?

Interior. Hall and stairs. Morning.
CHILDREN *rushing down the stairs, shouting.*

Exterior. House in St John's Wood. Morning.
JAKE *getting out of chauffeur-driven car at the front gate.*

Interior. Hall.
CHILDREN *flinging themselves at* JAKE.

JAKE. Hullo . . . hullo . . . hullo . . . Good God, – who's this? Ha-ha-ha . . . (etc.) . . . Where's Mum?

Shout from CHILD.

CHILD. Here she is!

Interior. Sitting-room.
Silent, empty. Shouts from hall. (Dialogue from previous scene repeated)

JAKE'S VOICE. Hullo . . . hullo . . . hullo . . . Good God, – who's this? Ha-ha-ha . . . (etc.) . . . Where's Mum?

CHILD'S VOICE (*shouting*). Here she is!

Sitting-room door is flung open.

Exterior. Front path.
CHILDREN *struggling with cases.*

Interior. Sitting-room. Morning.
JAKE *and* JO. CHILDREN. JAKE *gives* JO *a Moorish dressing gown.*

JAKE. It's meant to bring you luck.

CHILDREN *are opening cases with cries, unwrapping presents.* JAKE *claps his hands.*

Come on, come on, where's that drink? None of these are for you, you haven't been good enough.

CHILD ONE. We have!

CHILD TWO. They've got our names on!

A CHILD *hands* JAKE *a drink. He sips.*

JAKE. Who put all that soda in?

CHILD ONE. I got a green star for spelling.

CHILD FOUR. Where's mine?

CHILD TWO. What's this?

JAKE. What do you think?

JO *helps them unwrap packages.*

CHILD THREE. Did you see any lions?

CHILD FIVE. We went to the circus.

CHILD SIX. We went to the pictures.

CHILD THREE. Did you see any camels?

CHILD TWO. That's where I fell down.
CHILD FOUR. Was it a jet?
CHILD THREE. What about hyenas?
CHILD ONE. I've got a new book.
CHILD TWO. I had a bandage.

Interior. Sitting-room. Later same morning.
JO and JAKE with drinks. Paper and packages all over room. Sounds of children playing, from upstairs. A record playing. JAKE smiles, touches her.

JAKE. Darling . . .

She smiles.

JO. I'm all right now.
JAKE. Wish you'd been there. Marvellous place.
JO. Was it?
JAKE. Come here.

She sits with him. He kisses her. He settles down comfortably.

Of course, Hurst and Betty hated each other on sight.
JO. Did they?
JAKE. Well, first of all, there was some ridiculous business about a camel, he got her up on this camel, pure spite of course, anyway, she must have been dead drunk at the time, anyway –

A sudden crash from outside the door. A cry.
JO stands. Door bursts open. THREE CHILDREN run through, one crying. The crying CHILD chases the other two through window to garden.

JO. Hey!

Exterior. The garden. Their point of view.
In garden, we see the first TWO CHILDREN turn running, shooting at THIRD.

Back to scene.
Sudden silence in room.
A radio and gramophone suddenly blurt together from above. Shouts.

CHILD'S VOICE (*shouting*). I'm playing mine!

CHILD'S VOICE (*shouting*). I told you just now!

JAKE sinks in chair, blankly chuckles.

JO. What happened?

JAKE. Mmmmm? Well, what was so funny . . . you see . . . it was really what she was wearing, really . . . that's what was so funny . . .

JO. On the camel?

A scream from the garden. They look out of window.

The garden. Their point of view.
A CHILD lies prone on the grass.

JO (*through window*). Tim! What are you doing?

CHILD (TIM). Nothing!

Back to scene.
Silence in room.

JO. We've got lunch . . . ready soon . . . for you.

JAKE. Ah.

Music from upstairs.

JO. Bit of a racket.

JAKE. Saturday morning.

He yawns, sits. She goes to the door.

JO (*calling*). Turn one of those off!

CHILD'S VOICE. I had mine on first.

JO. I said turn one of them off, at once, now.

CHILD'S VOICE. Which one?

JO. Turn them both off!

JAKE. It doesn't matter, it doesn't matter.

She goes to him.

JO. What happened? Tell me.

JAKE. What?

JO. About . . . the camel . . . and . . .

JAKE. Oh, it's . . . all . . .

Closes his eyes.

. . . pretty uninteresting.

Opens his eyes.

What's the matter? What are you crying about?

JO. No.

JAKE. Nothing to cry about.

She rests against him.

Is there?

Pause.

JO. Look. Why don't we ask them round?

JAKE. Who?

JO. All of them. Tonight.

JAKE. Tonight?

JO. Yes. Why not? All of them.

JAKE. Who?

JO. Oh . . . the Conways, Hurst, all of them. Then I could hear all about it. Properly. Come on, why not?

JAKE. But why do you want all that lot round here to-night! They might not be free anyway.

JO. Ring and find out.

JAKE. But . . . do you want to . . .?

JO. Yes, I do. I'll ring. What's the Conway's number?

JAKE. Have you been having an affair with that doctor or something?

JO. Yes. How did you know?

JAKE. What are you up to?

She seizes his head. She kisses him hard.

Interior. Sitting-room. Night.
The party. The glass doors between sitting-room and dining-room are open. Both rooms are crowded with

people. Concentrated party noise. JO's *face.* CON-
WAY *is hemming her into a corner, talking.*

CONWAY. Professional people are all a lot of bloody parasites,
the lot of them. Doctors, lawyers – you know what
I mean – parsons, the whole bloody crew of them.
I call myself a tradesman because it's the only
thing left to respect in my honest opinion. In my
honest opinion, an honest tradesman is the only
thing left to respect in this world. A man like me,
for instance. The rest of them are just a bunch of
lousy frauds.

DINAH *signals to* JO *from another corner of the room.
As* CONWAY *turns,* DINAH *smiles radiantly.*
CONWAY *turns back to* JO, *nudges her, leans closer.*

What do you think? Come on, what do you think?
JO. Excuse me a second, I must . . .

(*She catches sight of* JAKE.)

Jake, I think Mr Conway wants another drink.

CONWAY *drains his glass.* JO *moves away. Camera
follows her as she moves. Snatches of conversation
overheard :*

GUEST ONE. Well, there was this man, you see, there was this
man, and all his life, the one thing he wanted more
than anything else was to beat a woman, you see.
No it's quite true, really. It's a true story. It was
the one thing he really wanted to do. But he never
met anyone who wanted him to do it . . .

GUEST TWO. But it's got nothing to do with you, darling.

GUEST ONE. He was a very nice chap, you see, very quiet sort
of bloke . . .

GUEST THREE. It has absolutely everything to do with me as a
matter of fact.

GUEST ONE. Well, one night at a party he met a woman. He was
telling her about it, you see, and she said what a
wonderful coincidence, there's nothing I'd love
more in the whole world. Well, he couldn't believe
his ears . . .

GUEST FOUR. He stands to make at least fifteen grand out of it, so what's the matter?

GUEST FIVE. Who said anything was the matter?

GUEST ONE. No, it's really true, really. She took him home to her flat. He was so excited he could hardly get up the stairs.

GUEST SIX. I had three showers a day – absolutely every single day.

GUEST SEVEN. What were the peasants like?

GUEST EIGHT. Extraordinarily interesting. Fascinating faces.

GUEST SEVEN. Lots of character, I suppose.

GUEST EIGHT. Oh lots, lots.

JO *joins* DINAH.

JO. How's things?

DINAH. Marvellous. Dad's really with it tonight, isn't he? I didn't know Beth Conway had red hair. I thought it was sort of blonde. She's lovely, isn't she? Isn't she smiling at you? Have you spoken to her?

BETH. DINAH's *point of view, lying on couch, talking to* JAKE *and surrounded by people.*
Back to scene.
MAN *comes up with a drink for* DINAH.

MAN. Here you are, my dear.

He peers at JO, *smiling.*

Who's this?

DINAH. She's my mother.

MAN. Really?

JO. Hullo. Just a minute.

She moves away, camera with her. Snatches of conversation:

GUEST ONE (*trying to make himself heard above laughter*).
. . . No, well, anyway, after all that, at last, at last, they stood there stark naked, looking at each other. He had the cane in his hand . . .

GUEST NINE. It'll be a smash, and believe me, when I say smash . . .

GUEST TEN. Who knows if you don't.

GUEST ONE. Suddenly, to his amazement . . . suddenly to his horror and amazement . . .

GUEST ELEVEN. How's your new house, Mr Gross?

GUEST TWELVE. Which one?

GUEST ONE. He saw that she was holding a cane too. 'What's all this?' he said.

GUEST THIRTEEN. Actually, you really are terribly masculine.

GUEST FOURTEEN. Am I really?

GUEST ONE. Suddenly she whacked him with all her might. 'Oww!' he screamed.

JO *joins* BETH, JAKE *and* CONWAY *and the group around the couch.*

JAKE. Beth wants your advice. I've told her you know all about children.

JO. I wouldn't say that.

CONWAY. What my wife needs is another half-dozen and quick.

JO (*to* BETH). Did you like Morocco?

BETH. Oh, it was quite fun. Quite fun really.

All the noise of the party dies away, as we dissolve to:

Interior. Sitting-room. Later same night.
The room dishevelled, full of smoke, overflowing ashtrays, bottles, glasses, but empty of people except for CONWAY, BETH, JAKE *and* JO.

CONWAY (*his voice coming out of the silence*).
I call myself a tradesman, because it's the only thing left to respect, in my honest opinion. In my honest opinion, an honest tradesman is the only thing left to respect in this world. That's my honest opinion.

JAKE. You'd say that in all honesty, would you?

CONWAY. In all honesty, Jake. In complete honesty, boy. Ask Beth. Ask Beth if I mean what I say. (*Pause.*) Ask her!

They look at BETH.

BETH. Oh, my husband always . . . means what he says. (*To* JO.) Does yours?

JO. You'd better ask him.

JAKE *laughs.*

BETH. He writes film scripts beautifully, anyway, doesn't he? He's got such extraordinary understanding, such . . . swift . . . you know . . . kind of illumination of people. Some of the scenes with John actually made me really cry.

JAKE. That was just the sand in your eyes.

CONWAY. Lots of sand in Morocco, was there?

JAKE. Uh.

Pause.

JO. Another drink?

BETH. I'm fine.

JO. Mr Conway?

CONWAY. No, I don't think I'll have another one, thank you very much.

JAKE. I'll have one.

JO *gets it.*

CONWAY. I looked after our baby girl while Beth was away.

JAKE. How did she respond to that?

CONWAY. How did she respond to it? I'm her father!

Pause.

Intelligent woman, your wife.

They all look at JO.

JO. Oh no. I'm not at all.

BETH. I think he's right. I think you look very intelligent.

CONWAY. I like intelligent women. They're stimulating, they're vital . . . vital . . . that's what makes them intelligent, I suppose.

JAKE. Yes, it depends which way you look at it.

BETH. Jake's got an idea for a new film, it takes place on the Italian Riviera. We could all go, all of us together, the four of us, think what fun we could have.

Silence. They all sit. Staring.

Interior. Main bedroom. Late night.
After the party. JO *and* JAKE *are undressing.*

JO. They've nearly finished the house.
JAKE. Have they? Oh, good, good.

Pause.

JO. You're a marvellous colour.
JAKE. It was hot.

Pause.

JO. Do you think she's attractive?
JAKE. Who?
JO. Beth.
JAKE. Mmmm–hmmm. I suppose so.

She pulls him on to the bed, caresses him, tracing his
body. JAKE *murmurs:*

I need you.
JO. What about the Arab women?
JAKE. Oh, I couldn't begin to tell you.
JO. Did they like you?
JAKE. Wouldn't leave me alone.
JO. Did they touch you like that?

He suddenly turns her over on her back and stares
down at her.

What is it?

Silence. He looks at her, as if about to speak, then
kisses her suddenly.

Exterior. Hillside. Day.
We see the new house in the background. It is of very
modern design, startling against the skyline.
JAKE *and* FOUR CHILDREN *are cycling up the path*
towards the house. One of the smaller children is on a
tricycle. When they near the house, the CHILD *on the*
tricycle begins to slide back down the hill. JAKE *gets*
off his bike, pushes CHILD *till they reach the straight,*
then remounts and rides on.

The other CHILDREN *ride in circles around large picnic rugs on the grass.* DINAH *is there with the* SMALLEST CHILD.
Another angle : the picnic laid out on the grass.

DINAH. Mummy's looking for some plates upstairs.
CHILD. Where's the big red ball?
JAKE. After tea.

JAKE *goes towards house, goes in door.* CHILD *shouts up to top window :*

CHILD. Mummy! Can I have the big red ball?

JO *appears at window.*

JO *(calling down).* What?
CHILD. I just want to put it on the grass. I won't play with it.

Interior. Upper floor of new house.
It is empty of furniture. JO *at window.* JAKE *enters.*
JO *(to* JAKE*).* Give me the ball.

He does so. She throws it out of window, leans on sill, smiling, as :

JO. Here it is.
CHILD. I'm going to throw it at Dinah.
JO. You'd better not.

JAKE *picks up a pile of dusty plates.* JO *glances at him and smiles. He comes to her. They both look out of window.*
Another angle : at window.
JO *and* JAKE *looking down over fields. Suddenly focus on barn, low down, broken, overgrown. (A momentary shot.)*
JO *and* JAKE *looking at each other.*

JAKE. I love you.

Interior. Bedroom. JO's *father's house. Day.*
MR JAMES *in bed,* JO *beside him. Her* MOTHER

sobbing by window. MR JAMES's *hands reach for* JO's, *grasp them, draw them to his eyes, hold them to his eyes. Hold them. Drop them. Stillness. Silence.* JO's *face.* MOTHER *sobs at window. Bed still. Body.*

Interior. Staircase. Father's house. Day.
Sheets and blankets being carried up by two old women.

Interior. Living-room. Father's house. Evening.
JO *and* MOTHER *drinking brandy.*

MOTHER. He was such a good man. Nobody knew how good he was. Have you told Jake yet? He was very fond of George. He was, I know. And George was fond of him. George really was fond of him.

JO. I know.

MOTHER. He didn't care for any of the others much, but I don't know . . . he was really *fond* of Jake.

JO. Jake was fond of him, too.

MOTHER. I know he was. (*Pause.*) I'll never see him again. I'm glad he wanted to be cremated. I wish I could believe I'd see him again. But I'm glad he'll be cremated. I couldn't bear to think of him buried . . . The thought of him under that . . . I mean just the thought . . .

JO. Mother . . .

MOTHER. Just to think, just to think of him . . .

JO. Mother, listen, I want to tell you something.

MOTHER *turns, looks at* JO. *Silence.* JO *goes over to table, picks up bottle of sedative and spoon.*

I'm . . .

MOTHER. What? No! You can't! You're not! You're not! You can't!

JO. Well, there it is . . .

MOTHER. But . . . but . . . what can Jake be thinking of?

JO *pours sedative into spoon, gives it to* MOTHER, *as:*

JO. He doesn't know. Nobody knows.

MOTHER. You must be mad! Aren't you ever going to get any rest?

JO. It'll be all right, really.

MOTHER. How can you be so careless, so thoughtless! It's lunacy! How can you want to start all that over again?

Interior. Living-room. JO's *father's house. Day.*
JAKE, JO, DINAH *and* JO's MOTHER. *They all wear coats.*

MOTHER (*to* JAKE). He was so fond of you. He was. He was so proud of you too. He really was. Only the other night he said we must go and see your new film. He did. Of course, he couldn't go . . .

JAKE. No . . .

MOTHER. No, oh no, he couldn't go.

Front drive of house. Their point of view through window.
The hearse draws up.
Back to scene.

MOTHER. Oh dear, there they are. There they are.

She holds JO's *hand.*
The UNDERTAKER *comes through the front door.*

UNDERTAKER. We can't . . . quite . . . get to the front door. Could the gentleman please move his car?

JAKE (*to* MOTHER). You go into the garden. I'll . . .

Exterior. Garden. JO's *father's house.*
JO, DINAH *and* JO's MOTHER, *walking.*

MOTHER. He loved his vegetables. We never bought a single vegetable until last winter. He just couldn't manage it any more. Remember the strawberries, Dinah? You loved his strawberries.

DINAH. Yes, they were marvellous.

MOTHER. I know you did.

JAKE *appears.*

JAKE. A few minutes.

They all walk.

JO. How's things at home?

JAKE. Fine.

DINAH. Chaos.

JAKE. Of course it isn't. All in control.

MOTHER. Oh, I don't know what George would have said if he knew.

JAKE. Mmmm? About what?

JO. You could let this off for allotments, couldn't you?

MOTHER. He loved the children, but he always thought there were too many. Always. I don't know what you're thinking of, Jake, really.

JAKE. What do you mean?

JO. Are they ready yet?

MOTHER. It's too much. I'm glad he didn't live to see it.

JO (*to* DINAH). Go and find out if they're ready.

JAKE. What do you mean? See what?

DINAH. Won't they tell us when they're ready?

JO. No, they won't. They might be waiting, or something. Go on, please.

DINAH. O.K.

DINAH *goes.*

MOTHER. At least he's going to be cremated. I'm so glad about that.

JAKE *looks at* JO.

JAKE. Live to see what?

Pause.

MOTHER. On top of everything else. As if she hasn't got enough. Mind you, he loved them, he loved the children.

JAKE *stands still and stares at* JO.
DINAH *appears around the corner.*

Exterior. Front of JO's *father's house.*
TWO TEENAGE BOYS, *gawky, standing in school uniform. The hearse.*
The group appears from the garden. JAKE *walks apart, smoking.*

MOTHER. Oh, look, the boys are here. The boys have come.

She goes to them. JO *stays a moment with* DINAH.

DINAH. Who are they?
JO. Your brothers.
DINAH. Good God!

DINAH *goes to them.* JO *looks round to* JAKE.
Close-up of JO.
Close-up of JAKE *not looking, collar up.*
Another angle : JO *walks towards the group.*
Another angle : The BOYS *watch her come.*
Close-up of JAKE.
The group.

PETE. Hullo, Mum.
JO. Hullo.
JACK. Hullo.
JO. Hullo.

Pause.
MOTHER *brings her handkerchief to her mouth.*
(*To* DINAH, *indicating her* MOTHER.)

Dinah . . .
DINAH (*looking at boys*). I wouldn't have believed it.

She draws MOTHER *away.*

JO (*to boys*). What do you think of your sister?
JACK. Pretty good.

Pause.

JO. Are you . . . everything all right?
JACK. Fine.

Pause.

PETE. Yes. Fine.

Pause.

JO. Good.

Exterior. Front of JO's *father's house. Another angle. All getting into cars.* JAKE *alone, in Jaguar, moves swiftly away.*

MOTHER (*to* JO). Poor Jake – he's so upset. He was always so very fond of George.

Interior. DINAH's *bedroom. St John's Wood. House. Night.*

DINAH, *dressed, on floor with book.* JO.

DINAH. It was when the coffin went in, when they pushed it in, you know, I think that's when it was. I suddenly thought, well, it might be possible. You know . . . God might be possible. Have you ever read Thomas Aquinas? I'm reading this book, it's marvellous. 'That the Divine Being cannot be specified by the Addition of a Substantial Difference.' See what I mean?

Interior. Landing outside DINAH's *room.*

JO *comes out of* DINAH's *room, closes door, starts down stairs – then suddenly changes her mind, turns.*

Interior. Top staircase.

JO *climbing up stairs to :*

Interior. Attic.

JO *enters. Junk everywhere.* JO *looks around, and walks slowly over to corner. She reaches out and pulls down a cot, a rubber bath.*

The rubber bath is perished. She stands looking at it, looks up.

A high chair, a pair of scales, stuck up in corner, out of reach.

JO *begins to clamber over suitcases to reach them –
stops, as she hears the front door slam, footsteps.
She turns in sudden panic, throws bath back on to
pile, makes for the door.*

Interior. Stairway.
JO *descending stairs to hall.*

Interior. Sitting-room. Night.
Fire in grate. JAKE, *having just come in, is settling
himself by it.* JO *enters.*

JO. You look awful.

JAKE. I feel awful.

*She sits on other side of fire. They look into it. She
kicks her shoes off.*

You must be tired.

JO. Mmmm.

Pause.

And you.

JAKE. Mmmm.

Pause.

JO. I'm sorry.

Pause.

JAKE. Sorry?

Pause.

JO. I know you don't want it. (*Pause.*) I know . . . you
don't want the baby.

JAKE. Do you?

Pause.

JO. I'm sorry . . . I'm sorry . . .

Pause.

JAKE. It can't be helped.

JO. It'll be all right, it will . . . I mean, you'll like it . . . I mean, perhaps it'll be a boy . . . you haven't got nearly enough boys. When we get the house ready we can spend the summer there. We can spread out a bit . . . I mean, you won't notice.

JAKE. All right. It doesn't matter.

JO. It does. It does matter. (*Pause.*) You mean you . . . you really don't want it?

JAKE. No.

She stands, walks.

JO. What do you want then?

JAKE. It doesn't matter, does it?

Pause.

JO. Why?

Pause.

JAKE. I don't want it. That's why. (*Pause.*) I wanted us to change. Now we can't change. You see? It's my fault. It's because of me, I know that. But I thought we could change . . . branch out . . . be free. (*Pause.*) Now there's no chance. (*Pause.*) We're back where we were.

She goes to him, holds him.

I'm not blaming you, I'm blaming myself. It's my fault, I know that. We haven't . . . lived together. But it's just that I've suddenly realized . . . that we could lead a more sensible life. It was possible. We haven't lived. (*Pause.*) We don't need it. It'll kill us. We could begin, you see, we could really begin . . . I know it . . . you know, to . . . You know what I mean. I mean there is a world, there is a world apart from birth, there's a world apart from . . . we don't want any more . . . how can we have any more?

Silence.

I know the idea of abortion is repellant to you, I know that. It is to me, too. You must admit I've never suggested it.

Silence.

It's ghastly, the idea of abortion, I know that. Ghastly. (*Silence.*) I wouldn't dream of suggesting it. (*Silence.*) But after all, it would be perfectly legal, you've just been treated for depression, I mean the Doctor said . . . there wouldn't be anything underhand about it.

Close-up of JAKE.

After all, I got you into this. I just want to make you happy. All those boring months, the pain at the end. I just want to get you out of it, I want to get us both out of it while there's still time, that's all.

Interior. SURGEON's *office. Nursing home. Day.*
SURGEON *and* JO.

SURGEON (*with papers*). Now, Mrs Armitage . . . I've had a talk with your husband . . . and I did suggest to him that . . . in your case . . . we might consider going somewhat further than this . . . operation. I recommended pursuing, shall we say, a more sensible, long-term policy. Has he spoken to you about it?

JO. I . . . don't think so.

SURGEON. No. Good. I thought it would be better to speak to you myself.

JO. What do you mean?

SURGEON. The reasons for recommending that this pregnancy be terminated, you see, would seem to apply with equal validity to any future pregnancy. Do you see what I mean? (*Pause.*) You've had a considerable number of children. Perhaps it would be wise for you not to have any more.

JO. How do you do that?

SURGEON. It's a matter of sterilization. Quite simple. You can lead a completely normal married life, but you'll never conceive.

JO. Oh. (*Pause.*) What did my husband say?

SURGEON. Oh, he left the decision entirely to you, of course. As we do.

Interior. JO's *room in nursing home. Night.*
JO *is lying in bed, silent, alone, eyes open, still.*

Interior. JO's *room in nursing home. Day. Close-up of* JO.
In nightdress, head flung back on pillow, laughing. She is still in bed. JAKE *sits on chair.*

JAKE. Be careful. You'll hurt yourself.

JO. I'm so happy.

JAKE. Good.

JO. You don't know what it's like to be sterilized. You've never been sterilized.

JAKE. Never.

JO. It's wonderful. I'm free, you see, free. Aren't I? Completely free.

JAKE. Yes. I know.

JO. We don't have to worry about it any more, you see. It'll just never happen again. We just don't have to worry about all that ever again.

He kisses her, leaning.

JAKE. No. Never.

JO. I'm going to get rid of that Nanny for a start. I've always hated her. In the summer, we'll be able to move to the country, won't we?

JAKE. Yes.

JO. We can live with the children again, properly, and then we can go away, just do anything, just do anything.

JAKE. Yes.

He takes her hand and kisses it.
Close-up of JAKE's *face smiling, gentle.*

Interior. JO's *room in nursing home. Evening.*
The room is full of flowers. JO *in bed.* DINAH *with a small bunch of violets.*

DINAH. I brought you these.

JO. Oh . . . thank you.

DINAH. They don't stand much of a chance with all these others.

JO. Oh yes they do.

DINAH (*examining flowers*). Look at this! Wow! Who are they all from?

JO (*laughing*). I haven't the slightest idea.

DINAH *sits on the bed.*

DINAH. You feeling all right now?

JO. Mmmm. Marvellous.

DINAH. It was a sort of . . . womb thing, I suppose, was it?

JO. Yes . . . something like that.

DINAH. Does it happen to everyone?

JO. No, of course not.

DINAH. Just happens to some women, does it?

JO. Mmmmmm.

A silence.

Look, come on, help me make this list, we're going to make a clean sweep.

JO *gives* DINAH *pencil and paper.*

DINAH. What list?

JO. There's going to be some changes made.

DINAH. Good. What?

JO. We're going to do things. First, sack that Nanny.

DINAH. Good!

JO. Sack Nanny, put it down.

DINAH. I am. When?

JO. Immediately.

DINAH. Right. Next.

JO. Start moving things to the new house.

DINAH. Wonderful. What things?

JO. Anything.

DINAH. All that junk in the attic?

JO. Yes, all that junk.

DINAH. It isn't all junk.

JO. Just put it down.

DINAH. How?

JO. Move junk to new house. Send everything to cleaners.

DINAH. We haven't phoned the removal people.

JO. Phone removal people.

DINAH. Get your hair cut.

JO. Sack the Nanny.

DINAH. We've got that.

JO. Throw away junk.

DINAH. But we're going to move the junk.

JO. No, we're not going to move the junk, we're going to move the things we want.

DINAH. Sort out the things we want.

JO. Make a clean sweep.

Another angle to include door.
JAKE comes in.

JAKE. Hullo, what's all this?

JO hides the list.

JO. Nothing.

JAKE. Let's have a look.

DINAH. You can't.

JAKE slips list out from under pillow, reads it.
JAKE writes.

JAKE. Here you are.

DINAH. What have you put?

She grabs it.

'Love Jake.'

A short laugh between JO and JAKE.
He goes to flowers and looks at them.

There's a pile of old sheets in the cupboard. We never use them.

JO. Throw them out.

JAKE. Beautiful flowers. Very nice of them all, isn't it?

DINAH *looks at* JO.

JO. Yes.

JAKE. Have you . . . written to them, thanked them?

JO. Yes.

JAKE. Good. Good. Written to the Conways?

JO. Mmmm.

JAKE. Good.

Interior. Main bedroom. St John's Wood. House. Day.
JAKE *putting suitcases down.* JO *comes into the room. They look at each other. She flings herself into his arms. Onto bed.*

Interior. Hall. Day.
JO, REMOVAL MEN, CHILDREN. JO *crisp, decisive, authoritative.* CHILDREN *are playing games in the hall.*

JO (*to* MAN). You will keep that upright, won't you?

MAN. Yes, Miss.

JO (*to* CHILD). Come on now, let the man get through.

As MAN *starts out through door with his load:*

(*to* FOREMAN.) Is that it?

FOREMAN. That tallboy, Miss . . .

JO. No, no. That stays here.

FOREMAN. That's about it then.

The phone rings. JO *goes into sitting room.*

CHILD (*to* MAN). I'll give you a hand.

MAN. I can manage, thanks.

Interior. Sitting-room.
JO *at phone.*

JO. Hello . . .

CONWAY. This is Bob Conway.

JO. Who?

CONWAY. Conway, you know, Beth's husband.

JO. Oh, Mr Conway, how are you? I'm afraid Jake's at the studio.

CONWAY. Actually, I wanted to . . .

JO (*interrupting*). Could you hold on for just a minute . . . (*To* REMOVAL MAN.) Mrs Teff will be waiting for you at the house.

REMOVAL MAN. Mrs Teff. Right Madam. Thank you.

JO. Thank you. (*To* CONWAY.) Sorry . . .

CONWAY. I was wondering if you could have tea with me tomorrow.

JO. What?

CONWAY. Something I wanted to talk to you about.

JO. Oh, I don't think I could really manage tomorrow. I'm taking the children to the zoo.

CONWAY. Splendid! What could be nicer?

JO. What?

CONWAY. I mean, why don't I see you there?

JO. All right. Why don't you meet us all at that place by the penguins – the tea place. Do you know it?

CONWAY. Perfect!

JO. Fine.

CONWAY. I shall look forward to it. Thank you.

JO. See you there about four o'clock.

CONWAY. Good-bye now.

JO. Bye-bye.

Exterior. Zoo café.

JO, CONWAY, FERGUS, ELIZABETH *and* NANNY *seated around tea table.* MARK *feeding penguins.*

CONWAY (*to* ELIZABETH).

Don't you look pretty in that dress?

(*To* FERGUS.)

What animals do you like best?

JO. Mark . . .

MARK *moves forward.*

CONWAY (*to* MARK).
What about you?
MARK. Penguins.

Laughter.

CONWAY. Aren't they delicious!
ELIZABETH. May we see the bears now?
JO. All right. But don't run away from Nanny.
NANNY. Elizabeth!

They run down the steps, NANNY *following* ELIZA-
BETH.

CONWAY (*warmly*). Well, how are you?
JO. Fine.
CONWAY. So nice of you to come. I'm very pleased you could
manage it, I must say. Was it very inconvenient?
JO. No, no, it's all right, don't quite know what . . .
CONWAY. No, it's a bit of a mystery, isn't it, never mind, let's
have some tea.

Calls.

Miss!

Then.

Got a surprise did you, when I phoned?
Ha-ha. Still, I think secret meetings are rather gay,
don't you?
JO. Well, it depends on what . . . they're all about.
CONWAY. Ah! Too true! What are you going to have, brown
bread and jam, or marmalade, scones, toasted tea
cakes, a lettuce sandwich, cucumber sandwich,
cakes, gateaux, pastries, Welsh rarebits, anything
you like.

A WAITRESS *has come up to the table.*

(*To* WAITRESS.) Isn't that true?
WAITRESS. What?
CONWAY. That we can have anything we like.
WAITRESS. Anything that's on there.
CONWAY. Well, what'll it be?

JO. Just tea.

CONWAY. Really? That all? Ah well, right, tea for two, and . . . (*looks at menu.*) . . . tea for two. Wait a minute, what about lemon tea? Look, it's on the menu.

JO. All right, lemon tea.

CONWAY (*to* WAITRESS). Lemon tea – for two.

WAITRESS *goes off.*

I nearly missed it. I nearly missed it on the menu, didn't see it, and then suddenly I looked and there it was – lemon tea! How are you? You look marvellous.

JO. Yes, I am. You seem in pretty good trim yourself.

CONWAY. I always am, quite frankly. I'm always on top of the world, as a matter of fact. Feel better after your stay in the Nursing Home, do you?

JO. Yes. Oh, thank you for the flowers.

CONWAY. Don't mention it. Beth and I thought of you a lot. Yes, we did. We thought of you a great deal. Especially quite recently.

WAITRESS *brings tea.*

(*To* WAITRESS.) Oh, thanks. Lovely.

Pause. WAITRESS *goes off.*

It's rather fun meeting you like this, isn't it? Just you and me. All alone. You're an intelligent woman. Why don't we make a habit of it, eh? (*He takes her hand, continues.*) What do you think?

She looks at his hand on hers – withdraws hers slowly.

JO (*with a smile*). I'd have to ask my husband.

CONWAY. Oh yes, of course, you're married aren't you. Yes. Yes, that reminds me of what I wanted to talk to you about. I'll tell you what it is. It's nothing much. It's just that a letter has come into my hands, you see. I won't bother to tell you how. But anyway, I've got this letter on me, you see. I mean, I've got

it on me now, you see, in my pocket . . . can I
read you . . . something of it . . . ?

Pause.

JO. Why?

CONWAY. It's from my wife. (*Takes out letter, opens it, reads.*)
'Jake baby, How are you, honey lamb, are you still
managing without me? Poor darling . . .'

Another angle on JO *listening,* CONWAY'S VOICE
continues, very dim, indecipherable.
Another angle on CONWAY *reading.*

'. . . Don't let your eyes stray to those luscious bits
hanging round the set, they're no good when it
comes to it as well you know. I'm saving myself for
you like you told me, although it's pretty difficult,
you understand . . .'

Another angle on JO *listening.*
Another angle on CONWAY *reading.*

'. . . waiting to soothe you, honey love. How
brave, courageous, and tough you are to face it all
alone . . .'

CONWAY *and* JO *at table.*

I've been checking up. He rang her this morning.
Did you know that? When they were in the studio,
he sent her flowers every day, did you know *that*?
He's crazy about her, duckie, he's mad about her.
He can't keep off it. He had that other one before
Beth, whats-her-name, it doesn't matter, until she
got fed up with him. He's not much good in bed, I
understand.

JO *stands up. He pulls her down. She holds her side.*

JO. I'm ill.

CONWAY. You had an abortion, didn't you? Shall I tell you
why? Because Beth's a good girl at heart, she
would have left him. He made you have it so that he
could keep Beth. She told me, for Christ's sake!

She's a lovely girl. She's going to starve for me. She's going to starve. I wouldn't touch her with a barge pole, not even if she came crawling . . .

JO. I want to go.

CONWAY. Listen, if he ever rings her or sees her again, I'll fry him. You understand? I'll boil him. You tell him that.

JO. No.

CONWAY. You'd better. He's not a grown man, your husband, he's a puking boy. He can't even lay a girl without the whole world knowing it. Beth says he makes her sick with his slop. I made her swear on the baby's head she was telling the truth. I brought the baby in and told her to swear on its head. Tell him to keep off, well off . . .

JO. You can tell him yourself.

CONWAY. If I hear his stinking voice I'll pull it out of his throat.

JO. Is that all? I want to go.

CONWAY. Listen. Tell me something. Is it true that when he's in bed he likes to . . .

JO *stands, runs out of the café.*

Exterior. Teashop.
JO, *clasping her side, running, past monkeys.*

Interior. Sitting-room. Night.
JAKE *and* JO.

JO. Did you sleep with Philpot?

JAKE. Oh, Christ, it's years ago, it's gone –

JO. Did you?

JAKE. Yes, of course I did.

JO. You told me you hadn't.

JAKE. I lied. So what? What else did you expect me to do?

JO. Here? In the house?

JAKE. I don't remember. Yes.

JO. Often?

JAKE. As often as we could. What's the point? What the hell does it matter?

JO. What about all the others?

JAKE. What others?

JO. The others.

JAKE. There weren't any others.

JO. How many?

JAKE. Half a dozen. A dozen. I don't know. What does the number matter?

JO. When you were away, or when you were here?

JAKE. When I was away! Is that what you want me to say?

JO. If it's true.

JAKE. Then it was while I was away.

Pause.

You live in a dream world, you know that?

Pause.

JO. Why did you marry me?

JAKE. You know why.

JO. What do you think of marriage?

JAKE. It doesn't exist, it doesn't exist, so what? What do you mean? It doesn't matter what I think about it. It exists, that's what I think about it.

JO. Why did you go to bed with Beth?

JAKE. Oh –

JO. Didn't you ever . . . try not to?

JAKE. Yes . . . Yes.

JO. When I was in the nursing home, didn't you mind?

JAKE. Mind? Of course I minded! I came to see you every evening, didn't I?

JO. And you met her afterwards.

JAKE. That's ridiculous, for God's sake, it's –

JO. Where did you meet?

JAKE. It's not true!

JO. Near the nursing home?

JAKE. Not very far. I don't know where it was. Anyway, it never happened. What are you doing? You haven't exactly been a model of faithfulness yourself, have you?

JO. I was never unfaithful to anyone. To anyone. Ever.

JAKE. Christ, what a bloody hypocrite you are.

JO. Did you stay the night, or just a few hours?

JAKE. Why don't you shut up? Why don't you die?

JO. How should I die?

JAKE. I don't know. Leave me.

JO. I can die here . . . What shall we do?

JAKE. Nothing. I love you. I've always loved you.

JO. He says you love her. He says you make her sick with your love.

JAKE. He's crazy, he's a madman.

JO. Was Philpot the first, or were there others before?

JAKE. Of course there weren't.

JO. How many? Who were they?

JAKE. What others?

JO. How often?

JAKE. There weren't any others.

JO. Did you bring them here?

JAKE. How could I bring them here?

JO. Where did you take them?

JAKE. It never happened.

Exterior. Garden of JO's *father's house, shooting from garden through house to front. Afternoon.*
We can see right through the house to the front gate where the Floride is parked. JO *and* MOTHER *are walking into house.* JO *is carrying an overnight bag. She walks uncertainly, nervously.* MOTHER *is talking without pause.*

MOTHER. I don't know what to do. I wish I knew what to do. I've been sitting here, thinking about it. And then you came. I had a feeling you'd come. I don't know what to do, but I think we ought to face it. You're shivering. Are you cold?

JO. No.

The MOTHER *continues talking and, as she does so, moves forward into foreground, into the garden.* JO *puts bag down, stands a moment in doorway alone before following.*

MOTHER (*as she comes into garden*). Put your bag down. It's not cold. But we've got to face it. George loved his garden. He wouldn't want strangers in his garden with spades and things digging up his garden. I'm not going to do it. I've made up my mind. Don't you think I'm right.

JO (*joining her*). Yes.

Another angle as they approach a table on the lawn where tea is laid out. Deck chairs.

MOTHER. When the boys get back we'll have tea.

JO. The boys?

MOTHER. Pete and Jack. They came to see me yesterday. They'll always come, they said. George was so fond of them. He was fond of Jake too. They'll be back in a minute, then we'll have tea. I was so pleased you had such a sensible operation. So sensible. It must be so wonderful for Jake, not to have that awful worry over his head any more. He's worked so hard for you.

In the distance by the back gate, behind some bushes, we see the boys, PETE *and* JACK, *meandering haphazardly, kicking a ball slowly between them.* JO *watches them approach.*

George would never forgive me. He loved his garden, but the boys will look after it.

The BOYS *appear on the lawn, approach slowly, kicking.*

They're here. They came in the back gate.

The BOYS *reach them, with the ball. They smile faintly at* JO, *who does the same.*

Did you come in the back gate?

PETE. Mmmm.

MOTHER. Did you see who's here?

The BOYS *mutter 'hullo'.* JO *does the same.*

PETE (*to* JO). You're looking very well.

JACK. Very well.

MOTHER. We'll have tea in a minute. Pete won the hundred yards. Did you tell your mother?

JACK *giggles.*

JO (*to* PETE). Did you?

PETE. Yeh. The two–twenty, too.

JO. Oh good.

Silence.

PETE. I like your car.

JACK. It's a Floride.

JO. Yes.

PETE. Good car. Fast.

PETE *kicks the ball to* JACK. *The* BOYS *sit on the grass.*

Did you have lots of traffic?

JO. Traffic?

PETE. On the way down.

JO. Oh. No.

Silence. JACK *turns on his front, whispers something to* PETE. *They giggle.* MOTHER *closes her eyes, murmurs:*

MOTHER (*murmuring*). I often think . . .

The BOYS *whisper and giggle.*

. . . the birds wake me up now . . .

PETE *balances the ball on his head.*

. . . every morning . . .

JO *sits in deckchair, clutching her arms.*

Interior. Sitting-room. Day.
JO *at window.*
She goes to table, looks in an address book, puts it down. Goes to mantelpiece. One bottle on it. She

pours a drink, looks at bottle. It is almost empty.
Knock at door.

JO. Come in.

Door opens. SMALLEST CHILD *comes in, on reins,*
held from outside. Young NANNY *can just be seen*
in hall.

NANNY. Say 'Good-bye Mummy'.

JO *and* CHILD *look at each other. Silence.* JO *looks*
at CHILD. CHILD *totters, smiles, is doubtful.*

Say 'Good-bye Mummy'.

JO *stands still.*
The reins tighten. The NANNY *remains outside.*
CHILD *scratches its head.*

JO. Have a nice walk.

CHILD *is pulled back, looks round for* NANNY.
CHILD *disappears. Hear bells on reins tinkling.*

Interior. Hall. Night.
Empty. Doorbell rings.
Another angle.
JO *opens door, drink in hand. A* JAMAICAN *in*
camelhair coat, beard.

MAN. Good evening.

JO. Good evening.

MAN. I hope you are not alarmed by my call.

JO. No.

MAN. May I introduce myself to you?

JO. Yes. Do.

MAN. I am the new King of Israel, appointed by Yahweh,
the Eternal Lord God. I have come to give you
my blessing.

Pause.

I have been anointed. I am the King of Judah.

JO. I see.

MAN. In the Emphasized Bible, the name of Yahweh appears over seven thousand times. I have been appointed to fulfil the prophecy in Ezekiel. The prophecy appears seventy-two times in the Book of Ezekiel.

Bows his head.

I bless you.

JO. Would you . . . come inside a second . . .

Interior. Hall. Another angle.
The MAN *stands.*

JO. Just a minute.

Interior. Sitting-room.
JO *goes to desk, looking for purse. The* MAN *can be seen in the hall.*

MAN. The people are unhappy because they give the gift of their love to unworthy men and unworthy women.

JO *finds purse on mantelpiece, takes out five shillings. When she turns the* MAN *is in the room.*

Continents are no obstruction, mountains are no obstruction, oceans are no impediment. The Word is the work.

She gives him the money.

JO. Here, please.

MAN. This will help me. My aim is to build a radio station in Jerusalem.

The phone rings. JO *half turns, uncertain.*

The music of the Word can emanate and issue out through the miracle of the medium of the modern channels of communication . . .

JO. Excuse me.

She picks up phone.

CONWAY'S VOICE (*over phone*). Mrs Armitage – ?

    JO. She's not in.

Pause.

CONWAY'S

    VOICE. That's you, isn't it?

    JO. I don't know what you mean.

CONWAY'S

    VOICE. All right. Give her a message. Tell her Beth Conway's pregnant.

Another angle on JO.
Silence.

It's not mine. I thought she might be interested.

    JO. I'll tell her.

CONWAY'S

    VOICE. Tell her my wife's going to have this kid in a public ward, and if there's any way of stopping her getting a whiff of gas I'll find it.

    JO. She can't have it.

CONWAY'S

    VOICE. She's going to have it all right. She's going to wipe its bottom and stare at its ugly mug for the rest of her life. No more gay life for my little Beth. This kid's going to make her curse Jake Armitage until she's dead . . . I'm going to grind the slime out of her. I'm going to see her oozing in her own slime. Until she's dead. She's going to hate that kid almost as much as I will. I'm going to see that she bleeds to death in Jake Armitage's dirt.

Another angle to include MAN.
JO *puts the phone down. She turns, looks at the* MAN. *He smiles.*

    MAN. You will be blessed for this.

Interior. Main bedroom.
Close on JO's *fist crashing into* JAKE's *face. A violent clash of wrists, gasps, sobs, broken sounds.*

JO's *feet kicking.*
JAKE's *arm and elbow thrusting her away.*
Her nails.
His hand striking her.
His shirt torn.
Her nails on his neck.
His hands at her throat.
Her body falling spread-eagled on the floor.
A bedroom stool hurtling across the room.
Dressing-table mirror as stool smashes into it. It shatters.
Silence. Moans. Breathing.
Long shot. Main bedroom. JO *and* JAKE.
They remain still, staring at each other, panting.

Interior. Bedroom in GILES's *flat. Evening.*
JO *and* GILES *in bed.* JO *is half dressed. They are smoking and drinking tea.*

JO (*murmuring*). You always were the sexiest of my husbands.

GILES. Was I?

JO. Hmmm.

Pause.

Why did I leave you?

GILES. I was too sexy.

JO. Yes, perhaps that was it. Perhaps I should try each of my old husbands in turn, see what it's like.

GILES. You could. One of them's dead, that's the trouble.

JO. Which one?

GILES. The one I took over from. Remember? You were a widow at the time.

JO. Oh yes, of course. He was in the army or something, wasn't he?

GILES. That's right. Killed in action.

JO. Well, I couldn't try him again then.

GILES. Old husbands are only good for a night. Dead husbands are only good for a night.

JO. Are they?

GILES. Yes.

JO. But you cried when I left you.

GILES. Did I?

JO. You were heartbroken.

GILES. Yes, I cried. I remember.

JO. That means you must still be mad about me.

GILES. I'm not.

JO. Why not?

GILES. You've changed. You go to bed with your clothes on.

JO. That's only because I have scars I don't want you to see.

GILES. You always had scars.

JO. I have a very new scar.

GILES. What about your husband? Does he mind?

JO. Oh, he doesn't mind. He did it himself, with a monkey wrench.

Interior. Bar of London Club. Evening.
JAKE sitting alone at the end of the long bar. A group of MEN are in foreground. CONWAY is one of them, although we don't immediately see him. The MEN are laughing. BARMAN moves down the bar towards JAKE with a drink, as:

FIRST MAN. Cyril? Now wait a minute, I haven't seen Cyril –

SECOND MAN. I haven't seen him since –

FIRST MAN. Just a minute, let me think –

SECOND MAN. Cyril?

Laughs.

My goodness!

FIRST MAN. Wait a minute, let me . . . Just a minute, let me think . . .

JAKE is given his drink and looks up. CONWAY raises his glass.

CONWAY (*calling*). Cheers! How's the wife?

(*To the two MEN.*)

Will you excuse me a moment. Friend of mine.

FIRST MAN. Yes, of course.

(*To* SECOND MAN.)

I'll tell you the last time I saw Cyril . . .

JAKE *and* CONWAY *together on bar stools.*

CONWAY. You don't mind my coming up to speak to you, do you? I mean, I know that script writers after a hard day's work at the studio like a little drink in peace. But when I saw you I said to myself, my goodness, there's Jake Armitage, I've been to his house, we've met, I wonder if he'd mind if I had a word with him.

JAKE. What makes you think script writers mind being spoken to?

CONWAY. Don't they?

JAKE. Script writers love being spoken to.

CONWAY. Really?

JAKE. Anyway, it isn't often I get a night out with the boys.

CONWAY. Oh, where's your little wife tonight then?

JAKE. She's opening the Chelsea Flower Show.

CONWAY. Go on!

Pause.

JAKE. By the way, do you play snooker?

CONWAY. I do, as a matter of fact.

JAKE. What a shame I don't.

CONWAY. What games do you play?

JAKE. What games? Do you know, honestly, I can't remember. What games do you play?

CONWAY. Snooker for one.

JAKE. I bet you're pretty good.

CONWAY. Not as good as you.

JAKE. But I don't play.

CONWAY. I don't believe a word of it.

JAKE. Cheers.

A MAN *passes.*

MAN. Hello, Jake.

JAKE raises his head and smiles.

CONWAY. Oh, you haven't heard the glad tidings, have you?
JAKE. What's that?
CONWAY. My wife's going to have a baby.
JAKE. Is that so? I say!
CONWAY. Yes, you and your wife must come round to see it. I understand she's very fond of children.
JAKE. Yes, we'd adore to. How is your wife, by the way?
CONWAY. Tip top. She's at a reception tonight for the Duchess of Dubrovnik.
JAKE. I thought she *was* the Duchess of Dubrovnik.
CONWAY. My wife? No, no, not at all. Not at all. Not at all.
JAKE (*laughing*). Well, you're not the bloody Duke anyway.

JAKE's glass slips from his hand, falls on CONWAY's lap and then to the floor. Whisky stains CONWAY's trousers.

CONWAY. You've made me wet.

They stare at each other, their faces close together, bending forward on their bar stools.

*Interior. Bedroom in GILES's flat. Evening.
GILES sits on bed. JO strokes his arm.*
JO. Shall I stay?

GILES smiles, ruffles her hair.

GILES (*gently*). No, you can't. Killer.

She stiffens.

JO. What do you mean? Killer? It's him. He's responsible. He is.
GILES. He phoned this morning.
JO. Did he? Why? Is his bed cold? He doesn't suffer. What has he suffered? It's happened to me. It's me. Look at me. Look at me.

GILES. I am.

They stare at each other for a moment. She slowly closes her eyes. Silence. She suddenly whispers.

JO. What should I have done? It was the only thing I ever really . . . that I ever really . . . I've lost it. There was something we had . . . It's gone.

Slight pause.

I don't know . . . how to keep things . . . whole.

Slight pause.

GILES. He phoned to say his father's dead.

Exterior. Cemetery. Day.
It is very windy and dull. A coffin is being lowered into a grave. There is a spare group of elderly men, obviously friends of JAKE's *father, around the grave.* JAKE *stands alone.*
As the PARSON *speaks a short prayer, which we can hardly hear through the wind, we see that* JO *has joined the group on the other side of the grave from* JAKE.
JAKE *steps forward and throws earth into the grave, then steps back to where he was.*
JO *moves round towards* JAKE. *As she does so, we see the old men begin to throw earth into the grave.*
JO *stands beside* JAKE, *takes his hand, looks at him. He glances at her and then away. His hand slips from hers. She looks at him. His gaze is fixed on the grave.*
JAKE *turns and walks out of the cemetery.*
The gravediggers begin to fill in the grave.
JO *is left standing.*

Exterior. Hillside leading to new house. Late after-noon.
JO *walking up towards new house.*

Interior. Main room of new house.
JO *enters. Enormous windows high up, looking down at the silent stillness of the fields. The sky a mist. Mist hanging in the valleys. Noise of birds.*
The rooms are empty except for isolated pieces of furniture. JO *pauses for a moment, then locks all the doors.*

Interior. Kitchen of new house.
JO *wanders in. No food. No sign of life. Empty. Unused. Bare.*

Interior. Main room.
JO *takes telephone off hook, sits down by window.*
The window.
Sun through mist.

Interior. Main room. Cats.
Snaking, on bare floorboards.

Interior. Bedroom. New house. Night.
JO *lying awake. The moon through the uncurtained windows.*
Cats asleep on bed.

Interior. Main room. Night. JO.
At window, smoking.
The window. Daylight.

Interior. Staircase.
JO *climbs stairs.*

Interior. Room at top of new house.
JO *enters, opens window, looks down towards barn.*

JO's face.
Another angle : JO at window.
She opens window wider. Stops.
JO's face.
Another angle : JO at window.
In the distance, through the window, see numbers of
CHILDREN *fanning out like trappers, converging*
on house, JAKE *bringing up the rear.*
Close-up on children's legs.
Sticks whipping grass.
Long shot. JAKE *and* CHILDREN.
JO *at window motionless. She shuts window. Calls*
from CHILDREN *as they reach house. Bangs on the*
locked doors. Glass breaking. Door opening. Sudden
flood of voices.

CHILD'S VOICE. Where is she ?

SECOND
CHILD'S VOICE. Upstairs.

THIRD
CHILD'S VOICE. Probably still in bed.

FOURTH
CHILD'S VOICE. I'm going to feed the cats.

JAKE'S VOICE. JO –

JO's face calms, becomes still.
High angle shooting down staircase.
JO *walks down the stairs towards them, stops midway.*
JAKE *stands at foot of stairs, arms full of parcels,*
surrounded by CHILDREN. *The* CHILDREN *look*
at JO *curiously, but do not go to her.*

JAKE. We thought we might join you for a while.

He goes towards the kitchen with some of the
CHILDREN, *also carrying parcels. Other* CHILDREN
rush past JO *up the stairs. She remains standing on*
the stairs.

Interior. Kitchen. New house.
JAKE *and* CHILDREN *undoing parcels.* JO *can be*
seen on the stairs in background.

JAKE. Where's that coffee pot?

CHILD (*shouting to* JO). We didn't know where you were.

JAKE. Let's give it a wash. Get the cups out, Dinah.

DINAH. Where are they?

CHILD. I know.

> *More* CHILDREN *rush in with cats. During the ensuing dialogue* JO *slowly descends the stairs and enters the kitchen. The* CHILDREN *speak to her from a distance, tentatively.*

JAKE. Did we bring any milk?

CHILD ONE. Where's the big red ball?

JAKE. Later. Who's got the milk? Where are all those bags?

DINAH. Let me do it.

CHILD THREE (*to* JO). I've got a bandage. Look!

CHILD TWO. I want some orange squash.

JAKE (*pulling cans of beer from bag*). Where's the opener?

CHILD ONE. I won't play with it. I just want to put in on the grass.

DINAH. Put all that paper in the bin.

JAKE. The opener . . .

CHILD THREE (*to* JO). Can I tell you a story?

CHILD TWO (*to* JO). I've got ten stars for reading.

> DINAH *hands opener to* JAKE.

DINAH. Here you are. Do you want cabbage or carrots?

> JAKE *opens beer can. It spurts.* CHILDREN *react noisily.*

I'll wipe it.

CHILD FOUR. I'll do it.

DINAH. Where's the tea–cloth?

> JAKE *offers can of beer to* JO.

JAKE. Want one?

JO. Yes, I'll have one.

> *She takes it, starts drinking from the can.*

The Quiller Memorandum

The Quiller Memorandum was first presented by
The Rank Organization on 10th November 1966
with the following cast:

KENNETH LINDSAY JONES	Herbert Stass
RUSHINGTON	Robert Flemyng
GIBBS	George Sanders
QUILLER	George Segal
POL	Alec Guinness
HENGEL	Peter Carsten
BARMAN	Hans Schwarz
DORFMANN	Victor Beaumont
HASSLER	Gunter Meisner
WENG	Robert Helpmann
SCHOOL PORTER	Konrad Thoms
FRAU SCHROEDER	Edith Schneider
INGE	Senta Berger
MAN, A	John Rees
MAN, B	Philip Madoc
MAN, C	Harry Brooks
GRAUBER	Ernst Walder
MAN, F	Bernard Egan
OKTOBER	Max von Sydow
DOCTOR	Paul Hansard
MAN, H	Sean Arnold
MAN, I	Janos Kurucz
BARMAN	Carl Duering
NIGHTPORTER	Philo Hauser
ASSISTANT	Brigitte Laufer
MAN, J	Nikolaus Dutsch
NAGEL	Ves Delahunt
MAN, K	Peter Lang
MAN, L	Herbert Fux
MAN, M	Peer Goldmann
MAN, N	Malte Petzel
MAN, O	Axel Anderson
MAN, P	Wolfgang Priewe
HUGHES	Claus Tinney

Directed by Michael Anderson

The Quiller Memorandum

Exterior. Berlin Tiergarten. Summer night.
A long road. Derelict buildings at either side.
It is late at night.
In the distance, KENNETH LINDSAY JONES *is walking towards the camera.*
Silence.
The camera moves sideways to disclose a brightly lit telephone box. It is the one hard source of light.
His face, as he stops by a lamp post. He lights one cigarette from another, flips the first one away and glances up at the buildings and along the road behind him.
There is no one in sight.
He continues to walk towards the telephone box.
From the telephone box see him approach.
His footsteps echo. He walks slowly past the telephone box and stops. He glances up the street again. No one. He drops his cigarette.
He moves suddenly and enters the telephone box.

Interior. Telephone box. Night.
JONES *inserts a coin, lifts receiver. He begins to dial. He dials one figure and a second figure.*
A sudden report. Window smashes. Glass falls in.
JONES *hits interior of box with great force. He falls in a heap, his head cracking against telephone.*

Exterior. Road. Night.
The telephone box, brightly lit. A shape on the floor.
No movement or sound along the road.

Interior. London club. Day.
A WAITER *is serving potatoes to two gentlemen.*

RUSHINGTON. Thanks. That's . . . quite sufficient, thank you.

The WAITER *nods and goes.*

GIBBS. Salt?

RUSHINGTON. Oh, thanks.

They salt their food and begin to eat.

GIBBS. What exactly is he doing now?

RUSHINGTON. He's on leave, actually. On vacation.

GIBBS. Ah.

They eat.

Well, perhaps someone might get in touch with him.

RUSHINGTON. Oh yes, certainly. No difficulty about that.

GIBBS. Ask him if he'd mind popping over to Berlin.

RUSHINGTON. Mmmm. I think so.

GIBBS. Good.

They eat.

Shame about K.L.J.

RUSHINGTON. Mmmm.

GIBBS. How was he killed?

RUSHINGTON. Shot.

GIBBS. What gun?

RUSHINGTON. Long shot in spine, actually. Nine point three. Same as Metzler.

GIBBS. Oh, really?

They eat.

How's your lunch?

RUSHINGTON. Rather good.

GIBBS. What is it?

RUSHINGTON. Pheasant.

GIBBS. Ah. Yes, that should be rather good. Is it?

RUSHINGTON. It is rather, yes.

Exterior. Olympic Stadium. Berlin. Day.
QUILLER *is walking towards the entrance, away from the camera. He passes through the gates.*

Interior. Olympic Stadium. Day.
A group of people pass in foreground.
As their voices recede, the camera remains on POL
who is sitting on the edge of one of the tiers below.
He is eating sandwiches.
QUILLER *comes into the foreground and stands for a*
moment looking down at POL, *his back still to the*
camera.
QUILLER *descends the steps and stops by the side of*
POL.
POL *does not look up. He continues eating.*

QUILLER. Excuse me. Do you have a light?

POL *looks up.*

POL. Certainly.

POL *takes out a lighter and lights* QUILLER's *cigar-*
ette.
As QUILLER *bends to the light his face is seen for the*
first time.
QUILLER *takes a packet of Chesterfields from his*
pocket.

QUILLER. Do you smoke this brand?
POL. No I don't think I know that brand.
QUILLER. Perhaps I might introduce it to you.
POL. Thank you.

POL *takes a cigarette from the packet and puts it in*
his top pocket. He moves his legs and indicates the
seat beside him. QUILLER *crosses him and sits down.*
POL *bites into his sandwich and grins at* QUILLER.
Ever been here before?

QUILLER. No.
POL. Impressive isn't it? Built by Werner in 1936. For
the Olympics. It holds one hundred thousand
people. (*He points.*) Certain well-known personali-
ties used to stand right up there. Must have been
quite noisy. One hundred thousand people – all
cheering. Wouldn't you say? Yes, quite noisy.

He offers the sandwiches to QUILLER.

Some leberwurst?

QUILLER. No thanks.

POL. Or some schinken? (*He examines the sandwich.*) No,
wait a moment, what am I talking about, this isn't
schinken, it's knackwurst. What about some
knackwurst?

QUILLER. I'm not hungry.

POL. Aren't you? I am.

*He bites into the sandwich, chews a moment and then
stands.*

You don't mind if I eat while we walk?

*He walks up to the circular covered passageway which
runs round the perimeter of the Stadium.*
QUILLER *remains seated for a second. He then stands
abruptly and walks up to join* POL.

QUILLER. What do you want?

POL. You've been on holiday, I understand.

QUILLER. I *am* on holiday.

POL. By the sea?

QUILLER. What do you want?

POL. Oh, my name's Pol, by the way.

QUILLER. What?

POL. Pol.

QUILLER. Mine's Quiller.

POL. I know that.

(*Pause.*)

I understand you've been working in the Middle
East for some time.

QUILLER. Yes, I've been working there.

POL. We've been engaged in some rather tough work
here. I think we're coping moderately well with the
situation in other parts of the country, but it's
getting a little out of hand in Berlin. They're
quite a tough bunch. Nazi from top to toe. In
the classic tradition. But not just the remains of the
old lot. Oh no. There's quite a bit of new blood.

Youth. Firm believers. Very dangerous. It won't do to underestimate them.

They walk.

Quite complex, of course, the over-all issue. Difficult to pinpoint. Nobody wears a brown shirt now, you see. No banners. Consequently, they're difficult to recognize – they look like everybody else. They move in various walks of life all over the country but they're very careful and quite clever and they look like everybody else. Intriguing. Don't you think? However, I agree with you – that's all politics. Not our job. I'll tell you what our job is. Our job is to get to the hard core – the extreme element – the ones you *can* recognize – if you get close enough to see them. The hard core. They have a base here. But we don't know where it is. We need, rather urgently, to find it.

QUILLER. I've read the files.

POL. The files till when?

QUILLER. Till June.

POL. Oh yes, of course, you've been on holiday. You read them while you were in London, did you?

QUILLER. That's right.

POL. Who was our leading operator here, in the last file you saw?

QUILLER. Metzler.

POL. He's dead. Another colleague of yours took over from him. Kenneth Lindsay Jones.

QUILLER. Uh-huh.

POL. He's dead too. He was killed two days ago. Long range nine point three, in the spine.

QUILLER's *face.*

We'd like you to take over.

POL *takes the cigarette from his top pocket and lights it.*

He was obstinate. He refused cover. If he'd allowed us to give him cover he might not be dead and we might have a little more idea of where he'd got to.

QUILLER. He was justified in using any method he thought fit.

POL. Not a very efficient method – in his case.

QUILLER. What do you know about it? You only talk to people.

They stare at each other.

POL. This is a very strong operation. Fully urgent. They have killed two of our men. We want you to take over from Jones.

Pause.

I've been asked to say that this is not an order but a request. Consider it, will you? At your leisure. I'll give you five minutes. Perhaps you would join me for coffee in Section E at – (*Looks at watch.*) – 11.26.

POL *strolls away.*

QUILLER *looks after him.*

Exterior. Hotel. Berlin. Day.
People passing. Taxis drawing up. Lights. Traffic.
QUILLER *walks down steps of hotel. He stops, lights a cigarette. He glances lightly across the street. His eyes run quickly along the windows opposite. Smoking, he looks along the street. Among all the people moving there is one person stationary. He is standing under a lamp post by a newspaper stand, reading a paper.*
QUILLER *walks up the street, past the man, buys a paper at the paper stand and walks back past the man.*

Exterior. Berlin. Day.
QUILLER *walking. Crowds of people.* QUILLER *looks behind him, casually. The* MAN *is standing some way along the pavement, reading a theatre bill.*

QUILLER *walks quickly towards a bookshop and goes in.*
The MAN *follows at a distance.*

Exterior. Side exit. Bookshop.
QUILLER *walks through the bookshop and out by the side exit.*
From the same point of view see the MAN *approach the main entrance.*
He peers through the window into the shop and enters.
He looks about, observes the side exit and walks quickly out by it.
He stands on the pavement and looks about.
There is no sign of QUILLER.
The MAN *walks quickly down the street.*
QUILLER *enters the shop and follows him.*

Exterior. Berlin. Day.
QUILLER *walking. He watches, from a distance, between moving figures. The* MAN'S *head twisting, looking about him. The* MAN *goes to the edge of the road and looks across it. He stands, looks at newspaper in his hand and throws it into the gutter.*
He goes into a small bar.

Interior. Bar.
The man, HENGEL, *is sitting at a table with a glass of beer. He is alone in the bar.*
QUILLER *enters, crosses to* HENGEL'S *table and sits.*
HENGEL *stares at him.* QUILLER *smiles.*
Silence.
The BARMAN *moves towards the table.*
QUILLER. I'd like a double Jack Daniels on the rocks. Do you have it?
BARMAN. Yes, sir.

The BARMAN *goes back to bar.*
QUILLER *smiles at* HENGEL.

QUILLER. Would you like to see the evening paper?

He passes his newspaper across to HENGEL.
HENGEL *does not pick it up.*
They look at each other.
The BARMAN *brings the whisky.* QUILLER *drinks.*
HENGEL *takes out a packet of Chesterfields.*

HENGEL. Do you smoke this brand?
QUILLER. No, I don't think I know that brand.
HENGEL. Perhaps I might introduce it to you.
QUILLER. Would you say they're milder than other brands?
HENGEL. They're milder than some other brands.
QUILLER. Okay, I'll try one.

They light their cigarettes.

HENGEL. I lost you.
QUILLER. Why? Were you following me?
HENGEL. You were playing a game with me. I didn't appreciate it.
QUILLER. Now come on, don't be silly, you might have been one of the adverse party.
HENGEL. They don't know you're here. Yet.
QUILLER. You don't think so?
HENGEL. No. I'm one of your cover, by the way.
QUILLER. Hi.

Pause.

HENGEL. I'd like to ask what method you intend to employ.
QUILLER. Well . . .

He clicks fingers at BARMAN, *gesturing to man and self.*

Same again.

He turns to HENGEL.

Well, I'll tell you. If you say they don't know I'm here, I think I'd better let them know I'm here. Otherwise how are we ever going to get together?
HENGEL. I see. That's your business. The fact is, I've been asked to give you certain fragments of information,

to do with some of KLJ's movements. We've no idea whether it's of any value.

THE BARMAN *brings the drinks, takes empties and goes.*
QUILLER *looks at* HENGEL.

QUILLER. What's your name?
HENGEL. Hengel.
QUILLER. Why are you so tense, Hengel?
HENGEL. Are you being funny?
QUILLER. Look at your hand. It's so tight. And look at your skin. Your skin's terrible.

Pause.

HENGEL. I have a feeling, Mr Quiller, that you won't find life here so funny for very long.
QUILLER. Why don't you drink your beer?
HENGEL. I don't want it.
QUILLER. I bought it for you.
HENGEL. You can't make me want it, Mr Quiller.

QUILLER *takes* HENGEL's *beer.*

QUILLER. Well, I need a chaser.

He drinks.

HENGEL. I worked with KLJ. I knew him.
QUILLER. Oh, really?
HENGEL. I was one of his cover until he insisted that all his cover was called off. I consider that to have been a very stupid decision, if I may say so, on his part. Once he was alone, of course, he was killed. I knew he would die. Did you know him?

Pause.

QUILLER. Yes, I did.
HENGEL. If he'd allowed me to stay with him I could have saved his life.

QUILLER *looks at him and finishes his drink.*

QUILLER. Give me the information.

HENGEL. What?

QUILLER. You said you had information. Give it to me.

> HENGEL *glances at* BARMAN, *takes an envelope out of his pocket and puts it on the table.*
>
> QUILLER *slits the envelope and takes out various pieces of paper.*
>
> *There are two torn tickets, one from a bowling alley and one from a swimming pool, and a German newspaper cutting, the headline of which is glimpsed: School Teacher Arrested – War Crimes.*
>
> QUILLER *puts these items in his pocket, stands and walks to the door.*
>
> QUILLER *goes out, leaving* HENGEL *at table.*

> *Interior. Bowling Alley.*
> *Lines of men bowling. Some lanes empty.* QUILLER *walking with manager* (DORFMANN).

QUILLER. Yes, I'm thinking of starting a big chain of these places in the States.

DORFMANN. Don't they have quite a few there already?

QUILLER. Yes. Oh quite a few. Quite a few. Thousands. But there's always room for a few more.

DORFMANN. Always.

> *They reach a lane and stop to watch about half a dozen men bowling.*

QUILLER. What kind of business do you do?

DORFMANN. Quite good. We have . . . many regulars.

> *They watch the game.*

QUILLER. Yes, a friend of mine was telling me about this place. He was in here a couple of nights ago. Don't know if you met him. Fellow by the name of Jones – Kenneth Lindsay Jones.

DORFMANN. Jones? No. I don't think so. No. I think I would remember the name.

QUILLER. Yes.

> *Pause.*

DORFMANN. Would you like to bowl?

QUILLER *looks at his watch.*

QUILLER. No. Not now thanks. But maybe I'll come back another night.

DORFMANN. Please come back. Show me how to bowl.

They laugh.

QUILLER. Right. Bye Mr Weiss.

DORFMANN. Auf wiedersehen.

QUILLER *goes.*
The last pin is knocked over.

Interior. Indoor swimming bath. Day.
A young man dives from the diving board into the pool. Young men are diving, swimming, sitting at the pool edge. There is a continual echo.
From pool level see QUILLER *appear on the changing room gallery. He is fully dressed. He stands, looking down.*

Interior. Swimming bath gallery.
QUILLER'S *view of the pool. Shining water and bodies. Two men leave the pool and walk up the steps. They look at* QUILLER *curiously and pass him, brushing close.* QUILLER *brushes water from his arm. An* ATTENDANT *approaches him.*

ATTENDANT (*in German*). You are not swimming?

QUILLER. Sorry. I don't understand.

ATTENDANT (*in English*). You are not swimming?

QUILLER. No.

ATTENDANT. This is for swimming, this place.

QUILLER. I'm a coach, back in the States. I teach swimming at Williamsburg, Virginia. I heard some of the best swimmers in Berlin come here. A friend of mine was telling me. An Englishman. Name of Jones.

ATTENDANT. This place is for swimming. You cannot watch. It is not allowed to have onlookers.

QUILLER. Oh, what a pity. I'd hoped I'd have been able to watch.

ATTENDANT. No.

> QUILLER *looks again at the swimmers.*
> *They are diving and swimming with great grace.*

QUILLER. Pity. Well . . . danke.

> *He walks along the gallery and out of the exit.*
> *The* ATTENDANT *watches him go.*

> *Exterior. Swimming bath. Day.*
> QUILLER *comes out of swimming bath into the street.*
> *Across the street a man,* WENG, *leans against a wall.*
> QUILLER *walks to the corner, to a taxi rank, followed by* WENG.
> *He gets into a taxi. It drives off.*
> WENG *gets into a taxi. His taxi follows* QUILLER's.

> *Exterior. Hotel. Day.*
> *Two taxis draw up at hotel.*
> QUILLER *gets out of one, goes up steps into hotel.*
> WENG *gets out of other, looks up at hotel.*
> QUILLER, *at top of hotel steps, glances round at* WENG.
> WENG *walks slowly along.*
> QUILLER *goes through swing doors.*

> *Interior. Hotel lobby.*
> QUILLER *comes through swing doors. He looks out to the front of the hotel. There is no sign of* WENG.
> QUILLER *turns.*
> *In the corner of the lobby* HENGEL *is sitting.* HENGEL *starts to get up.* QUILLER *goes towards him.* HENGEL *sits.*
> QUILLER *sits by him.* HENGEL *is drinking coffee.*

QUILLER. What do you want?

HENGEL. I have been asked to inquire if you carry anything useful.
QUILLER. I don't carry anything.
HENGEL. I think they'll be disturbed to hear that.
QUILLER. Let them be disturbed.
HENGEL. Certain objects can be valuable to a man in your position.
QUILLER. I decide that. You don't.

Pause.

QUILLER. I'm going somewhere. Have another cup of coffee.
HENGEL. It's my job to accompany you.
QUILLER. I don't need you today.
HENGEL. I am your cover. I must keep with you.
QUILLER. Go and see a good movie. Take the day off.
HENGEL. You want a bullet in your spine, too?
QUILLER. There's a spy film on at the Palace.

HENGEL *leans forward.*

HENGEL. I shall report this.

QUILLER *stands and clicks his fingers at the waiter.*

QUILLER. A cognac for the gentleman.

QUILLER *walks out of the hotel.*

Exterior. Hotel. Day.
QUILLER *standing on steps a moment. No sign of* WENG.

Exterior. Hertz garage. Day.
Sign saying 'CAR HIRE' in a number of languages.
QUILLER, *seen from street, walking from office with car keys. He gets into an Auto-Union and drives into the street.*

Exterior. School. Outskirts Berlin. Day.
Children playing in the front playground.

QUILLER walks into the shot, stands a moment look-
ing at the school and then walks towards it.

Exterior. School. Day.
QUILLER enters the school. He can be seen speaking to
a PORTER. The PORTER lifts a telephone, speaks into
it and then points up the stairs.
Children are changing classes. QUILLER walks up the
stairs.

Interior. Headmistress's Study.

QUILLER. My name's Cooper. I'm a journalist.

HEADMISTRESS I speak English, I am afraid, not so very well . . .
(FRAU
SCHROEDER).

QUILLER. Don't speak German at all.

They both laugh, and sit.

HEADMISTRESS. How can I . . . help you?

QUILLER (*briskly*). I'm writing an article for the *Philadelphia World Review*.

HEADMISTRESS. Uh . . . huh?

QUILLER. You haven't heard of it?

HEADMISTRESS. Oh . . . no.

QUILLER. That's because it hasn't started yet. This is going to be the first number.

HEADMISTRESS. Ah.

QUILLER. We in Philadelphia are convinced that current affairs in Europe have a great deal of bearing on the lives of the citizens of Philadelphia – you know, the people back home in Philly.

HEADMISTRESS. Uuh . . . I don't understand . . . exactly . . . what . . .

QUILLER (*speaking very deliberately*). I'm collating material for an article about the Nazi situation in Germany.

HEADMISTRESS. Nazi?

QUILLER *takes out newspaper cutting.*

QUILLER. That's right. We understand that you had a school teacher here recently, name of Steiner, who was discovered to have been a war criminal. Is that right.

HEADMISTRESS. That is . . . so.

QUILLER. Well – we'd like a little more information for our Philly readers.

Pause.

HEADMISTRESS. It was all reported.

QUILLER. I didn't think it was reported in any great detail. The man hanged himself, I believe.

HEADMISTRESS. Hanged?

QUILLER. Yes, you know . . .

QUILLER *mimes a rope round the neck, and jerks it.*

HEADMISTRESS. Oh, hanged . . . yes but I am so sorry, my English . . . I have a teacher here, who has . . . replaced . . . this man. She knows English. Perhaps . . . you would like to speak to her?

QUILLER. Sure. Thanks.

HEADMISTRESS. If you will come with me. I will see if she's still here.

They stand.

Interior. School. Corridor and classroom.
The HEADMISTRESS *leads* QUILLER *down a corridor. Children pass them. They reach the open door of a classroom.* INGE *is within, talking to a little girl.*

Interior. Classroom.
INGE *looks up.* HEADMISTRESS *and* QUILLER *at the door.*
HEADMISTRESS *speaks German.*

HEADMISTRESS. Have you a moment.

INGE (*in German*). Yes, of course. All right, Hilde.

The little girl bobs to them all and goes.

HEADMISTRESS. Inge – this is Herr Cooper – Fräulein Lindt.

They nod to each other and smile.

Herr Cooper is a journalist. He is writing an article about Herr Steiner. Perhaps you might be able to help him – in English.

INGE *(in German)*. Yes, of course.

HEADMISTRESS. Good. (*To* QUILLER.) Good-bye.

QUILLER. Thank you.

She leaves the room.

INGE *and* QUILLER *look at each other for a moment.*

INGE. So – you are writing an article about Herr Steiner?

QUILLER. No, no . . . he's just an item. The article is about the present day Nazi question in Germany. I don't know much about it myself, I've been a sports writer all my life.

INGE. Oh.

QUILLER. But you know what boxing is these days.

INGE. No? What?

QUILLER. The golden days are over. You're not a boxing fan?

INGE. No, I'm not.

QUILLER. Ah.

Pause.

Well listen, this man Steiner, can you tell me anything about him?

INGE. Not very much, I'm afraid.

QUILLER. I mean, what was he like?

INGE. He was a very good teacher.

QUILLER. Was he?

INGE. Oh yes. We were . . . so surprised . . . when we heard about his past. We couldn't believe it. I mean he was so wonderful with the children.

QUILLER. Is that a fact?

INGE. Yes, he seemed to feel . . . I don't know . . . a great responsibility towards them. It's funny, how little you know about people, however closely you work with them. But I . . .

Pause.

QUILLER. What?

INGE. Oh, I think it is true to say that, at heart, he was part of the old Germany.

QUILLER *takes out a notebook.*

QUILLER. That's quite an interesting angle. The old Germany and the new Germany. (*Writing.*) Yes . . . that's quite an interesting angle.

He looks at her.

What would you say were the aims of the new Germany?

INGE. Oh, that's a very big question.

QUILLER. What are your aims?

INGE. Mine?

QUILLER. As a school teacher.

INGE. Oh . . . I think, perhaps . . . to try to teach the children a broader attitude towards Europe, a broader attitude towards the world.

QUILLER. Uh-huh. (*Lifts pencil.*) Mind if I quote that?

INGE (*laughing*). I'm not an important person, really. I'm just a school teacher.

QUILLER. But you're a young German woman. That's what's going to interest the readers back home. The feminine point of view.

INGE. You seem to approach your work with a lot of enthusiasm.

QUILLER. Well listen, that's the kind of man I am. It's all or nothing with me.

They smile.
She puts a few books into her bag and goes for her coat. He watches her.

You've been most helpful.

He helps her with her coat.

Do you live near the school?

INGE. No, I live in Bundesallee.

QUILLER. Why don't I give you a lift?

She looks at him.

INGE. That's very kind of you.

Exterior. Block of flats. Afternoon.
The Auto-Union draws up. INGE *and* QUILLER *get out and stand on the pavement.*

INGE. Thank you.

QUILLER. Thank *you*.

INGE. Good luck . . . with your article.

QUILLER. Yes . . . umm . . .

They stand a moment.

I might like to . . . reach you again . . . about the article. Can I call you?

INGE. I'm at school every day.

She puts out her hand. He shakes it.

Good-bye.

She walks to the door of the block.
He stands, uncertain, suddenly calls to her.

QUILLER. Hey, wait a minute.

He joins her at the door.

That bag looks heavy.

He tests it for weight.

Very heavy.

He looks at her.

Why don't I help you carry it?

INGE *laughs.*

INGE. All right.

Interior. INGE'*s flat. Afternoon.*
QUILLER *is sitting with a drink, stretched out.*

QUILLER. The point about Louis was Louis's co-ordination. Louis had wonderful co-ordination. He was really – (*puts fists into a boxing posture*) – you know – he was really of a piece, that guy. And he had a killer inside him. I mean look what he did to Schmeling.

INGE. Who?

QUILLER. Schmeling. German fighter. Louis killed him.

INGE. I thought Schmeling beat him.

QUILLER. He beat him the first time. But Louis killed him the second time.

INGE. Ah.

QUILLER. He massacred him. Yes, I don't know what it is, but the Germans have been a great disappointment – I mean from the boxing point of view. I mean, you know, you'd think, that the way the German mind goes – I mean the old German mind, not the new German mind – you'd have thought they'd have done well in the fight game. But it ain't worked out like that. We got them beat.

INGE *looks at him with a half smile.*

INGE. So it seems.

QUILLER. But that's the way it goes.

Pause.

INGE. A little more?

QUILLER. Oh, thanks.

INGE *rises, takes his glass, fills it, adds ice.*
He watches her.
She brings glass back to him.
He watches her.
She smiles at him.

INGE. Here you are.

He takes glass.
She turns, fills her own glass.
He watches her.
She sits.

QUILLER. Cheers.

They drink.

What kind of men do you know?

INGE. I don't know many.

QUILLER. Why not?

INGE. Oh, I'm . . . busy.

Pause.

QUILLER. You know, someone was telling me that there are some people who don't think like, for instance, you do.

INGE. How do you mean?

QUILLER. Well, someone was telling me that there are some people here who wouldn't agree with your attitude – about Europe, about education – you know, about things like that.

INGE. That's true, I suppose.

QUILLER. That's what this man was telling me.

INGE. Yes.

Pause.

QUILLER. You mean there are certain people here who believe that this country should be . . . very strong, that it should be dominant?

INGE. That's right.

QUILLER. They still believe that?

INGE. Oh yes. Still.

QUILLER *drinks.*

QUILLER. Well listen, I don't think there's anything basically wrong with that, is there? I mean we believe the same in the States. We believe our country should be strong. I wouldn't say dominant – I mean we don't want to dominate anybody – but I would say strong. Yes, I'd say that.

Silence.

But listen . . . what kind of people are they exactly? Nazis?

INGE. Well, they are . . . I would say. But of course they don't call themselves that any more.

QUILLER. They don't?

INGE. No.

QUILLER. You know, this fits in with what this man was telling me. He was saying that these boys don't show themselves, they keep themselves pretty much under cover.

INGE. Yes. So I believe.

QUILLER. Yes . . . he was saying they've got a kind of long term policy, that they want to infiltrate themselves into the mind of the country, over a period of years. But they're not in any kind of hurry, this time . . . you know . . .

He laughs.

INGE. Yes.

QUILLER. But that they're very convinced men. Very convinced.

INGE. I would say that, yes.

QUILLER. Yes, that's exactly what this man was telling me.

Pause.

INGE. Who is this man?

He looks up from his drink.

QUILLER. What man?

INGE. The man . . . who was talking to you.

QUILLER. Oh, just a guy I met in a bar.

INGE. Oh.

Pause.

Are you going to write about this . . . question . . . in your article?

QUILLER. No, no, it's outside my range. I'm not political. I haven't got a political brain.

INGE. Ah.

They drink.

QUILLER. It's very pleasant here.

INGE. Yes. I like it.

QUILLER. You like living alone?

INGE. I've been alone for a long time. My family was killed in the war.

Pause.

I live for my work now.

Pause.

How long are you staying in Berlin?
QUILLER. Until I've finished my assignment.

Pause.

Why don't we go out one night?
INGE. That would be very nice.

Exterior. Block of flats. Afternoon.
QUILLER *emerges from the building. He stops in the porch and arranges his tie. He then walks in the direction of his car, parked at the side of the road.*
For no apparent reason he walks past his car, without looking at it, and continues round the corner.

Exterior. Other side of block.
QUILLER *suddenly turns on his heel and walks straight back in the direction he has come.*
A man is walking slowly along by the shops.
QUILLER *walks up to him and stands in front of him.*
The man stops, looks at QUILLER *with surprise.*
QUILLER. Are you following me?

Silence.
Then in fluent German.

I said are you following me?
MAN (A) (*in German*). I am not.

The rest of the scene is played in German.

QUILLER. Why are you following me?
MAN. I am not. You are mistaken.

The MAN *attempts to move.* QUILLER *blocks his path.*

MAN. Excuse me.
QUILLER. Where are you going?
MAN. To meet a friend.

QUILLER. Where?
MAN. Here.

QUILLER *turns. Another man stands behind him.*
FIRST MAN *speaks to the* SECOND MAN (B).

FIRST MAN. This man has accused me of following him.
SECOND MAN. Following? Why?
FIRST MAN. I do not know.
SECOND MAN (*to* QUILLER). Why do you say such a thing?

A THIRD MAN (C) *joins the group.*

THIRD MAN. What is the matter?
FIRST MAN. This man is being offensive.
THIRD MAN. Offensive?

THIRD MAN *moves closer to* QUILLER.

THIRD MAN. Are you being offensive?

QUILLER *is closed in by the three men by the shop window.*
He smiles, and speaks to the THIRD MAN.

QUILLER. Don't come any nearer, will you?

Silence. The THIRD MAN *is still.*
QUILLER *smiles at the* FIRST MAN.

Well, perhaps I was mistaken.

Pause.

Perhaps you weren't following me.

The men are silent.
He looks at each of them in turn.
He points at THIRD MAN.

You're in my way.

THIRD MAN *moves back.* QUILLER *walks through them and back down the street. The three remain at the window.*

Exterior. Block of flats.
QUILLER *gets into his Auto-Union and drives off.*

Exterior. Hotel. Early evening.
QUILLER *running up steps of hotel.*
A porter is collecting cases from a taxi and arranging them on the pavement.

Interior. Hotel lobby.
QUILLER *walking through lobby. He stops, grimaces. He has seen* HENGEL *sitting in the corner. He walks over and sits by* HENGEL, *who has a glass of beer in front of him.*

QUILLER. How was the movie? Instructive?

HENGEL. There are two things to tell you. Firstly they do not understand why you carry no kind of instrument.

QUILLER. What's the second thing?

HENGEL. I am still your cover. I will tag you. I am to keep with you.

QUILLER *looks at him.*

QUILLER. You carry instruments, I suppose?

HENGEL. I do.

QUILLER. Yes. Then I'll probably feel more secure with you around.

HENGEL. You should.

QUILLER. You'll see I don't come to any harm.

HENGEL. That's my job.

QUILLER. Well thanks, Hengel. Thanks a lot.

HENGEL *looks at him suspiciously.*

HENGEL. We see that you've hired a car.

QUILLER. That's right.

HENGEL. How is your operation proceeding? We'd all like to know.

QUILLER. It's difficult to say, Hengel.

Pause.

Well, I'm just going for a little ride about the town, to see the sights.

HENGEL. I'll tag you.

QUILLER. Okay.

> QUILLER *stands.*

Don't lose me now.

Exterior. Hotel. Early evening.
QUILLER on steps. He lights a cigarette.

Interior. A window opposite.
A hand on a curtain. Curtain slightly shifts.
QUILLER can be seen standing. A PORTER ascends
hotel steps, with suitcases.

Exterior. Hotel.
QUILLER begins to descend the steps.
The PORTER is going up. As they pass, the PORTER
hoists a suitcase up in his arm. The edge of the case
hits QUILLER on the thigh. QUILLER grimaces, holds
his thigh.

QUILLER. What the hell –

PORTER. Oh, I am sorry, sir.

> QUILLER *rubs his thigh.*

I do apologize, sir.

> HENGEL *comes out of hotel.*

QUILLER. What's your name?

PORTER. Grauber, sir.

> QUILLER *moves down the steps and gets into his car.*
> HENGEL *moves down steps and gets into a Volks-*
> *wagen.*
> *They drive off.*

Interior. Window opposite.
The hand drops the curtain.

Exterior. Berlin streets. Dusk.
QUILLER's *Auto-Union turns sharp left, quickly.*
HENGEL's *Volkswagen follows.*
Auto-Union turns sharp right.
Volkswagen follows.
Auto-Union crosses crossroads at speed.
Volkswagen just makes lights, following.

Interior. Auto-Union.
QUILLER *looking in rear mirror. The Volkswagen just in sight.*
QUILLER *grins.*

Exterior. Streets. Dusk.
Auto-Union turns left, right and right again and comes out into a wide avenue. The Volkswagen is no longer in sight.

Interior. Auto-Union.
QUILLER *chuckling to himself, as he drives.*
He glances in the rear mirror. No sign of the Volks-wagen.
He glances in his wing mirror. A Mercedes 300 is approaching.
QUILLER *lessens his speed and looks out casually at the tree-lined avenue.*

Exterior. Avenue.
The Auto-Union and the Mercedes 300 proceeding sedately along the avenue.

Interior. Auto-Union.
QUILLER *glances back from the window.*
His eyes blink. He shakes his head, grunts.
He pulls up at traffic lights.
He moans lightly. The red traffic light winks foggily.

Exterior. Avenue. Traffic lights.
The Auto-Union at the traffic lights. The Mercedes
beside it.
Three other cars behind the Auto-Union. The lights go
to green. Auto-Union remains still. Cars begin to hoot.
One car pulls round and goes past.
The Mercedes remains. The Auto-Union remains.
The other cars pull away and go past, hooting.

Interior. Auto-Union.
QUILLER *grunting, blinking.*
The green light winks.
QUILLER's *hand is on the gear lever. He presses but is*
unable to put the car into gear. His hand falls to his
thigh, clutches it.
The driving door opens. A man steps in.
MAN (D). I'll drive. Move over.

QUILLER *tries to resist, is too weak. The* MAN *shifts*
QUILLER *into the passenger seat.* QUILLER *slumps.*
The MAN *drives off.*

Exterior. Avenue. Dusk.
The Auto-Union and the Mercedes proceeding
sedately along the avenue.

Interior. A large reception room.
QUILLER's *point of view.*
A large brilliantly lit chandelier.
Camera descends to see an oil painting of a nude
blonde, leaning across a chair, on the far wall.
Below the painting a pair of white and golden double
doors.
A man, F., *in a dark suit stands by them.*
The room is large, high-ceilinged, well-furnished.
QUILLER *in a silk brocade chair.*

QUILLER *sits, a cushion behind his head.*
He clenches his eyes, looks at his watch.
His point of view.
A carpet stretches from his chair to the doors.
A man, GRAUBER, *walks across from the curtained window to join the other at the doors.*
A third man, OKTOBER, *stands by an enormous fireplace.*
A fourth, in a white surgeon's gown, walks towards QUILLER.
QUILLER'*s eyes close.*
The DOCTOR *raises one of* QUILLER'*s eyelids.*
The DOCTOR *steps back.* QUILLER'*s eyes open.*
The DOCTOR *turns his head towards the fireplace.*
OKTOBER *leaves the fireplace and walks slowly to* QUILLER.
QUILLER *looks up at him and shivers.*

OKTOBER. Are you cold?

QUILLER *looks at him.*

QUILLER. What is it? Day or night?

OKTOBER *studies him.*

OKTOBER. My name's Oktober. What's yours?

Silence.

QUILLER. What's the time?
OKTOBER. You've just looked at your watch.
QUILLER. It may be slow. Or fast. What time do you make it?
OKTOBER. Oh, time isn't really very important.
QUILLER. It is to me. I have an appointment.

He points at painting.

She looks something like that, too. So . . .
OKTOBER. She'll wait.

Pause.

QUILLER. Listen, can I make a suggestion?
OKTOBER. Surely. But we would like to know your name first.
QUILLER. Let me make this suggestion first.

OKTOBER. No. Tell us your name first.

Pause.

QUILLER. They call me Spike.

OKTOBER. Not your nickname. Your surname.

QUILLER. Canetti.

Pause.

OKTOBER. What is your suggestion?

QUILLER. I think this is a case of mistaken identity. I work for Doubledays in New York. I came to Berlin looking for rare books.

OKTOBER. Have you found them?

QUILLER. Well no, not quite yet. I haven't found them yet.

OKTOBER *smiles.*

OKTOBER. What is your real name?

QUILLER. My mother's maiden name was O'Reilly.

OKTOBER. What is your real name, please, Mr Quiller?

QUILLER. Well, originally I had to walk around with a double-barrelled name. O'Reilly Canetti. But I found it a bit heavy. (*Turns to* DOCTOR.) Wouldn't you find it heavy? So I dropped the O'Reilly and kept the Canetti.

OKTOBER. What does your father do, Mr Quiller?

QUILLER. He's dead.

OKTOBER. And your mother?

QUILLER. She's dead too.

OKTOBER. And your sister?

QUILLER. She's dead too. What I mean is I never had one. I was an only child.

OKTOBER. You must be lonely.

QUILLER. No, no . . . no.

OKTOBER. You must feel lonely now, sitting here amongst strangers.

QUILLER. No, I like meeting people. You know . . . new faces . . .

Pause.

OKTOBER. How's your leg?

QUILLER. My leg? Oh yes. Someone scratched it – with a
suitcase.

OKTOBER *clicks his fingers to* GRAUBER *at the door.*
GRAUBER *comes forward, down the carpet.*

OKTOBER. He did it.

QUILLER *looks at* GRAUBER *and waves, vaguely.*

QUILLER. Oh, hi. Hullo.

GRAUBER *goes back to the door.*

OKTOBER. We know . . . a little about you.
QUILLER. Me?
OKTOBER. A little. But we would like to know a little more. I
shall tell you quite simply. We would like to know
the exact location of your local Control in Berlin.
We would like to know a little more about your
current code systems. We would like to be able to
appreciate the extent of your knowledge about us,
and also what information, if any, your predecessor
managed to pass to your Control. We would like to
know the exact nature of your present mission in
Berlin.

Pause.

You are a sensible man, and you know perfectly
well you must give us this information since you
have no alternative.

Pause.

QUILLER. Have you got a telephone here?

He looks inquiringly about.

I think I should call my lawyer in New York. Guy
called Cuspensky. I'll make it collect. So don't
worry about that.
OKTOBER. You don't work in New York, Mr Quiller. You
work in Europe and the Middle East.

OKTOBER *turns and moves a few paces away.*

The TWO GUARDS, GRAUBER *and* F, *move from the doors and approach* QUILLER'S *chair.*
They stand with their hands in their jacket pockets.
A THIRD MAN, C, *comes into view from behind his chair, hand in pocket.*
The DOCTOR *wheels a small table towards chair. On it is a hypodermic kit. The* DOCTOR *selects equipment.*
Silence.
DOCTOR *fills a syringe. A colourless fluid.*

Take off your coat.

QUILLER. Sure.

All the men watch him begin to take off his coat.
QUILLER *takes his coat off.*
Very fast, he whips it into OKTOBER'S *face and kicks him in groin, and in a continuing move swings the small table at the head of* C *at his right. It hits him. The man's gun, out, falls. The hypodermic kit scatters.*
OKTOBER *has fallen.* C *clutches his head.*
QUILLER *swivels. A gun descends on his shoulder as he ducks.*
QUILLER *seizes* GRAUBER'S *leg, his shoulder on his knee, his left hand behind his ankle, and breaks* GRAUBER'S *leg.* GRAUBER *screams.*
F *kicks at* QUILLER'S *head.* QUILLER *grasps his foot and twists.* F *is thrown off balance.*
QUILLER *begins his run to the door.*
He is tackled and brought down by F.
They sprawl.
F *grips* QUILLER'S *leg.*
QUILLER *kicks him in the face with his free leg.*
F *continues to grip and twist leg.*
QUILLER, *writhing, kicks him again in the face.*
C'S *arm locks round his throat.*
QUILLER'S *head jerks back as the pressure tightens.*
F'S *face, bloodied, comes into picture.*
He hits QUILLER *in the face.*
All this has taken place in silence.
A sharp word from OKTOBER.
Sound of doors shutting.

Shoes move by QUILLER's *locked head. A shoe kicks his head. The arm loosens on his neck.*
QUILLER, *nose bleeding, looks up at bloodied face of* F. *The arm is taken from his neck.* F *and* C *stand. Legs stand above him.* OKTOBER's *voice:*

OKTOBER. You may get up.

QUILLER *stands, tucks his shirt in and looks about. Four men,* A, B, H *and* I, *stand by the door, guns out.* F *stands, breathing heavily.*
C *stands still, a cut on his forehead.*
GRAUBER *lies on the floor, still, his leg at an odd angle.*
OKTOBER *stands stiffly, slightly sweating.*

OKTOBER (*to* QUILLER). Sit down.

QUILLER *looks at the faces of the men surrounding him.*
He walks down the carpet to the chair and sits.
QUILLER's *point of view.*
A, B, C *and* F *walk down the room towards him, guns out. They stop.*
The DOCTOR *rolls up his sleeve, cleanses the skin and picks up the syringe.*
QUILLER *glances at the* DOCTOR.
His face twists.

Exterior. Terrace. From room. Night.
Cigar smoke rising on the terrace. The long windows are ajar.
OKTOBER *stands on terrace, looking down into the dark garden.*
A man, B, *comes through the curtain and stands.*
OKTOBER *turns and walks back into the room.*
QUILLER's *point of view.*
His eyes flicker, open.
FOUR MEN, A, B, C *and* F, *stand by the doors, indistinct, blurred, in soft focus.*
OKTOBER *stands in the middle of the room, looking at him.*

Behind him, TWO OTHER MEN, H *and* I, *by the windows. No guns in sight.*
The DOCTOR *straps a constrictor on* QUILLER's *arm, for blood-pressure. He feels* QUILLER's *pulse.*
OKTOBER *walks forward.*
He smiles.

OKTOBER. My name's Oktober. What's yours?
QUILLER. Quiller.
OKTOBER. And your first name?
QUILLER. Inge.
OKTOBER. Your name is Inge? Really?

QUILLER *breathes heavily, hisses through his teeth.*

That's a girl's name. It's the name of a girl. She must be a very beautiful girl. Tell us about her.

Pause.

You're not worried, are you? There's nothing to be worried about. Is there?
QUILLER. No.
OKTOBER. You can talk to me quite easily, can't you?
QUILLER. No.
OKTOBER. Of course you can. You need to relax. They work you too hard. That boss of yours, what's his name?

Pause.

What's his name?
QUILLER. Inge.
OKTOBER. No, she's a girl. She's not your boss.

QUILLER's *eyes close, his head droops.*

Open your eyes.

The eyes remain closed.

Open your eyes.

The eyes open.

Sit up. You seem to be sleepy. Don't fall asleep. Not yet. Jones hated your boss. They betrayed him and killed him. What was his name?

QUILLER. She has long legs.

OKTOBER. Really? I'm so glad to hear that. You're very lucky. After you leave us you can go to her. She's waiting for you.

QUILLER. White . . .

OKTOBER. She adores you.

QUILLER. No.

OKTOBER. Oh yes. Adores you. She wants you only. She longs for you only.

QUILLER. Longs . . . adores me . . .

Pause.

Wants me . . . only . . .

OKTOBER. Don't sleep. It's too early.

QUILLER's *head drops onto his chest. He is asleep.*
OKTOBER *looks at the* DOCTOR.

DOCTOR. He forced himself . . . to sleep.

OKTOBER. Wake him up.

The DOCTOR *fills another syringe and injects* QUILLER's *sleeping body. He signals to a* GUARD (A). A *moves to the chair, holding some leather straps. He bends at the chair.*

QUILLER's *point of view.*
The chandelier, abnormally ablaze, swimming on ceiling.
The room seems larger than it is.
Everything is in sharp focus, to infinity.
QUILLER's *eyes are open, bright, very alive.*
From his point of view figures, furniture, etc. are etched with an abnormal distinction.
The DOCTOR *stands close to him.*
A basin of water stands on the side table. Lights shine brilliantly in the water.
The ripple of the water is deep. The tick of the watch is sharp.
He looks up. The chandelier jolts, dazzles.

> *He takes his eyes from it.*
> OKTOBER *stands in front of him.*

OKTOBER. That was a good sleep you had. How do you feel?

QUILLER (*loudly*). Great.

> QUILLER *speaks involuntarily, compulsively, on every cue.*
> *He is sweating.*
> *He jerks forward, is stopped. He looks down.*
> *His ankles and wrists are strapped to the chair.*
> *He jerks forward again and falls with the chair.*
> TWO GUARDS, B *and* C, *from behind, set the chair upright and remain holding it.*

OKTOBER. Talk to me.

QUILLER. Nothing to talk.

OKTOBER. Oh come on, Quiller, we don't want to keep you here all night. Your Control will be worried about you. You haven't reported for a long time.

QUILLER. Don't report. I'm my . . .

OKTOBER. What?

QUILLER. My own master.

OKTOBER. But you mustn't lose touch with them. Why don't you phone them? Or we can take a message for you? What's the address?

QUILLER. Not waiting.

OKTOBER. Of course they're waiting, and Inge's waiting. Who is Inge?

QUILLER. Who?

OKTOBER. What's her second name? Inge what?

QUILLER. Who?

OKTOBER. Inge who?

QUILLER. What?

OKTOBER. Inge what?

QUILLER. Lin – link – link –

OKTOBER. Is she your link?

QUILLER. No link.

OKTOBER. Of course you have a link. You have colleagues. She's with your colleagues now.

QUILLER. No colleagues.

OKTOBER. You have a cover man. What's his name?

QUILLER. Heng – Hang – hang him –

OKTOBER. That's unkind. He's your friend. What's his name?

QUILLER. Jones.

OKTOBER. Jones knows Inge. He's with Inge now.

QUILLER. Dead.

OKTOBER. With her now. He's in bed with her now. He's enjoying her now. You must tell your base.

QUILLER. He's dead.

OKTOBER. You mustn't let her touch him, he's a corpse. Where's your base? Tell us your base. She's your colleague, how does she get signals from local Control?

QUILLER. She's not –

OKTOBER. Where's your base?

QUILLER. Secret! It's secret! Pol doesn't –

OKTOBER. Who is Pol?

QUILLER. Pop it in the box.

OKTOBER. Who is Pol?

QUILLER. Polly, pol, good polly –

OKTOBER. A pet shop? Which pet shop? Is that where your Control is now? Which pet shop?

QUILLER. In the Zoo.

OKTOBER. Who is your cover?

QUILLER. Getting in my way, never out of my way, do you smoke this brand?

OKTOBER. What brand?

QUILLER. Don't know it – too strong –

OKTOBER. Would you like a cigarette?

QUILLER. Not right brand.

OKTOBER. Which is your favourite brand?

QUILLER. No smoking. Call the guard.

OKTOBER. The next station is Kurfurstendam. What number do you want?

QUILLER. No number.

OKTOBER. Don't be silly. Your Control is in Kurfurstendam. We know that. You must get a message to your chief. But we've lost the number. What is it?

QUILLER. Too late –

OKTOBER. It's never too late. They're waiting for you. They're worried. They want to know where you are. What is the number?

QUILLER, *for the first time, does not answer.*
He breathes, is silent. From this moment his replies become gradually slower, more controlled.

The number.

QUILLER. What?

OKTOBER. The church. The churches. Where are we?

QUILLER. In your base.

OKTOBER. Don't be stupid, Quiller, you're not a baby. Inge what?

QUILLER. Lin – lie – lying low –

OKTOBER. What is the number of your base? Three? Five? Eight?

QUILLER. Nine. Ten. Out.

QUILLER *lets out a long breath, draws in his shoulders, relaxes back in the chair.*

OKTOBER. We've just had a call from your Control. You are ordered to make an immediate report.

QUILLER *is silent.*

Begin your report, Quiller.

QUILLER's *eyes turn to* DOCTOR's *watch. It is one o'clock.*

Can you hear me? Begin.

QUILLER *looks at him, speaks slowly.*

QUILLER. Do anything.

Pause.

It' won't matter.

OKTOBER. No. You've wasted my time. (*To the* DOCTOR.) Inject him. (*To* GUARDS B *and* C). When he's unconscious kill him.

Interior. London club. Evening.
GIBBS *walks down a long room towards the bar. He is dressed in full evening attire, with medals.* RUSHINGTON *is at the bar. He looks round.* GIBBS *sits on stool.*

RUSHINGTON. Hullo. Where are you off to tonight?

GIBBS. Midsummer Banquet.

RUSHINGTON. Oh yes? Who's giving that?

GIBBS. The Lord Mayor, old boy.

RUSHINGTON. Oh yes, of course.

GIBBS (*to* BARMAN). Vodka, please.

Pause.

RUSHINGTON. You've been before, have you?

GIBBS. Where?

RUSHINGTON. The Lord Mayor's Midsummer Banquet.

GIBBS. Oh yes.

The BARMAN *gives* GIBBS *his drink.*

RUSHINGTON. I've never been asked.

GIBBS. Haven't you?

GIBBS *drinks.*

Any news from Berlin?

RUSHINGTON. No. Not really.

GIBBS. Chase them up in the morning, will you? Find out what's going on.

RUSHINGTON. Yes. I will.

Pause.

GIBBS. I always enjoy the Banquet. It's a very splendid occasion.

RUSHINGTON. Yes, I'm sure it is.

The camera withdraws, leaving them at the bar.

Exterior. River. Night.
QUILLER's *face. His body lies on the river's edge. The water laps along it. Very gradually, his face lifts up.*
The lights of the bridge.
There is no one on the towpath.
QUILLER's *body in the mud.*
He raises himself up. He touches his neck, looks down at his body and touches it, with a certain surprise.
He slowly climbs the steps to the road.
He walks, soaked and dripping, along the road.

Interior. Small bleak bar. Night.
A BARMAN *is sitting with coffee reading a paper.*
The chairs are up on the tables.
The door opens. QUILLER *walks in.*

BARMAN (*in German*). We're shut.

QUILLER. Give me a drink.

BARMAN (*in English*). We're shut.

QUILLER. Rum.

QUILLER sits on a bar stool.
The BARMAN *goes behind the bar and slowly pours a rum.*
QUILLER looks at it.

QUILLER. A double.

BARMAN *pours another into glass.*

BARMAN. Four marks.

QUILLER *takes out wallet and waves some notes.*

QUILLER. Just a little wet.

He throws notes on bar, drinks.
BARMAN *watches him.*

I'd like a taxi.

BARMAN. Get one.

QUILLER. What?

BARMAN. There's a phone. Get one.

QUILLER. You get one.

BARMAN. This place is shut.

QUILLER *looks at him quietly.*

QUILLER. You get one.

BARMAN. Drunk Americans. I will call the police.

QUILLER *stands and goes round the other side of the bar.*
The BARMAN *reaches under the counter.*
QUILLER *points to his hand.*

QUILLER. Don't do that.

They stare at each other.

Call a taxi.

BARMAN picks up telephone on bar and dials.
They listen to the line buzz. A voice.

BARMAN. Taxi. Friedhof Bar.

He puts phone down. QUILLER *goes back to stool, drinks.*
BARMAN slowly begins to wipe a glass.
A clock ticks.

Interior. Zentral Hotel. Night.
QUILLER enters.
The lobby. It is very shabby, dusty. A NIGHT-PORTER walks towards QUILLER. He looks at him without interest.

PORTER. Bitte?
QUILLER. I'd like a room.

Interior. Hotel room. Night.
Clothes drying in front of electric fire.
QUILLER in hotel bathrobe at door. He locks it.
He lies on bed, looks at ceiling, then at telephone.
He picks it up.
Pause.
A voice answers.

QUILLER. 346897.

Pause.
Ringing tone. INGE's *voice.*

INGE (*in German*). Yes?
QUILLER. I'm sorry – it's very late.
INGE. Who is this?
QUILLER. Me. Cooper.

Pause.

INGE. I was in bed.
QUILLER. Did you . . . get out of bed?
INGE. No, I'm still there. What is it? What's the time? It's so late.

QUILLER. Are you alone?
INGE. I'm asleep.

Pause.

Are you all right?
QUILLER. I want to see you.
INGE. Not now, I'm afraid.
QUILLER. When then?
INGE. Tomorrow, if you like. After school. Come and have a drink.

Pause.

QUILLER. All right. I'll be there. Good night.
INGE. Good night.

Interior. INGE's *bedroom. Night.*
INGE, *in bed, in a nightdress, replaces the telephone receiver on its hook, and draws the bedclothes about her.*
The light goes out.

Exterior. Hertz Garage. Day.
A car roars up the ramp and out into the street.
QUILLER *stands in fumes from the exhaust, looks up and down street, sees no one, goes into garage and walks towards glass fronted office. One woman can be seen in the office.*
QUILLER *enters.*
Camera shifts to reveal a telephone box in the wall near to the entrance. A man is speaking into the phone. He replaces reciever.
QUILLER *leaves the office and walks into the depth of the garage.*
The back of the man leaves the phone box.

Interior. Hertz Garage. Top landing.
Lines of cars.

QUILLER *seen in the distance, sitting in a Mercedes-Benz 230 SL.*
A MAN'S *back moves towards the car.*

Interior. Mercedes-Benz.
QUILLER *watches torso of man passing from bonnet to passenger window.*
The MAN *opens door.* QUILLER *looks at him. The* MAN *holds a packet of Chesterfields in his hand. He is* WENG. *He sits next to* QUILLER.

WENG. Do you smoke this brand?

QUILLER (*wearily*). Oh Christ. No, I don't think I know that brand.

WENG. Perhaps I might introduce it to you.

QUILLER. All right, all right. What do you want?

Pause.

WENG. They're milder than some other brands.

QUILLER. I know they are. What do you want?

WENG. Would you like to try one?

QUILLER. God, you boys are tough, Yes, I'd love to try one. May I? Please?

WENG. Certainly.

QUILLER *takes a cigarette.*

QUILLER. Won't you join me?

WENG. I don't smoke.

WENG *watches* QUILLER *as he lights his cigarette.*

You don't look too well.

QUILLER. Listen, don't try to be an intellectual. What do you want?

WENG. I've been waiting for you here. Your car was found abandoned. I was posted here in case you turned up for a new one. Hengel is very annoyed, by the way. You led him a dance and lost him. We really don't know what you're up to.

QUILLER. Uh-huh. I see.

WENG. I have to take you to meet someone.

QUILLER. You do, eh?
WENG. Yes. I do.

Interior. Toy Department. Large store.
HENGEL *looking intently at something.*
It is a toy mountain train set. He is absorbed.
QUILLER's *voice:*
QUILLER. Why don't you blow the track up? Go on. You're a
spy.

HENGEL *turns.* QUILLER *and* WENG *stand by him.*
The crowds move about them. The three speak very
quietly, almost in whispers.

WENG. That's a very odd kind of remark to make.
QUILLER. What's odd about it?
HENGEL. I have to take you somewhere.
QUILLER (*to* WENG). What exactly do you find odd?
WENG. You.
QUILLER (*to* HENGEL). What do you mean, take me some-
where?
HENGEL. I have to take you to meet someone.
QUILLER. I was brought here to meet you.
HENGEL. You were brought here to meet me in order for me
to take you to meet someone else.
QUILLER. Now who would that be?
HENGEL. I have not been told to tell you.
QUILLER. I'm ordering you to tell me.
HENGEL. You can't order me.
QUILLER. Of course I can. You're just a cover man. I'm the
leading operator.

Pause. A lady assistant approaches.

ASSISTANT. Can I help you?

They look at her.

WENG. I don't think so, thank you. We're just looking.

She smiles – goes.

HENGEL. It's Pol.

QUILLER. Yes. (*Pointing to* WENG.) Well, he can come too.

HENGEL. He has not been invited.

QUILLER. But I'm ordering you to bring him along.

Pause.

HENGEL. Come on, Weng.

They all move to the door.

QUILLER (*to* WENG). What are you, Chinese?

WENG. In a way.

Interior. Café. Day.
POL *is sitting at a corner table, with coffee and a selection of cream cakes.*
QUILLER, HENGEL *and* WENG *walk to his table. He looks up.*
They all sit.
POL *looks at each in turn.*

POL. I'm sure the adverse party would be thrilled to see us all together. (*To* HENGEL.) Surely you can find Mr Weng some coffee somewhere else?

HENGEL. Mr Quiller ordered us to join you.

POL *looks at* QUILLER.

POL. Hullo, Quiller. How are you?

QUILLER. Great. I want to make a public announcement. I don't want any more cover.

Pause.

POL. You don't want any more cover?

QUILLER. No.

POL. You can't be said to have *had* very much cover, really, can you? You've made your cover's work rather hard.

QUILLER. That was just play. It's over.

QUILLER *looks at them.*

No more cover.

POL. Will you have coffee?

QUILLER. I'd like you to call them off. Please.
POL. I'm glad you said please . . . Quiller.

> POL *sips his coffee. He looks at them all.*
> *Silence.*
> POL *puts his cup down. He speaks quietly to* HENGEL
> *and* WENG.

All cover called off until further notice.

A pause.

QUILLER. I would like my car to be taken to the Hotel Zentral
lock-up garage and left there.
POL. Could you see to that, Hengel?
HENGEL. Certainly I'll see to it.

> *Silence.*

QUILLER. I would be glad if I could talk to you privately.

> POL *cuts into his cake. Eats a piece and nods to*
> HENGEL *and* WENG.
> HENGEL *and* WENG *stand and go out.*
> *Silence.*

POL. I'm sorry. Did you say something?
QUILLER. I would like some black coffee.

> POL *looks at him.*

Please.

> POL *signals to waiter.*

POL (*in German*). One black coffee, please.

> POL *slices another piece of cake and eats.*

QUILLER. I've been to their base.
POL. Oh yes?
QUILLER. But I don't know where it is.
POL. You were sleepwalking.
QUILLER. I was taken there.
POL. Ah.

> *Pause.*

QUILLER. Met a man called Oktober.

POL. Oh yes.

QUILLER. Know him?

POL. We've never actually met.

QUILLER. At the end of our conversation he ordered them to kill me.

POL. And did they?

Pause.

QUILLER. No.

POL. Odd.

Pause.

Do you think they disobeyed him?

QUILLER. I wouldn't think so.

The waiter brings coffee, sets it down, goes.

They didn't take me through the full course, either.

POL. Didn't want to hurt you unduly, I'm sure.

QUILLER. They hurt KLJ.

POL. He got too close.

QUILLER. I was close.

POL. You were helpless.

Pause.

QUILLER. I'm alive, anyway.

POL. I'm so glad.

POL *takes out a small cigar.*

QUILLER. They wanted to know where our base was.

POL. Did you tell them?

QUILLER *chuckles, looking at* POL.

POL *lights cigar.*

QUILLER. They obviously think –

POL *coughs as he inhales.*

POL. I'm so sorry. What did you say?

QUILLER. You're smoking the wrong brand.

POL *looks at him.*

POL. No I'm not.

QUILLER. They obviously think they can find our base – through another method.

POL. Do you know I think you're right? But what other method?

QUILLER. I can find *their* base – by another method.

POL. Can you really? Good. How? Would you like to tell me?

QUILLER. No.

POL. Oh.

POL puffs his cigar. QUILLER drinks coffee, lights cigarette.

QUILLER. Mind if I smoke?

POL. I've agreed to withdraw cover – for twelve hours. But I shall want a full report from you – very shortly. In the meantime, of course – without cover – you may die. I would like to emphasize that you're not on a routine mission.

QUILLER. Go ahead. Emphasize.

POL. I'll want my report shortly.

QUILLER. You'll get it.

POL. Why don't you carry weapons?

QUILLER. You'll get your report.

POL. You haven't answered my question.

QUILLER. I don't have to. I use my own judgement. If you don't like it, call me off. That's all you can do.

Pause.

You'll get your report.

POL. You're on a delicate mission, Quiller. Perhaps you're beginning to appreciate that. Let me put it this way.

He takes two large cream cakes and arranges them on the table.

There are two opposing armies drawn up on the field. But there's a heavy fog. They can't see each other. They want to, of course, very much.

He takes a currant from a cake and sets it between the cakes.

You're in the gap between them. You can just see us, you can just see them. Your mission is to get near enough to see them and signal their position to us, so giving us the advantage. But if in signalling their position to us you inadvertently signal our position to them, then it will be they who will gain a very considerable advantage.

He points to the currant.

That's where you are, Quiller. In the gap.

He pops the currant in his mouth and eats it.

Interior. INGE's flat. Early evening.
QUILLER is with INGE. He is pouring drinks. He takes INGE's glass over to her but does not give it to her.
He stands looking at her.

QUILLER. Did you get to sleep?

INGE. What?

QUILLER. Did you get to sleep again, after I phoned?

INGE. Yes.

QUILLER gives her her glass.

Not immediately. Did you?

QUILLER. Not immediately.

Pause.

INGE. It was a strange time to call.

Pause.

You seem different.

QUILLER. Do I?

INGE. Quieter.

QUILLER. I've been thinking about you.

Pause.

INGE. How's your article? The one you were going to write?

QUILLER. I haven't written it.

Pause.

Actually . . . that wasn't exactly true. There's no such thing as the Philadelphia World Review.

INGE. Then who are you writing for?

QUILLER. No one. I'm not a writer.

INGE *stares at him and laughs.*

INGE. What are you?

QUILLER. I'm a kind of investigator.

INGE. What do you mean?

QUILLER. I'm investigating those people we were talking about last time.

Pause.

INGE. Those people? What do you mean?

QUILLER. Those people.

INGE. But you said you were a journalist.

QUILLER. I'm not.

INGE *moves away from him to the window, stands with her back to him, eventually turns, looks at him.*

INGE. Why are you telling me?

QUILLER. I thought you ought to know.

Pause.

INGE. But do you realize . . . what kind of people they are? They're quite ruthless . . . they're . . . ruthless. Everyone here knows about them. They've killed people.

QUILLER *goes to her.*

QUILLER. You don't have to worry about me. I just thought you ought to know, that's all.

He holds her shoulders.

INGE. Do you . . . have a gun?

QUILLER. No, no.

INGE. Why not? Shouldn't you?

QUILLER. If you don't carry one you're less likely to get yourself killed. Believe me.

He draws her towards him.

I've missed you.

He touches her mouth.

Ssshh.

He kisses her.

I've missed you, all the time.

He draws her onto the sofa and caresses her face.

INGE. No. Please.

QUILLER. I've been wanting to touch you.

He kisses her throat.

You're so white.

He kisses her deeply.
She does not resist.
He murmurs, very close to her.

Have you been waiting for me?

INGE. Yes.

QUILLER. Yes.

Pause.

I know you have.

They look at each other.

Interior. INGE's *flat. Later. Evening.*
INGE *and* QUILLER *lying on the carpet, with cushions, smoking. Evening light through the window. Silence.*
INGE *at length turns on her elbows and looks down at him.*
She kisses him, tenderly.

INGE. I am worried about you, you know.

QUILLER. No need.

INGE. Oh yes there is. A friend of my father's . . . he's told me about them.

QUILLER. About who?

INGE. Those people . . . He was with them.

QUILLER. A friend of your father's?

INGE. Yes. I know what they're like. He's told me what they're like.

Pause.

QUILLER. He knew them, eh?

INGE. Oh, he knew them. Yes.

Pause.

QUILLER. Where is he . . . this man?

INGE. What?

QUILLER. Do you know where he is? Can you reach him?

INGE. Yes, I . . . I think so. Why?

QUILLER. I think I'd like to speak to him.

INGE. But why?

QUILLER. Just a word.

INGE. But I've told you, he's not with them any more.

QUILLER. He might be able to help.

INGE. He might not want to.

QUILLER. Listen. I want to know where their base is, you see.

INGE. But he wouldn't know.

QUILLER. If he was with them he might know.

Pause.

Can I see him?

INGE *is silent. She looks at him.*

INGE. You . . . really want to?

QUILLER. Yes.

She turns away from him.

INGE (*quietly*). All right.

Interior. Swimming bath. Night.

*INGE and QUILLER enter by a side door, into a
passage.
The passage is dark.
They walk up it. Their steps echo.*

*Interior. Swimming bath. The pool.
The pool bathed in soft night light from a large sky-
light.
There is no water in the pool.
Silence.
QUILLER and INGE enter by door onto the changing
room gallery.*

INGE. He must be here. The door was open.

*QUILLER walks down the stairs to the side of the pool.
He looks about, and gives a cheerful whistle of call.
The whistle echoes. There is no other response.
INGE joins him at the side of the pool.*

QUILLER. Well . . . let's wait.

*He walks down into the empty pool.
She follows. Their steps echo.*

Want to dance?

INGE. No, thank you.

Pause. She moves a few steps.

QUILLER. Let's go down to the deep end.

*They walk down the slope and stand in the deepest
corner of the pool. He puts his arm around her.*

We could do an underwater ballet.

He kisses her.

Ever done that?

*She looks up at the diving board, looming above them.
A changing room door creaks. She looks at QUILLER.*

Draught. What's his name?

INGE. Hassler.

Long shot of pool.
Their figures in the far corner.
QUILLER *shouts.*

QUILLER. Hassler!
INGE. Don't!

The shouts of 'Hassler' and 'Don't' echo round the
bath and die.
QUILLER *walks into the middle of the pool.*
He feints a few football moves, stops.

QUILLER. Maybe the bar's open.

A door bangs. They hear steps.
HASSLER (*the swimming bath attendant*) *appears on*
the gallery, hurries down the stairs to the pool side
and down into the pool.
They all meet in the middle of the pool.

HASSLER. I had to be late.
INGE (*to* HASSLER). This is the man.
QUILLER. We've met.
HASSLER. I had to be late. I had to make some inquiries. I
wanted to give you this information. I am glad you
are someone to do something.
QUILLER. Uh-huh.
HASSLER. I was checking. But I have to tell you . . . they
have moved . . . some months . . . from the old
house. I do not know the new house. I keep away
from things, you see.
QUILLER. Ah.
HASSLER. But I think . . . I know someone who does.

QUILLER *looks at him.*

QUILLER. Who?
HASSLER. The name is Schroeder.
QUILLER. What does he know?
HASSLER. I don't know. I think . . . I think . . . perhaps
. . . where they are.

Pause.

QUILLER. Can I see him?

HASSLER. I can try. I can ask. There is a telephone.

HASSLER looks at them both.

Shall I ask?

QUILLER. Where's the telephone?

HASSLER. In the back.

QUILLER walks towards the steps.
Silence.
A changing room door creaks. INGE *looks up.*

It's only a draught.

QUILLER. We'd better get you home.

INGE. No. I want to stay with you.

QUILLER looks at her a moment. They then all move up the steps, and disappear along the gallery.
The diving board looms above the pool.

Exterior. Road by canal. Night.
HASSLER's car draws into the side of the road, by the trees.
The engine cuts off.
Silence.
Suddenly another car draws up.
A WOMAN *gets out of it and walks towards* HASS-LER's *car.*

Interior. HASSLER's *car.*
The WOMAN *gets into* HASSLER's *car.* QUILLER *looks at her.*
It is FRAU SCHROEDER.

SCHROEDER (*to* INGE). You are surprised to see me?

INGE. Yes, I am.

SCHROEDER. I told the police about Steiner.
(*To* QUILLER). I am glad to see you again. I am glad to be of help. I tried to help your friend, but . . .

QUILLER. You know the house?

SCHROEDER. Yes.

QUILLER. Where is it?

SCHROEDER (*pointing*). That's it.

QUILLER *looks*.

QUILLER. Is anyone in there?

SCHROEDER. I don't know. I just know that's the house.

Silence in the car.

HASSLER. We must all go now. Come on. You can tell your people.

QUILLER. Oh no. I have to check whether she's right.

INGE. How?

QUILLER. I've got to go over there, to check whether she's right.

SCHROEDER. I am right.

INGE. Others can check. Why do you have to do that?

QUILLER. Well . . . it's part of my job, you see.

SCHROEDER. I'm going. I've shown you the house. That's all I can do.

HASSLER. It's stupid to stay here. We must get out.

QUILLER (*to* INGE). You go with them.

Pause.

INGE. No. I'll wait for you.

HASSLER (*to* INGE). You're stupid. (*To* FRAU SCHROEDER.) I'll go with you.
(*To* INGE.) You keep the car.

HASSLER *gets out*. FRAU SCHROEDER *opens his door*.

QUILLER (*to* FRAU SCHROEDER). Thank you.

SCHROEDER. Don't mention it.

FRAU SCHROEDER *gets out*.
QUILLER *and* INGE *look at each other*.

QUILLER. Don't worry. I'm just going to check, that's all. Now listen, I want you to remember a telephone number. All right?

INGE. Yes.

QUILLER. Now. Fix it. 21.89.62. Got it?

INGE. 21.89.62.

QUILLER. If I'm not back in twenty minutes ring that number. Tell them you've run out of Chesterfields. Tell them where you are. Okay?

INGE. Yes.

QUILLER. What's the number?

INGE. 21.89.62.

QUILLER. Stay here. Twenty minutes.

QUILLER opens the car door, gets out.

INGE. Listen –

He bends in.

I love you.

QUILLER looks at her and smiles faintly.

He walks across the road.
She watches him, sitting still in the car.

Exterior. House. Night.
QUILLER walks towards it. He comes to a garden gate.
He opens it and goes through.

Interior. Garden. Night.
QUILLER is in a large dark garden. Many overgrown shrubs.
Ahead of him, a dark, dim house.
He walks softly through the garden towards the back of the house.
He reaches it and stops.
Silence.
He tries a window. It is locked.
He examines other windows. One window is slightly ajar.
He squeezes his arm through the gap and unhooks the window from the inside.

Interior. House. Scullery. Night.
QUILLER, *with difficulty, climbs through the small window into the scullery.*
He looks about. The scullery is bare, dirty, damp, bleak.
QUILLER *opens the inner door.*

Interior. House. Hall.
QUILLER *walks into the hall.*
The floorboards are cracked, broken. Plaster is broken on the walls.
The house appears to be derelict.

Interior. House. Staircase.
QUILLER *ascends the stairs.*
Silence.
Sudden shot, with QUILLER's *eyeline.*
A MAN, J, *standing by a wall in shadow.*
QUILLER *looks sharply to his right.*
Another MAN, B.
Another MAN, C.
QUILLER *looks up to the first landing.*
Another MAN, A, *is standing on the landing.*
All the MEN *are still, but stand in quite relaxed postures.*
QUILLER *looks about him.*
There is no way out.
The MAN *on the landing speaks.*

MAN (A). Come up, please.

Slowly, QUILLER *begins to walk upstairs.*

Interior. First landing. Night.
QUILLER *reaches the landing and looks back.*
B *and* C *are following him up the stairs.*
A *walks to a door and opens it.*
A burst of light.

MAN (A). This way, please.

> QUILLER *walks into the room.*

> *Interior. House. Reception room.*
> QUILLER *enters.*
> *It is the room he has been in before.*
> B *and* C *follow him into the room and stand.*
> OKTOBER *is alone in the large room.*
> *He turns.*

OKTOBER. Hullo, Quiller. Do come in.

> *He waves to chair.*

> Sit down. What a surprise. What will you have to drink?

QUILLER. A double Jack Daniels on the rocks.

OKTOBER (*to a* MAN, B). A double Jack Daniels on the rocks.

MAN. We have no Jack Daniels, Reichsführer.

OKTOBER. No Jack Daniels? Tch, tch, tch. (*To* QUILLER.) What would you say to some old Kentucky Grandad?

QUILLER. Make it Scotch Malt.

OKTOBER. Ah. I wish we could help you there but unfortunately I know we can't.

QUILLER. What kind of a bar is this, for Christ's sake?

OKTOBER. I am not a barman Mr Quiller.

> *He walks to the door.*

> I am a German gentleman.

> *He opens the door and gestures to* QUILLER.

> Please.

> QUILLER *remains still.*

QUILLER. Where are we going?

OKTOBER. Downstairs.

> QUILLER *does not move.* OKTOBER *stands by the door.*
> B *and* C *move a few steps towards* QUILLER. *They stop, close to him.*
> QUILLER *goes to the door.*

Interior. House. Landing.
OKTOBER, QUILLER *and* B *and* C *walk along landing
to back stairs.*
They stop by an old service lift.
One of the men opens the doors. They all get in.

Interior. Lift.
The lift goes down.
It has an open top.
The four stand in silence.
OKTOBER *speaks sharply in German to the two men.*

OKTOBER. Would you mind not standing so close.

B *and* C *move away.*

Interior. House. Basement.
The lift arrives. They get out.
*There is a long corridor of whitewashed stone. There
are a number of doors at either side, closed.*
They begin to walk down the corridor.
A door opens suddenly and a MAN *in a boiler suit
comes out, wheeling a trolley. On the trolley is a large
filing cabinet.*
*He wheels the trolley down the corridor, round a
corner and out of sight.*

QUILLER. He's working late.
OKTOBER. We're moving tomorrow.
QUILLER. Oh?
OKTOBER. Yes, we have a busy night ahead of us. We're
moving all our equipment. We're changing our
base.
QUILLER. Oh.

They continue walking.
QUILLER *pauses in his step and stops.*
He glances at the two men behind him.
They all stop.

Where are we going?
OKTOBER. In here.

He goes towards a door.

Oh, I hear you've called off your cover by the way. That was an odd thing to do.

He opens the door and goes in.
QUILLER *follows, flanked by the two men.*

Interior. Cellar.
The cellar is a long low-ceilinged room. A long metal-framed, hooded strip light shines from the ceiling.
The rest of the room is in shadow.
INGE *is sitting in a chair under the light.*
Two men, DORFMANN *and* NAGEL, *well dressed, sit at a distance from her in half shadow, in easy chairs.*
The room appears to have been stripped.
There are two or three closed crates, a rolled carpet and two chairs piled on top of each other.
INGE *looks at* OKTOBER, *not at* QUILLER.
OKTOBER *gestures to the two men.*

OKTOBER. Herr Dorfmann. Herr Nagel. Mr Quiller.

Neither QUILLER, DORFMANN *or* NAGEL *respond to this introduction.*

OKTOBER *looks at* INGE.

And this is Fräulein Lindt.

Turns to QUILLER.

We have just found her sitting in a car, quite near here. Her first name is Inge.

Pause.

QUILLER. So what?
OKTOBER. She's your friend.
QUILLER. I've never seen her before.
OKTOBER. Yes, yes. She's your close friend. Inge.

Pause.

I remember the name well. (*To a* MAN.) You. Do you remember the name?

MAN (C). Yes, Reichsführer.

The recorded voices of QUILLER *and* OKTOBER *are suddenly heard in the room. They listen, still. So does* INGE.

OKTOBER *looks at* QUILLER *and then, gradually, his gaze rests upon* INGE.

INGE *glances at him.*

QUILLER *is aware that* OKTOBER *and* INGE *are looking at each other throughout the recording.*

The recorded voices:

OKTOBER. That boss of yours, what's his name?

QUILLER. Inge.

OKTOBER. No, she's a girl. She's not your boss. What was his name?

QUILLER. She has long legs.

OKTOBER. After you leave us you can go to her. She's waiting for you.

QUILLER. White . . .

OKTOBER. She adores you.

QUILLER. No.

OKTOBER. Oh yes. Adores you. She wants you only. She longs for you only.

QUILLER. Longs . . . adores me . . .

Pause.

Wants me . . . only . . .

The tape recorder is switched off.

Silence. QUILLER *and* INGE *still do not look at each other.*

OKTOBER (*gaily*). And here she is.

QUILLER. No, no. Not at all. The Inge I was talking about was fat. Very fat. Gigantic.

He looks at INGE.

I don't know this girl.

OKTOBER (*to* INGE). For a nice innocent German girl you pick very bizarre friends. Do you understand English? (*Sharply, in German.*) Do you understand English?

INGE. Nein.

OKTOBER *laughs*.

OKTOBER. You must find him very attractive. What's it like to be so sexually attractive, Quiller?

Pause.

Mmmnnn?

Pause.

Anyway, I'm glad you were able to drop in tonight. You're quite free to go now.

Silence.

Really. You can go – now.

QUILLER *remains still*.

But there is just one thing. We're still very interested in the location of your base. We feel . . . that there might be some information there which could be of importance to us.

Pause.

So let me make a proposal to you. If you would like to tell us where your base is you can take . . . her . . . with you. Truly. You will be quite safe, quite free.

Pause.

If not, she will stay here, with us.

Pause.

But do go, if you like, and consider the matter. Take a walk. Think about it. But please don't forget you have complete freedom to return here at any time, give us the information we require and leave . . . with this lady.

Pause.

We'll give you till dawn.

He looks at INGE, *then back at* QUILLER.

If you're still undecided by dawn – we'll kill you both.

Pause.

How's that? Fair?

QUILLER. Sure.
OKTOBER. Good.

Pause.

QUILLER. Right. I'll get some air.
OKTOBER. Yes, why don't you? I hope to see you a little later tonight. In fact I'm sure I will.

OKTOBER *turns to* B *and* C.

Take Mr Quiller up in the lift will you? He knows the way out.

QUILLER *without looking at* INGE *leaves the room.*

Interior. Corridor.
B, C *and* QUILLER *walk towards the lift.*

Interior. Lift.
QUILLER, B *and* C *enter the lift.*
The doors close.
The lift goes up, very slowly.
Silence in the lift.
The lift stops.

Interior. Hall.
The lift doors open. QUILLER, B *and* C *walk into the hall.*
The two men stand. QUILLER *looks at them.*
They remain still.

Interior. House. Stairs and hall.
QUILLER *walks to the door.*
A *is standing by the door. He opens it.*
QUILLER *goes out.*

Exterior. House. Front. Night.
QUILLER *walks down the steps of the house, along to
the front gate, and out on to the road.*

Exterior. Berlin Tiergarten. Night.
A long road. Derelict buildings at either side.
It is late at night.
In the distance, QUILLER *is walking towards the
camera.*
Silence.
*The camera moves sideways to disclose a brightly lit
telephone box. It is the one hard source of light.*
*His face, as he stops by a lamp post. He lights a
cigarette and glances up at the buildings and along the
road behind him.*
There is no one in sight.
He continues to walk towards the telephone box.
From the telephone box see him approach.
He walks straight past it and up the road.
As he passes it a MAN, K, *emerges from the shadow of
trees on the opposite side of the road and walks slowly
along, in the same direction.*

Exterior. Corner of road. Tiergarten area. Night.
QUILLER *approaches street corner.*
There is a MAN, L, *at the opposite corner, standing.*
QUILLER *looks up at the moon and glances back.*
Two men, M *and* N, *are walking slowly down the road,
on opposite sides of it.*
A fourth MAN, K, *is standing by a dark café.*

Exterior. City. Night.
QUILLER *walking.*
Three men, L, M *and* N, *one in front and two behind,
also strolling.*
Their steps resound on the road.
Apart from them, the street is empty, silent.
QUILLER *pauses a moment by a telephone box.*
The others halt.
Silence.
QUILLER *walks on. So do the others.*

Interior. All night café.
Steam. Lorry drivers talking loudly.
QUILLER *walks in, walks to bar, asks for coffee.*
He looks at telephone behind the bar.
In the mirror he sees the door open and K *walk in.*
K *sits down.*
QUILLER *receives his coffee, sips.*

Exterior. All night café. Night.
QUILLER *comes out of the café.*
*He strolls casually towards an overhead railway
station.*
L, M *and* N *saunter, at a distance, behind him.*
QUILLER *stands a moment by the entrance. A signal
is heard from the platform.*
Suddenly QUILLER *dashes into the station and up the
stairs.*

Exterior. Platform. Night.
The train is pulling out.
The camera moves to see, in the street below, L, M *and*
N *jumping into a car. The car pulls away with great
speed and follows the direction of the train.*

Exterior. Platform.
QUILLER *comes into shot.*
He steps carefully across the tracks and disappears down the opposite stairway.

Exterior. Other side of station. Night.
QUILLER *comes out of the station and stops.*
A MAN, O, *is standing by a lamp post.*
Another MAN, P, *is standing at the corner.*
QUILLER *looks at* O *and walks slowly towards him.*
O *stares at him.*

QUILLER. Do you have a light?

Another man walks into QUILLER's *vision.*
He is K. QUILLER *glances at him.*

MAN (O). No.
QUILLER. Non-smoker, eh?

The three men stand looking at him.
QUILLER *walks past them, down the street.*
The three men walk slowly after him.

Exterior. Tree-lined avenue. Night.
Shot through foliage onto street of QUILLER *walking along very slowly, a very small figure.*
The three men, at intervals, are glimpsed through the trees, walking in the same direction.

Exterior. Brandenburgerstrasse. Night.
QUILLER *walking slowly down the long deserted avenue, followed by the three men.*

Exterior. Hotel Zentral. Night.
QUILLER *comes down street, followed by men.*
He walks up the steps, into the hotel.
The men stay, singly, at the other side of the road.

Interior. Hotel lobby.
In the lobby the nightporter is brushing shoes.
He goes to the desk.

PORTER. What number?

QUILLER. Twenty-one.

PORTER *gives him key.*
QUILLER *moves up the stairs.*
PORTER *calls after him.*

PORTER. Do you want a morning paper?

QUILLER *turns and looks at him. At length he speaks.*

QUILLER. No.

Interior. Hotel. QUILLER's *room.*
QUILLER *shuts the door and looks at the room.*
It has been ransacked.
He locks the door, goes to the phone, lifts it, listens.
A regular sound of tapping.
He holds it a moment, replaces it.
He looks at his watch. It is five o'clock.
He goes into the bathroom.

Interior. Bathroom.
QUILLER *looking at his face in the mirror.*
His face is streaked, creased, grimy, strained. He throws water on his face.
Reaching for a towel, he suddenly finds himself looking out of the small bathroom window.
The window overlooks the garages, garage yard and gates to street at the back of the hotel.

Garage yard. QUILLER's *point of view.*
It is dawn.
Light filters gently over the yard.
Camera concentrates on the garage.

Interior. Room.
QUILLER *walks into room, wiping his face.*
He throws towel on the bed, bends and takes off his shoes.
He switches the light off and goes to the door.
Very slowly, he turns handle and pulls door softly towards him.

Interior. Hotel corridor.
The corridor is dimly lit.
QUILLER *emerges from room. He turns the door-handle soundlessly and closes door. He carries his shoes.*
Sound of a shoebrush from below.
QUILLER *walks down the corridor to a back flight of stairs.*
He walks in time to the sound of the shoebrush, freezing when the brushing pauses.

Interior. Side door. Hotel.
He approaches door. There is a key on the inside.
He unlocks the door and steps out into the yard.

Exterior. Garage yard.
The dawn light is growing.
He puts on his shoes.
He stands in the yard, facing the lock-up garages.
In front of him the yard gates leading to a narrow back street.
There is one lamp on the street, by the gate.
Silence.
QUILLER *walks to garage. He unlocks garage door quietly and pulls it.*
A stone jammed under the door screeches. The door jars.
He looks quickly behind him and up at the dark hotel. No movement of any kind.

He frowns and, still looking towards the hotel and the gates, pulls the door again, harshly. It scrapes.
No movement. No sound.
QUILLER *listens to the silence and feels the stillness.*
His eye begins to twitch.
He walks to the gate.

Exterior. Back gate. Street.
QUILLER *stands in the light of the lamp, on the street.*
There is no one in sight.
He opens the gate. It swings back with a slight clang.
The street is empty.
A car is parked in the street, empty.
All doors and windows are empty, silent.
The roofs are bare.
There is no figure in any shadow.
QUILLER *stands frozen in the lamplight.*
Far away the throb of a Diesel truck.

Exterior. Garage yard.
QUILLER *goes back into yard, and looks about him.*
An oil drum, timber, dustbins. Nothing more.
He goes into garage.

Interior. Garage.
QUILLER *takes out a pencil torch and flicks it over the garage. He then goes to his car, the Mercedes 230 SL. He looks at his watch.*
It is 5.24.
He examines the doors. No marks.
He opens the boot and examines it. Nothing.
He gets into the car.

Interior. Car.
He examines the interior of the car quickly but meticulously.
He releases bonnet and gets out.

Interior. Garage.
His torch probes the engine. He finds nothing.
He stands upright and still, sweating.
He presses his hand against his forehead.
His torch points down to the cement floor.
He glances down. A chip of stone, some splinters.
He suddenly squats, gets on to his back and pulls himself under the car.

Underneath of car.
QUILLER *shines his torch up.*
A small bomb, six inches by three, is attached to the underside of the car.
He wipes the sweat from his hands, takes bomb from its perch, holds it to his chest and slides out from under car.

Interior. Garage.
QUILLER *stands with bomb.*
He looks at the partitions in the garage. They are six feet high. There is a back door at the far end.
He leans into car, checks the gears for neutral and starts the engine.
He goes to the bonnet, looks at it.
He rests the bomb about a third of the distance from the front edge. The engine throbs.
He looks at his watch, flicking torch to catch the second hand.
He shines torch on the bomb.
The bomb is still. Then it begins to slide.
He catches it. Looks at his watch.
He places the bomb some inches higher on the bonnet. It rests there.
QUILLER *climbs first partition and drops.*
He climbs second partition and drops.
He kicks over an oil tin, nearly falls.
Climbs third partition and drops. Runs to back door

of garage. Pulls it. It is stuck. He pulls it violently.
It still will not open.
He looks down and sees bolt, unbolts it, goes out.

Exterior. Garage. High wall. Trees overhanging.
It is now light. Sound of birds.
Sounds of distant traffic.
QUILLER *crouches by the wall, tense.*
The engine of car can be heard throbbing faintly.
He looks at his watch. It is 5.55.
He waits. The car still throbs.
His eyelid twitches. He claps his hand over it.
He grits his teeth.
Starts to cough, stops.
The car still throbs.
QUILLER *is hunched. He suddenly stands upright,*
moves to the corner of the garage.
The ground shakes. The wall shudders.
QUILLER *swings back and throws himself flat on the*
ground.
The roof bursts open. Doors break off and crash across
the yard.
Silence. QUILLER *remains down.*
Another explosion. A sheet of hot air and flame.
Silence.

Exterior. The garage yard. Dawn.
The yard in chaos. Hotel windows broken.
Shouts.
QUILLER *is out of sight behind the garage.*
K *runs in from the gate to the wide open garage.*
The Mercedes is consumed with flame and smoke.
K *peers.*
K *turns away and walks back to the gate.*
O *and* P *join him.* K *nods to them.*
They walk out into the street.
It is daylight.

Exterior. City centre. Berlin. Early morning.
Two churches, one ruined, one new. A solitary taxi
passes them.
The taxi draws up at an office building.
QUILLER *gets out, pays the driver.*
The taxi drives off.
QUILLER *enters the building.*

Interior. Room. Local control.
The lift arrives. QUILLER *gets out.*
HENGEL, WENG, HUGHES *and two others are in*
the room.
They are in shirtsleeves, unshaven, bleary-eyed.
Cigarette ends in trays. Numbers of coffee cups.
HENGEL *picks up the phone and presses button.*

HENGEL (*into phone*). He's here. Yes. Right.

He puts phone down.
They all look at QUILLER.
He too is unshaven, his face creased with dirt.

QUILLER. Any coffee?
WENG. I think so.

WENG *looks into a jug and pours.*

QUILLER. Where's Pol?
HENGEL. He's been on all night. He's just gone to bed. He's
coming.

WENG *gives* QUILLER *coffee.*

WENG. Sugar?
QUILLER. No thanks.

Silence.

HENGEL. We've been up all night too.
QUILLER. Have you?

QUILLER *drinks his coffee, clasps the cup.*
He shivers.

HENGEL. Do you want the fire on?

QUILLER. No. That's all right.

They all sit in silence.
POL comes through an inner door, in a dressing gown.

POL. Hullo, Quiller.

QUILLER. Tiergarten. Number six. That's their base. Big house by the canal. Looks derelict.

POL. Will they be there?

QUILLER. Yes. They're not worried. They think I'm dead. They think I was blown up in a car.

POL (*to* HUGHES). Get Ziegler.

HUGHES dials.
Silence.
A voice.

HUGHES (*into phone*). Just a second, please. This is Local Control, Berlin.

POL takes the phone.

POL. Hullo Ziegler. Our man's back. Tiergarten. Number six. By the canal. You can go in now. (*He listens.*) Right.

He puts the phone down.

I'd like a full report as soon as possible, Quiller.

QUILLER looks at him.

QUILLER. You'll get it.

POL. Have a little rest first, of course.

QUILLER. Oh, thanks.

POL. I'm going to change.

POL goes out.
QUILLER sits looking at his cup.

Interior. Room. Local control. Forty minutes later.
QUILLER is standing by the window, looking down into the street below.
The street is crowded with people going to work.

There is a great deal of traffic.
It is a beautiful morning.
QUILLER *turns into the room.*
HENGEL *is sitting with his feet up.*
HUGHES *is sitting by the telephone.*
QUILLER *walks across the room, sits down.*
POL *comes through the inner door, shaved and dressed.*

POL. Any word?

HUGHES. No.

The telephone rings. HUGHES *picks it up.*

LCB.

HUGHES *listens a moment.*

Hold on, please.

HUGHES *nods at* POL. POL *takes phone.*

POL (*to* HUGHES). Take it.

HUGHES *lifts extension and takes shorthand trans-*
cript of the conversation.
There is a clatter of a voice at the other end of the
line.
POL *grunts occasionally. The voice stops.*

POL. Thank you. Good-bye.

POL *puts the phone down.*
QUILLER *looks at him through slit eyes.*
POL *stands.*

They've got them all. Good.

He waves to the door.

Where's my breakfast?

As POL *reaches the door* QUILLER *speaks.*

QUILLER. Where's mine?

POL *turns to him.*

POL. Oh. Are you hungry?

They regard each other.

Why don't we have breakfast together? Upstairs.
In about . . . eight minutes?

QUILLER. I'm too tired to go upstairs.

POL. We'll have it sent to you, Quiller. Don't put yourself out. Will you join me, Hengel?

HENGEL. With pleasure.

POL *and* HENGEL *go out.*
QUILLER *and* HUGHES *are left alone.*
Pause.

HUGHES. Well . . . that's that . . . for the time being.

QUILLER *lights a cigarette.*

QUILLER. What are the details?

HUGHES. Not many. They got them all. Got Oktober.

Pause.

QUILLER. Did they find a girl there?

HUGHES. No. No mention of a girl. They got Dorfmann
and Nagel.

Pause.

QUILLER. Are you sure they didn't find a girl?

HUGHES *examines his transscript. He looks up.*

HUGHES. Yes. Quite sure. No girl.

QUILLER *lifts his cigarette to his mouth and draws
on it.*

Exterior. Playground. School. Day.
Children playing in the playground.
In background, the school.
QUILLER *comes into shot.*
He walks towards school. A few children look at him.

Interior. School. Day.
QUILLER *walking down corridor. Children pass.*

He reaches INGE's *classroom. He stands at the door
and looks in.*
INGE *is there, talking to a boy. She looks up, sees*
QUILLER.
She speaks to the boy, who leaves the room.
QUILLER *goes in.*

Interior. Classroom. School.
QUILLER *shuts the door. He stands. They are alone.
Silence.*

INGE. Hullo.
QUILLER. Hullo.

Pause.
QUILLER *walks down the classroom, flips a book on
the desk.*

How are you?
INGE. I'm – all right –

QUILLER *flips open another exercise book and reads it.*

I was very lucky.
QUILLER (*shutting book*). What? Sorry?
INGE. I said I was very lucky.
QUILLER. Oh? How?
INGE. They let me go.

Pause.

QUILLER. Did they?
INGE. Yes.

Pause.

Yes, they suddenly . . . told me to go.
QUILLER. Well . . . you must have felt pretty relieved.
INGE. I did.

Pause.

QUILLER. We got all of them.
INGE. Oh, really?

Pause.

Oh, good.

QUILLER. Well . . . not all of them, perhaps. Most of them.

Pause.

INGE. You seem tired.

QUILLER. I had a heavy night.

Pause.

INGE. Oh, I tried to phone that number, by the way. After I got out. You remember? The number you gave me.

QUILLER. Oh yes.

INGE. Yes, I tried. But it didn't exist.

QUILLER. Oh, really? I must have made a mistake.

Pause.

Anyway . . . I'm glad to see that you're all right.

INGE. And you.

He walks up the classroom.

QUILLER. Well, I'm leaving Berlin.

INGE. Are you?

QUILLER. I'm a little tired.

INGE. You work too hard.

QUILLER. Well, you too. I'm sure you could take things a little easier, you know.

INGE. Oh no. I have my work to do. I must do it. I want to do it.

Pause.

QUILLER. Uh-huh. Well, if I ever get back to Berlin I'll look you up.

INGE. Yes. Please.

They look at each other.

That would be nice.

He puts out his hand. They shake hands.
Pause.

QUILLER. By the way, did you ever meet a man called Jones?

INGE. No. No, I don't think so.
QUILLER. Good-bye.
INGE. Good-bye.

He goes to the door. As he closes door, he sees her placing books into her bag.

Exterior. School. Playground.
QUILLER *walks away through playing children.*
INGE *comes to the top of the school steps.*
She calls to the children.
They collect around her.
They talk eagerly to her. She listens to them, smiling.
She glances up.
QUILLER, *in the distance, walks through the school gates.*

Accident

Accident was first presented by London Independent Producers (Distribution) Ltd on 9th February 1967 with the following cast:

STEPHEN	Dirk Bogarde
WILLIAM	Michael York
ANNA	Jacqueline Sassard
POLICEMAN	Brian Phelan
SECOND POLICEMAN	Terence Rigby
CLARISSA	Carole Caplin
ROSALIND	Vivien Merchant
TED	Maxwell Findlater
CHARLEY	Stanley Baker
PROVOST	Alexander Knox
HEDGES	Nicholas Mosley
RECEPTIONIST	Jane Hillary
SECRETARY	Jill Johnson
BELL	Harold Pinter
MAN IN BELL'S OFFICE	Freddie Jones
FRANCESCA	Delphine Seyrig
LAURA	Ann Firbank

Directed by Joseph Losey

Accident

Exterior. The house. Night. Summer.
Long shot.
The camera is still, looking at the house from outside the gate, up the short curved drive, across the circular gravel court.
In a meadow behind the house, dim shapes of animals.
The camera moves slowly forward to a position inside the gate. It comes to rest.
The house is silent, dark. One lower front window is curtained. Light filters through it on to the gravel.
Gradually, over picture, the hum of a car, in the distance.
The hum grows.
Closer but still distant, a sudden screech, grind, smash and splintering.

Silence.

Light goes on in the hall of the house.
The front door opens.
STEPHEN *is silhouetted in the light.*

Exterior. Lane. Night.
Camera jolting down the lane.
Sound of footsteps running.
Dark lane winding.
Tree shapes crossing, retreating, advancing.
Glimpsed fields through hedge. Shapes of cows.
A horse moving, head up.
Camera to sky. Stars.

Exterior. Foot of lane. Night.
Stephen halting.
Moonlight hits his face, sharply and briefly.

Exterior. The car.
Close shot from underside of car.
The smashed mass of the car, shooting at passenger seat front-section, lying on camera.
Broken metalwork, jagged shapes of glass.
Two bodies heaped together, still, forming one shape.
Silence but for the ticking of ignition.

Exterior. Lane.
Long shot from corner of the lane, which forms part of a road junction.
The car seen clearly lying on its side in the middle of the road. Mounds of earth rise at either side of the road, by the hedges.
Trees stand sharply against the sky.
Moonlight passes gently over glass of the car.
Camera moves slowly towards car, until it is quite close to it.

Long shot across top of car (which has its driving seat uppermost) to corner of lane. STEPHEN seen standing.
STEPHEN walks towards car. Camera closes in.
He is lost behind it.
His hands appear, grasping the car top.
His face.

Exterior. Lane. Moonlight.
Long shot of STEPHEN climbing on to the top of the car.

Exterior. Car.
STEPHEN looking down through driving window.
Bodies heaped within.
Ticking of ignition.

Long shot across bonnet from hedge of STEPHEN
trying to wrench car door open.
He does, with great effort.
The door crashes back against bonnet.
He almost falls off car.

Interior. Car.
The car jolts. The bodies jolt. A bottle of whisky rolls.
Looking up.
STEPHEN *at open door, above him the sky, looking
down.*
Foreground of skirt, legs, shoes.
STEPHEN *shifts his body, the car sways, his legs and
feet descend into car.*
Legs descending slowly. Ignition ticking.

From above. Close.
WILLIAM's *face. Blood and glass.*
STEPHEN's *feet placing themselves carefully by it.*
Ignition key is heard to be switched off. Silence.
The car jolts. WILLIAM's *head shifts.*

Exterior. Car.
Top shot.
STEPHEN's *hand clutching door frame, moving along
it.*

Exterior. Car.
From underside.
Jagged glass. Back of WILLIAM's *head.*
Camera moves through broken glass to WILLIAM's
temple.
STEPHEN'S VOICE. William?

STEPHEN's *feet searching for surer support, avoiding bodies.*
Moonlight sharp and splintered through smashed windscreen.
ANNA's *legs move. She groans.*

STEPHEN'S VOICE. Anna?

ANNA's *voice whimpering.*
Camera moves up her body. Her face is clenched. She whimpers, yelps. Her eyes open. She begins to push herself up. She mutters, her teeth chatter. She pushes herself up. STEPHEN's *hands seize and help her.*

Exterior. Lane.
The car, rocking, in the middle of the road.

Interior. Car.
ANNA's *shoes on* WILLIAM's *chest.*

Exterior. Lane.
Long shot of ANNA *rising slowly from car.*
Her head and shoulders rise against a background of stars.
She tosses her head.
A sudden scream from STEPHEN *over picture:*
STEPHEN. Don't! You're standing on his face!

Exterior. Car.
Close shot:
STEPHEN.
Medium shot of STEPHEN *and* ANNA. *They are standing by the side of the car. He is holding her under her shoulders, staring at her.*
His face.
Her face, still, eyes closed.

Exterior. Lane.
STEPHEN *walking through moonlight with* ANNA *in his arms.*
He carries her to a grass bank at side of lane and lowers her on to it.
ANNA *alone, lying on bank.*
Her legs.

Interior. Car.
WILLIAM's *face. Shining glass splinters on it and around it.*
STEPHEN's *head, listening, at* WILLIAM's *neck.*
The car shakes. He looks up.
ANNA *above him, at open door, reaching into car.*
Her face large, hair falling.
STEPHEN's *and* WILLIAM's *faces, close, both staring.*
ANNA, *supporting herself on steering wheel, reaching down into car to pick up her handbag.*

Exterior. Lane.
ANNA *walks to bank with handbag and sits.*
She takes handkerchief and mirror from bag and wipes her face.
STEPHEN *standing, looking down at her.*

ANNA *tracing smudges with her finger.*
STEPHEN'S VOICE. You can walk.

ANNA *does not look at him.*

I'm going to telephone.

ANNA *takes out a comb and combs her hair.*

STEPHEN (*looking down at her*). Can you walk?

ANNA *quietly completes her combing, puts comb, mirror, handkerchief into bag, closes bag.*
She sits still.

He puts his hands under her elbows and lifts her up.
They stand, apart.
Behind them in background the car.
He puts his hand on her elbow. She withdraws her elbow, not sharply.
She begins to walk alone up the lane. He follows.

Long shot.
They walk slowly up the lane towards the house.
STEPHEN *is no longer following. He is equal with her, but* ANNA *keeps a distance between them.*
They walk slowly at opposite sides of the lane, which slopes gently uphill, in the bright moonlight, the trees black above them, the sky large.

Interior. House. The hall.
(The interior of the house is untidy and rambling, comfortable. Some of the walls are rough plastered. There is a careless mixture of contemporary and antique furnishing, none of it expensive. The air of the house is casual, relaxed.)
The camera rests in the rear section of the hall, by the open door of the sitting room.
The staircase rises up.
Under the staircase, half in half out of an open cupboard, broken toys, a child's wheel barrow, a large hoop.
The ting of a telephone receiver replaced.

Interior. Sitting-room. Night.
ANNA *sitting still in an armchair.*
Her handbag lies on a coffee table close to her chair.
An old dog pokes his head in the sitting-room door.

Interior. The hall.
The dog turns from sitting-room door, walks up the

hall, sits, looks up at STEPHEN.
STEPHEN *sitting, by telephone, at hall table, looks down at the dog.*

Interior. Sitting-room.
STEPHEN *comes in. He walks slowly to* ANNA, *puts his hand on her forehead.*

Large close-up.
His hand on her forehead. Her eyes.

STEPHEN (*standing over* ANNA). You were lying on top of him.

Pause.

Were you driving?

ANNA *leans back in armchair.*
He touches her hair.

Don't worry.

Interior. House. Kitchen.
STEPHEN *walking to kitchen table with teapot. He pours tea into cup.*

Interior. Sitting-room.
STEPHEN *bending over* ANNA *with cup.*
STEPHEN. Drink it.

He places cup by handbag on side table.
ANNA *remains still in armchair.*
STEPHEN *sitting, watching her.*
Silence.
Sound of a car drawing up.
He turns to window.

Exterior. House. Front gate. Night.
Police car driving slowly down drive towards house.
STEPHEN *comes out of front door. The door swings half shut behind him.*
The car stops. TWO POLICEMEN *get out.*
STEPHEN *and the* POLICEMEN *stand a moment, talking.*

Interior. Sitting-room.
STEPHEN *enters the sitting-room, the* POLICEMEN *following.*
He stops, blinks, turns his head to the POLICEMEN.
POLICEMAN *settling himself in the armchair in which* ANNA *sat. He places his helmet on his lap, takes out notebook.*
STEPHEN, *standing, turns to other* POLICEMAN.

STEPHEN. Sit down.

SECOND
    POLICEMAN. No, it's all right.

STEPHEN *sitting, with cigarette.*

POLICEMAN'S Yours is the only house for some distance. So he
    VOICE. must have been coming to see you.
STEPHEN. He was.
POLICEMAN. You were expecting him?
STEPHEN. Yes.

STEPHEN *glances at* SECOND POLICEMAN.
SECOND POLICEMAN, *standing, expressionless.*
POLICEMAN *in chair, writing in notebook, suddenly coughs violently. He takes out handkerchief, wipes his mouth.*

POLICEMAN. Sorry.

He places his helmet on the table where ANNA'S *handbag and the teacup had been.*
The coffee table.
The helmet is placed on the coffee table.
STEPHEN'S *face.*

THE POLICEMAN *opening his notebook.*
SECOND POLICEMAN *looks out of french windows into the black rear garden.*

Did you know him well?

SECOND POLICEMAN *turns from window.*

STEPHEN. He was my pupil.

SECOND POLICEMAN *strolls back to his place in the room.*

POLICEMAN. He was your pupil at the university?
STEPHEN. Yes.

STEPHEN's *face.*

He wanted to talk to me about something.

The room.
Silence.

POLICEMAN. You found –

A sound, from no specific place, from somewhere in the house. It is very brief. The POLICEMAN *continues.*

POLICEMAN. You found the car at one forty-five?
STEPHEN. He was going to a party, then coming on to me.
SECOND   It looks as though he was pretty drunk. There was
POLICEMAN. whisky all over the car.

STEPHEN's *face.*

STEPHEN. I don't know what it was all about. (*Pause.*) I mean I don't know what he wanted to talk to me about.

The room.
The TWO POLICEMEN. *One sitting, the other standing.*
Silence.
STEPHEN's *face.*
STEPHEN. He probably wanted my advice about something.

Interior. Sitting-room.
Empty. No sound.

Interior. Kitchen.
STEPHEN *at long bare kitchen table.*

STEPHEN. Anna?

Interior. Landing. Bedroom door.
STEPHEN *rushes up stairs and enters bedroom.*

Interior. Bedroom.
It is STEPHEN *and* ROSALIND's *bedroom. It is*
attractive, with clear feminine characteristics.
The bed is a fourposter.
ANNA *lies on the fourposter bed.*
Her legs are curled. Her skirt is above her knees.
She is asleep.
Her handbag and the teacup are on a bedside table.
Stillness.
The camera, with STEPHEN, *moves slowly towards*
ANNA *on the bed.*
STEPHEN *standing by window, looking at bed.*
ANNA *asleep. Her body curved.*
STEPHEN *at foot of bed.*
ANNA's *feet.*
One shoe is on.
The other lying on bedcover.

Interior. Car.
ANNA's *shoe, standing, digging into* WILLIAM's *face.*
STEPHEN's *hands on her legs.*

STEPHEN's VOICE. Don't!

Close-up. WILLIAM's *face. Dead.*

Interior. STEPHEN's *study, college. Morning.*
WILLIAM's *face, smiling.*

WILLIAM *and* STEPHEN *are sitting by the open window. The window looks down to a quadrangle. On the grass a white goat is tethered. The scene is framed between them, below.*

STEPHEN. You haven't spoken to her?

WILLIAM. No.

STEPHEN. You've just seen her.

WILLIAM. I've just seen her. Walking about. A little.

STEPHEN. And you like the look of her?

WILLIAM. Yes. I do.

Pause.

STEPHEN. And what am I supposed to do about it?

WILLIAM. Nothing at all.

STEPHEN. Oh. Good.

WILLIAM. I'd just like to know what you think of her, that's all.

STEPHEN. You realize I'm her tutor?

WILLIAM. Naturally. I also realize you're my tutor.

STEPHEN. And that being her tutor, her moral welfare must be my first consideration.

WILLIAM. Ah. You mean besides being her tutor you are also her protector.

STEPHEN. I mean that I refuse to countenance or encourage male lust as directed against any of my woman students.

WILLIAM. Well said.

STEPHEN. Thank you.

WILLIAM. Anyway, what's her name, for God's sake?

STEPHEN. Her name? Her name. Ah yes, I remember her name. Her name is Anna von Graz und Leoben.

Pause.

WILLIAM. German.

STEPHEN. Austrian.

Pause.

WILLIAM. Well, come on! What do you think of her?

STEPHEN. I don't think.

WILLIAM. I thought thinking was your job!

STEPHEN. Not about *that*.

WILLIAM. You're not past it, are you? Already?

From the same viewpoint, ANNA *appears in the quad-*
rangle. She stops and talks to the goat.
WILLIAM *stands.*

It's her.

STEPHEN. She's coming for her second tutorial.

WILLIAM. You didn't tell me.

STEPHEN. Wait. I'll introduce you.

WILLIAM. She's talking to the goat.

STEPHEN. They speak German.

ANNA *stroking goat. The men at window.*
WILLIAM *at door.*

WILLIAM. No, not now. Really.

STEPHEN. You intend to go it alone, eh? Without introduction?

WILLIAM. That's right.

STEPHEN *alone in middle of study.*
He turns to window and looks down.
STEPHEN's *head at window.*
He watches ANNA *walk across lawn towards college.*
WILLIAM *crosses lawn, at a distance from her.*
ANNA *disappears under window.*
WILLIAM *stops by the goat and bends his head to it.*

Interior. Study.
ANNA *sitting, knees together, with notebook.*
Her face, listening.

STEPHEN'S VOICE. Philosophy is a process of enquiry only. It does not
attempt to find specific answers to specific ques-
tions.

Close-up. His face, looking at her.

Interior. House. Sitting-room. Afternoon.
Large close-up of CLARISSA's *face (three years old).*
She turns from camera, runs, jumps on her mother's
lap, looks over her mother's shoulder at camera.

STEPHEN *standing at door.* ROSALIND *sitting,* CLARISSA *on her lap.* TED (*seven years old*) *lying on floor with book, looking up. The dog, asleep on floor.*

STEPHEN. She loves her Dad.
ROSALIND. She hasn't eaten anything today.

ROSALIND *is pregnant. She is sewing. On the floor are paintboxes, papers in strips, scissors, children's books, a doll, cars.*
STEPHEN *looks at the floor and then walks across the room. He kicks* TED *as he passes.*

STEPHEN. Hullo.
TED. Hullo, Dad.

STEPHEN *sits.*

STEPHEN. What has she eaten?
ROSALIND. Some milk pudding at lunch.
STEPHEN. Well, that's all right.

STEPHEN *calls 'Hoy!' to* CLARISSA *and claps his hands.*
CLARISSA *runs to him, clasps his legs.*

Hullo.
TED. How many moons has Jupiter got?
STEPHEN. I don't know.
TED. Twelve.
STEPHEN. Twelve moons?
TED. Yes.
CLARISSA. Twelve moons.
STEPHEN (*to* TED). Do you want to get that book about the elephant?
TED. Yes!

TED *rushes to far end of room, to pile of books, and starts to rummage.*
ROSALIND, *sewing.*
STEPHEN, *with* CLARISSA *on his lap.*
STEPHEN. I've got a new pupil.

ROSALIND. Uh?

STEPHEN. She's an Austrian princess.

ROSALIND. *Is* she?

CLARISSA. A princess?

STEPHEN (*whispering to* CLARISSA). I think so.

TED'S VOICE. I can't find the book!

ROSALIND. How do you know she's a princess?

STEPHEN. She's got a very long name.

ROSALIND. Has she got golden hair?

STEPHEN. Uuuh . . . No.

ROSALIND. Then she's a fake.

> TED *at pile of books, looking at book.*

TED. I've found it! (*Frowns.*) I think.

> STEPHEN *cuddling* CLARISSA.

STEPHEN. She's very sunburnt.

ROSALIND. Then she's definitely not a princess.

STEPHEN. Why not?

CLARISSA. She is!

ROSALIND. Princesses keep their skin . . . quite white.

STEPHEN. Your skin is quite white.

ROSALIND. I know it is.

> TED *runs down the room, with book, sits on* STEPHEN'*s lap.*

TED. I knew I'd found it.

> STEPHEN *holds both children.*

STEPHEN. Where do you want to start?

TED. You start.

STEPHEN. Where?

TED. Here.

ROSALIND. Has she made advances to you?

STEPHEN. Oh no. I'm too old.

ROSALIND. You're not too old for me.

STEPHEN. I know that. (*To children.*) Now come on. Who's going to start?

> ROSALIND *stands and moves across to them.*

CLARISSA. I'll start.

TED. She can't read!

ROSALIND *bends over him.*

ROSALIND. And I'm not too old for you.

Interior. Study. College. Day.
ANNA *sitting with notebook. She is writing in it. Camera spreads to find* STEPHEN. *He is lying back in his chair, feet on desk.*
Silence.

STEPHEN. Write me an essay on what the problem is . . . or rather . . . on what the problem seems to you to be.

He lifts his head, looks at her.

Will you?

ANNA *smiles.*

ANNA. I'll try.

Interior. Don's Common Room. College.
STEPHEN, CHARLEY, *the* PROVOST *and* HEDGES, *a scientist, sit in armchairs, reading.* CHARLEY *reads a newspaper; the rest, books.*
Silence.

CHARLEY. A statistical analysis of sexual intercourse among students at Colenso University, Milwaukee, showed that 70 per cent did it in the evening, 29.9 per cent between two and four in the afternoon and 0.1 per cent during a lecture on Aristotle.

Pause.

PROVOST. I'm surprised to hear Aristotle is on the syllabus in the state of Wisconsin.

Silence.

CHARLEY (*still reading from paper*). Bus driver found in student's bed.

Pause.

PROVOST. But was anyone found in the bus driver's bed?

Pause.

Did you ever hear the story of my predecessor, Provost Jones, and the step-ladder?

Pause.

It's a bizarre story. It'll amuse you. Provost Jones and his good lady decided one day to buy a step-ladder.

Exterior. Riverbank. Day.
Heat, punts, canoes on river.
STEPHEN *walks along towpath.*
Young girls and men call to each other from boats.
STEPHEN's *head.*
He walks quickly.
Flashes of light on water.
Girls turning in boats. Distant laughter.
A call: 'Stephen!'
STEPHEN *stops, turns.*
Under a willow in a punt are WILLIAM *and* ANNA.
ANNA *wears a white dress with large woven holes in it.*
STEPHEN *stares.*

WILLIAM. Hullo.

STEPHEN *bends to them, under the willow.*
The punt rocks gently, surrounded by pinpoints of light. ANNA *smiles, lying back.*

You can't wear a suit like that on a day like this. It's ridiculous.

STEPHEN. I didn't know you two had met.

WILLIAM. We have. (*To* ANNA.) Haven't we?

ANNA. Mmmnn.

WILLIAM. Jump in.

STEPHEN. Me?

WILLIAM. Come on. We're going up river.

Long shot of STEPHEN *stepping into punt.*
The punt rocks. WILLIAM *pushes off.* STEPHEN
squats by ANNA.
The punt.
STEPHEN *settles into a half leaning, crouching posi-
tion by* ANNA's *legs.*
The punt.
WILLIAM's *legs.*
Through them ANNA *sitting,* STEPHEN *reclining
along punt, his head on the cushion by her hip.*
STEPHEN's *head at her hip.*
Her legs are bare, crossed.
Vapour on her legs.
Left foreground STEPHEN's *head. Above him*
ANNA's *back. Her hair glinting. Light in her hair.*
Beyond them WILLIAM *standing, punting.*
Her arm, still.
Her arm, moving.
Her armpit. Fuzzy hair.
Hole at the side of her dress.
STEPHEN's *body, stretched.*
Her hip. His head.
Her eyes closed.
The punt pole, dipping.
The back of STEPHEN's *head. His ears.*
WILLIAM *bending and straightening, with pole.*
Long shot.
The punt draws towards an island.
STEPHEN *standing, leaning from punt to grasp the
branch of a tree.*

Exterior. Quadrangle. Day.
STEPHEN *and* WILLIAM *appear from under arch
into quadrangle.*
STEPHEN *walks straight-backed in a soaking suit.*
WILLIAM *carries his gown.*

WILLIAM. You look very dignified.
STEPHEN. I feel *wet.*
WILLIAM. You don't look wet.

STEPHEN stops, looks at him.

STEPHEN. I don't *look* wet?

WILLIAM. Nobody looked at you as though you were wet, did they? They thought you were quite normal.

They walk across lawn, STEPHEN *pulling at his trousers.*

It was all my fault. I stayed too far out.

Interior. Arched door off quadrangle.
They enter out of sun.
STEPHEN *snarls at* WILLIAM.

STEPHEN. I'm getting old! Don't you understand? Old. My muscles. The muscles.

Interior. Stairway. College.
They climb stairway.

STEPHEN. No judgement. No judgement of distance. It's all gone. Vanished!

His voice echoes in the stone stairway.

Interior. STEPHEN's *study. College. Afternoon.*
STEPHEN *is changing into sweater and light trousers.*
WILLIAM *stands by window.*

WILLIAM. I thought forty was the prime of life. I mean, I wouldn't say you looked old. You've still got a pretty good figure. But I tell you what, why don't you do an hour's squash every morning? It'll do you the world of good.

STEPHEN *hitches his trousers.*

Do you want to borrow my belt?

STEPHEN (*coolly*). If you're going to be a farmer when you leave University, why the hell are you taking philosophy?

WILLIAM. I've got to be able to talk to the cows properly, haven't I?

Interior. STEPHEN's *study. Early evening.*
STEPHEN *and* WILLIAM *sit at the window, looking down, with glasses of whisky.*

WILLIAM. It's nice knowing you really, you know. You're not a bad fellow, for a teacher of philosophy. (*Pause.*) I haven't got many friends.

STEPHEN. That's because you're an aristocrat.

WILLIAM. Ah.

STEPHEN. Aristocrats were made to be . . .

He pauses.

WILLIAM. What?

STEPHEN. Slaughtered.

Pause.

WILLIAM. Oh.

He looks at STEPHEN's *face, slightly shadowed in the evening light.*

STEPHEN. Do you like her?

WILLIAM. Yes.

Pause.

STEPHEN. Why don't you bring her down for the day on Sunday? To my house.

WILLIAM. Great.

STEPHEN. Come for lunch.

WILLIAM. Marvellous. Shall I ask her?

STEPHEN. No. No, I'll ask her.

Interior. STEPHEN's *study. College. Morning.*
ANNA *sitting on floor by bookshelves, examining books on the bottom shelf.*
STEPHEN's *legs stand by her.*
STEPHEN *looking down at her, book in hand.*

STEPHEN. This might interest you.

She looks up.

It expresses another point of view . . . altogether. It's by Charley Hall. Do you know him?

ANNA. Yes, I think . . .

STEPHEN. The zoologist.

ANNA. Yes. I have met him.

STEPHEN. But this is a novel. He writes novels as well, you see. And appears on television.

ANNA. Does he?

STEPHEN (*grinning*). He's a versatile man. Read it. I don't think much of it, but you might.

He stretches his hand down.

Here.

He clasps her hand and draws her lightly to her feet. ANNA *takes the book.*

ANNA. Thanks.

She collects her notes from the desk, puts book and notes in her bag. He watches her.

STEPHEN. Would you like to come to my house for lunch on Sunday?

ANNA. That would be lovely.

STEPHEN. You could meet my wife. And the children.

ANNA. Yes.

Pause.

ANNA *clears her throat.*

STEPHEN. Perhaps William can bring you.

ANNA. Ah. Yes.

STEPHEN. I'll ask him.

Interior. House. Bedroom. Late afternoon.
ROSALIND *lying on fourposter bed.*
The curtains are drawn.
STEPHEN, *with camera, moves slowly towards the bed. He sits on the bed. She opens eyes, smiles.*

ROSALIND. Hullo.

STEPHEN. How are you?

ROSALIND. All right.

She draws his head down, kisses him swiftly.
Children's voices raised from garden.

What are they up to?
STEPHEN. They're all right.

He kisses her fingers.
Sound of dog barking.

Have you been able to rest . . . with all this racket?
ROSALIND. Yes.

He continues kissing her fingers.

STEPHEN. Oh, I've asked some people over on Sunday. (*He looks at her.*) Is that all right? (*Pause.*) Mnnn?
ROSALIND. What people?
STEPHEN. Well . . . William . . . you know . . .
ROSALIND. Mmn-hmmn?
STEPHEN. And this Anna von Graz. (*Pause.*) You know, that girl –
ROSALIND. The Princess.
STEPHEN. Yes. She's William's girl friend. (*Pause.*) What do you think?
ROSALIND. I'm not very good at mixing with royalty.
STEPHEN. She's not really a Princess. Don't be silly.
ROSALIND. I'm not silly.

Pause.

STEPHEN. Just for lunch, that's all. But I can easily put them off.
ROSALIND. Mmmn.

She gets out of bed.

STEPHEN. What are you doing?
ROSALIND. I'm going downstairs.

She takes a negligée from the back of the door. The negligée has frilled cuffs. She puts it on.

Interior. House. Stairs.
ROSALIND *walks down the stairs, followed by*
STEPHEN.
Silence.

Interior. House. Kitchen.
ROSALIND *goes to kettle, fills it with water.*
STEPHEN *stands inside the door, watching her.*
She puts the kettle on the stove and lights the gas.

STEPHEN. Well, what do you think?
ROSALIND. About what?
STEPHEN. About Sunday. I can put them off.
ROSALIND. Why should you put them off?

ROSALIND *cuts bread on the breadboard.*

STEPHEN. Well . . . the cooking and everything . . . if you don't feel up to it.
ROSALIND. I'm fine. Why do you keep going on about it? Let them come.

Pause.

STEPHEN. All right.

She goes to the back window and calls: 'Ted, Clarissa! Teatime!'

Exterior. Lane. Road junction. Morning.
Spot of accident.
Dog runs across road to earth mound.
STEPHEN's *voice: 'Mike! Come on!'*
TED *runs after dog.*

TED. Come on!

TED *chases dog off the mound. They run on to grass bank.* STEPHEN *comes into view, walks after them.*
Long shot.
Heat.
STEPHEN, TED *and the dog walk slowly up the lane towards the house.*

Exterior. House. Garden gate.
They pass through the gate and begin to walk up drive,
flanked by bushes.
WILLIAM's *car can be seen parked in the gravel*
court.
The dog burrows in a bush. TED *stops with him, bends.*

TED. What is it, Mike?

STEPHEN *walks ahead.*
He turns the corner of bushes, the house and court now
in full view.
He stops still.
By the hedge to the left of the house a white sports car
is parked.
ANNA, *in dark glasses, and* CHARLEY, *stand by the*
car, talking quietly.
Light vibrates on the car. An intense shimmer and
glint. The two figures and the car trapped, still, in
light, heat.
STEPHEN's *face, blinking in the sun, looking, his face*
creased.

Exterior. The court.
The scene, unmoving. The two figures by the car.
STEPHEN *standing.* TED *and dog rush past, run down*
side of house.
CHARLEY *and* ANNA *turn, see* STEPHEN.
CHARLEY *raises his hand in salutation.*
STEPHEN *walks across the gravel towards them. He*
reaches them. CHARLEY *is smiling.*

STEPHEN. Hullo Anna. William here?
ANNA. Yes, he's inside. What a lovely day.

Exterior. Front of house.
TED *and dog round corner of house.*

ANNA. Is that your son?
STEPHEN. Yes.

ANNA *walks over to* TED *and dog.*
STEPHEN *and* CHARLEY *remain by car.*
CHARLEY *sits on bonnet, stretches his arms.*

ANNA'S VOICE. What's your name?
       TED. Ted. What's yours?
      ANNA. Anna. What's his?
       TED. Mike.

STEPHEN and CHARLEY grin at each other.

STEPHEN. What are you doing here?
CHARLEY. I was just passing, so I thought I'd drop in.
STEPHEN. Passing?
CHARLEY. Yes, just passing. Just floating by.

Sounds of TED and dog.
CHARLEY chases TED and dog round corner of house.

Hi! Hi! Hi!

ANNA is no longer there.
STEPHEN stands by car.

Interior. House. Kitchen.
ROSALIND and WILLIAM peeling vegetables.
WILLIAM. Hullo.
STEPHEN. Hullo, William. Charley's here.
ROSALIND (*laughing*). We know.
STEPHEN. Is he staying for lunch?
ROSALIND. Of course.

Through the window into the back garden they watch
CHARLEY throwing a large ball. TED, CLARISSA and
dog run after it. CHARLEY runs after them, crawls on
his hands and knees among them.
ANNA appears on the lawn. CHARLEY kicks the ball
to her. She bounces it.

STEPHEN (*to ROSALIND*). Can I do anything?

Exterior. Lawn. Back garden. Afternoon.
The camera moves slowly up a slight rise and along
the lawn.
The garden is long, stretching down to trees. It is
mainly grass, with a few flowerbeds.

It is after lunch. Coffee cups, brandy glasses on the grass, some lying on their side. Very hot.
WILLIAM is lying, leaning on an elbow, picking at the grass, near CHARLEY. CHARLEY is lying on his back. ROSALIND is lying in a garden chair, feet up. ANNA sits, making a daisy chain with CLARISSA. TED and STEPHEN are doing some casual weeding at the verge.
Silence.

WILLIAM *and* CHARLEY.

WILLIAM. What are you writing now?
CHARLEY. A novel.

Pause.
The dog strolls, sniffing, between them, wanders towards ANNA.

WILLIAM. I'd like to write a novel.
CHARLEY. You would, eh?
WILLIAM. But I can't.
CHARLEY. It's child's play. You just need a starting point, that's all.
WILLIAM. Oh.

Pause.

CHARLEY. Here, for instance.
WILLIAM. Where?
CHARLEY. Here on this lawn. What are we up to?
WILLIAM. I know what I'm up to.
CHARLEY. What?
WILLIAM. Anna and I were invited here for lunch. We've just had it.
CHARLEY. Ah.

Pause.

WILLIAM. What are you up to?

ANNA *and* CLARISSA.

CLARISSA. We're going to Granny's on Tuesday.

ANNA. Are you?

CLARISSA. Teddy and Mummy and me.

ANNA. Are you going for a long time?

CLARISSA. We're going for three weeks. Mummy's going to have a baby, you see. If you're going to have a baby you've got to have a rest.

ANNA. Of course.

WILLIAM *and* CHARLEY.

CHARLEY. Describe what we're all doing.

WILLIAM *looks about the garden.*

WILLIAM. Rosalind's lying down. Stephen's weeding the garden. Anna's making a daisy chain. We're having this conversation.

CHARLEY. Good. But then you could go further. Rosalind is pregnant. Stephen's having an affair with a girl at Oxford. He's reached the age when he can't keep his hands off girls at Oxford.

WILLIAM. What?

CHARLEY. But he feels guilty, of course. So he makes up a story.

WILLIAM. What story?

CHARLEY. This story.

WILLIAM. What are you talking about?

CHARLEY *sits up, swats violently at flies.*

CHARLEY. Oh, these flies are terrible.

WILLIAM. What flies? There aren't any flies.

CHARLEY. They're Sicilian horse flies, from Corsica.

CHARLEY *shouts across lawn.*

Have you heard our conversation?

STEPHEN *weeding.*

STEPHEN. Yes!

ROSALIND *lying, eyes closed.*

ROSALIND. Yes.

> ANNA *carefully places daisy chain around* CLARISSA's *neck.*

> *Exterior. Tennis court.*
> WILLIAM *whipping ball fiercely over net.*
> *The tennis court is situated beyond the back garden. It is in a state of ruin. There are holes in the net. Weeds all over the ground.*
> CHARLEY *and* ANNA *play against* WILLIAM *and* STEPHEN. CHARLEY *is in bare feet.*
> ROSALIND *sits in a chair by the side, watching.*
> *The ball goes to and fro.*
> WILLIAM *drives, beating* CHARLEY.
> CHARLEY *serving.* ANNA *stands by the net. The ball hits* ANNA *in the back.* CHARLEY *laughs.*
> STEPHEN *serving, into net.*
> STEPHEN *rushing the net.* ANNA *bobbing about on the other side.*
> *Sun.*
> WILLIAM *drives between* CHARLEY *and* ANNA.
> ANNA *hits wildly, sends ball into bushes.*
> STEPHEN *lobs ball over net.* CHARLEY *heads it back.*
> CHARLEY *serves, hits* ANNA.
> WILLIAM *serves powerfully, beats* CHARLEY, *who falls flat on his back.*
> *Long shot, across tennis court.*
> ROSALIND's *chair, empty.*

> *Interior. House. Kitchen.*
> ROSALIND *cutting sandwiches.* STEPHEN *comes in.*

STEPHEN. What are you doing. ?

ROSALIND. Making tea.

STEPHEN. I've just asked them to stay for dinner.

> *She looks at him.*

ROSALIND. *Dinner?*

STEPHEN. No. Supper. Cold supper.
ROSALIND. Are they staying?
STEPHEN. I don't know. But I'll do it. I'll . . . do the supper.

The kettle boils.

ROSALIND. The kettle.

STEPHEN *goes to it.*

Exterior. Lawn. Back garden. Late afternoon.
Shadows beginning. Tea trolley standing.
ANNA *and* STEPHEN *reclining on the grass, amidst*
cups and plates, leavings of sandwiches and cakes.
WILLIAM *standing near them, practising strokes*
with a boy's cricket bat.

STEPHEN. Do you have any . . . sisters or brothers?
ANNA. One sister.
STEPHEN. Is she beautiful?
ANNA. Very.

WILLIAM *bends down to* ANNA.

WILLIAM (*to* ANNA). Come for a walk. Mmmn?
ANNA. Oh, I'm so comfortable.

WILLIAM *stands upright, is still a moment. He then*
picks up a tennis ball, bounces it, and slams it with bat
down the side of the house. He strolls after the ball.
ANNA *looks at* STEPHEN, *smiles.*

It's so lovely here.
STEPHEN. Yes . . . it is.

Pause.

I think I'll go for a walk.
ANNA. I'll come too.

STEPHEN *stretches his hand down. She jumps up by*
herself. She giggles.
He leads her across the lawn towards the trees.

Exterior. Path through grass.
STEPHEN *and* ANNA *walking through long grass beyond the tennis court, going uphill.*
Their legs swish through grass. Their voices:

STEPHEN. Are you fond of William?
ANNA. Why do you ask?

Silence. Their legs moving.
ANNA's *face.*

Are there many dons like you?
STEPHEN. Certainly not.

Exterior. A copse.
Long shot.
They appear, through fading light, through trees, into copse. Shafts of dying sun still bounce off the wood. Silence.
Sound of their feet on the brush. Birds. Creaks in undergrowth.
ANNA *stops, holds the branch of a tree.*
Silence. Sounds.

STEPHEN. Mind. There's a spider's web.

ANNA *looks at him.*

ANNA. It won't hurt me.

She walks slowly away. He follows.

Exterior. A stile.
The stile looks down upon a valley.
They stand at the stile.

ANNA. What a beautiful view.
STEPHEN. I thought you'd like to see it.

Their hands, close but not touching, on the stile.

ANNA. It was so kind of you to ask me here.

Silence.
STEPHEN's *hand grips the stile.*
He looks at her.

STEPHEN. No, it wasn't. It's been lovely to see you.

They stand, silent. He looking at her. She gazing at the view. She turns, looks at him.

ANNA. Shall we go back now?

STEPHEN. Yes.

Interior. Kitchen.
CHARLEY *opening a bottle of beer.* ROSALIND *comes in.*

ROSALIND. Oh hello.

CHARLEY. Hello. How are you?

ROSALIND. Fine. How's Laura?

CHARLEY. Great. All right . . . you know . . . I don't know really . . . I haven't seen her.

Pause.

I've been pretty busy. You know . . . one thing and another.

ROSALIND. You look terrible.

CHARLEY. Me? I feel wonderful.

ROSALIND *pours beer into his glass.*

ROSALIND. Well, this'll kill you.

CHARLEY. I know.

Exterior. Path through grass.
They are returning.
Long shot.

STEPHEN. Will you stay for supper?

ANNA. I'd love to, but I don't know about William.

STEPHEN. He'll stay.

Interior. House. Kitchen. Early evening.
CHARLEY *with beer.* STEPHEN *comes in.*

STEPHEN. Have you seen William?

CHARLEY. No. How are you getting on?
STEPHEN. Fine. What do you mean?

CHARLEY *pours beer.* STEPHEN *opens a bottle.*

CHARLEY. What does Rosalind think about it?

STEPHEN *pours beer.*

STEPHEN. What does Rosalind think about what?

WILLIAM *looks in at the door.*

WILLIAM. Have you seen Anna?
CHARLEY AND
STEPHEN. No.

They look at each other. CHARLEY *leaves the kitchen.*

STEPHEN. You're staying for supper, aren't you?
WILLIAM. We ought to go.
STEPHEN. It's all arranged.

Interior. House. Dining-room. Evening.
STEPHEN *opening wine bottle at sideboard. He places salad bowl, containing salad, on table. He goes quickly to sideboard, takes out bottle of whisky, pours himself a large one and drinks it.*
Voices from the front of the house.
He goes to window.
In the dusk, ROSALIND *and* ANNA *are walking up the drive to the house, with dog, talking quietly.*
STEPHEN *leans out of the window.*
STEPHEN. Where are the children?

The women stop.

ROSALIND. They're not back yet. They went out to tea.
STEPHEN (*to himself*). I didn't know that.
ROSALIND. How's the supper?
STEPHEN. Nearly there.

STEPHEN *takes whisky bottle and goes out door.*

Interior. The hall.
STEPHEN *crosses hall to sitting-room.*
ROSALIND *and* ANNA *come in front door.*

ROSALIND. I think it's about ten years.

ANNA. You're a wonderful couple.

Interior. House. Sitting-room.
CHARLEY *and* WILLIAM *are lying in chairs with beer.* STEPHEN *enters with bottle.*

STEPHEN. Whisky.

Interior. House. Dining-room. Night.
The men are at the table.
ANNA *and* ROSALIND *clearing soup plates, setting ham plates.*
One empty bottle of whisky on the sideboard. Two and a half empty bottles of red wine on table.

STEPHEN. Who made that soup? I didn't make any soup.

CHARLEY. Your wife! Your beautiful wife made the damn soup! It was beautiful soup. My wife's beautiful too, isn't she, Rosalind?

ROSALIND. Yes.

CHARLEY (*to* ANNA). She's as beautiful as that soup.

WILLIAM *sways in his chair.*

(*To* ANNA.) She's rich and intelligent and beautiful. And we've got three kids. Don't forget *that*. And she understands me. *And* . . .

STEPHEN. And.

CHARLEY. *And* . . . we're all very old friends. Him and his wife. And me and my wife. Don't forget that.

STEPHEN. But he's more successful than me because he appears on television.

ANNA (*to* CHARLEY). Do you talk on television?

CHARLEY. What do you think I do, play the flute?

ANNA. What do you talk about?

CHARLEY. You name it I'll talk about it.

STEPHEN. He talks about history, zoology –

CHARLEY. Anthropology, sociolog . . . sociologigy –

STEPHEN. Sociology!

CHARLEY. Codology.

STEPHEN. And sex. In that order.

ROSALIND. He suits the medium.

STEPHEN (*to* ROSALIND). Do you mean you don't think I would suit the medium?

CHARLEY. They wouldn't let you within ten miles of the medium!

STEPHEN *points a long arm across the table at* CHARLEY.

STEPHEN. I have an appointment with *your* producer next week.

CHARLEY. With *my* producer?

STEPHEN. *Your* producer.

WILLIAM *slumps on to the table.* ROSALIND *rises, goes to* ANNA. *They whisper.*

CHARLEY. What, with old Bill Smith?

STEPHEN. He's asked to see me.

CHARLEY. You're going to be on *my* television show?

STEPHEN. I'll run you out of town, kid.

ROSALIND. Stephen, he wants to drive back.

STEPHEN. Who does?

ROSALIND. William.

STEPHEN. Impossible. He's drunk.

ANNA. I'll drive.

CHARLEY. You haven't got a licence.

ANNA. William, can I drive?

ROSALIND. No. You'll have to stay.

WILLIAM. I'll drive.

ANNA. Oh, we'd better stay.

STEPHEN. I'll drive.

ROSALIND. No you won't.

STEPHEN. Charley can drive!

WILLIAM *stands. His chair falls.*

WILLIAM. Oh, to hell . . .

STEPHEN *stands, goes to him.*

STEPHEN. Listen, old boy. You're slightly drunk. You can stay.

WILLIAM. Why the bloody hell do you want us to bloody well stay?

ROSALIND takes WILLIAM's arm.

ROSALIND. Oh, come on.

She leads him out. ANNA follows.
STEPHEN leans on to the table. He stares across the table at CHARLEY, who stares back at him.
Silence.
STEPHEN walks to the door.

STEPHEN. Will you excuse me?

CHARLEY. But of course, my dear fellow.

Interior. Kitchen. Night.
Tap in sink turned full on.
STEPHEN's head bends underneath it.
He turns tap off, holds towel to his head, sits heavily in chair.
CHARLEY comes in, sways slightly, leans on door frame.

CHARLEY. They're staying.

Silence. .

Which room . . . is everyone in?

Pause.

STEPHEN. How the hell should I know?

Pause.

CHARLEY. Splendid day.

STEPHEN (*carefully*). It gives me great pleasure to know that you have enjoyed your day with us. Good night.

CHARLEY. Good night.

CHARLEY goes out of kitchen door.

Interior. Kitchen. Later.
Dog, looking up.
STEPHEN, *slumped in kitchen chair, wakes suddenly,*
looks at watch.
He stands, clenches eyes, goes to door.

Interior. The hall.
STEPHEN *switches out hall light.*
He looks up the stairs.
In the faint light at the top of the stairs he sees a
woman ascending in a negligee with frilled cuffs. He
stares after her. She goes out of sight.

Interior. Bedroom.
He enters, closes door. Stops dead.
A woman lies in the fourposter.
He stares with disbelief and delight.
He mouths softly :
STEPHEN. Anna.

He goes to bed, looks down. It is ROSALIND.

Interior. Bedroom.
STEPHEN *climbing onto the bed. He touches his wife.*
STEPHEN (*whispering*). Rosalind. (*Pause.*) Darling?
ROSALIND (*blurred*). What?
STEPHEN. I love you.

Interior. Television building. Day.
STEPHEN *sitting by low table in third floor ante-room,*
glass-panelled.
A RECEPTIONIST *sits at a distance from him, at a*
desk.
STEPHEN *flips through magazines.*
He opens a trade magazine.
Photograph of Charley and others with cameras,
entitled 'Conversation Piece'.

The phone rings. RECEPTIONIST *lifts it.*

RECEPTIONIST. Reception? . . . Yes . . . I see . . . Thank you.

She puts phone down.

(*To* STEPHEN.) Mr Smith isn't here, I'm afraid. Will you see Mr Bell?

STEPHEN. Uuh . . . yes, all right.

RECEPTIONIST (*pointing down corridor*). It's the fifth door on the left.

Interior. Corridor.
STEPHEN *walks down corridor.*
Box cubicles on either side of wood and glass. Voices, as he passes, from offices.
A door marked : MR BELL. ASSISTANT. TALKS.

Interior. BELL's *office.*
BELL *rising from desk.* SECRETARY *in corner, typing. Loud indecipherable voice from next office. Behind* BELL, *through small window, a building site. Cranes, bulldozers, etc.* BELL *wears a cardigan.*

BELL (*shaking hands*). Hullo . . . I'm Bell. Remember me? I'm Bell.

STEPHEN. Uuuhh . . .

BELL. I was at Oxford.

STEPHEN. Of course. How are you?

BELL. Bill Smith's ill. He's in hospital.

STEPHEN. Oh, I'm sorry.

BELL. I've got to go and see him. Sit down. (*To* SECRETARY.) Got that file?

SECRETARY *goes to filing cabinet.* STEPHEN *sits.*

STEPHEN. I don't . . . actually know him.

BELL. You don't *know* him?

SECRETARY *gives* BELL *file. He flips through it.*

What did he want you for, do you know?

STEPHEN. I think he . . . mmn . . .

BELL (*flipping*). Do you ever see Francesca?

STEPHEN. Who?

BELL. Francesca. The provost's daughter. The daughter of the provost.

STEPHEN. Ah . . . yes. No, I don't.

BELL (*swift smile*). You knew her well.

STEPHEN. I've been married some years.

BELL. Well done. (*Finding letter.*) Ah . . . yes. Bill was thinking of you for 'Conversation Piece'. I've got to go and see him in a minute. He's very ill.

A man enters the office hurriedly.

MAN. What's the matter with Bill?

BELL. He's very bad. He's in hospital.

MAN. What!

The MAN *sits heavily. The phone rings.*

SECRETARY (*on phone*). Mr Bell's secretary.

STEPHEN. Yes . . .

SECRETARY (*on phone*). Who?

STEPHEN. I think he was thinking of me.

MAN. He was perfectly all right yesterday. I had a drink with him.

SECRETARY *puts hand over receiver.*

SECRETARY. Mr Dyce.

BELL *waves hand irritably.*

MAN. I can't believe it.

SECRETARY (*to phone*). No, I'm afraid he's not.

BELL. Listen, the point is I don't know what his plans were, you see.

MAN. What happened to him?

SECRETARY (*on phone*). Yes, I'll see he gets the message.

BELL *stands.*

BELL. Perhaps I could let you know. (*To* MAN.) He collapsed last night. Look, why don't you come and see him? I'm going over there now to see him.

MAN. What time you going?

BELL. I'm going now. (*Shaking hands with* STEPHEN.) Well, all right. Sorry about this. Give my love to Francesca.

STEPHEN. I haven't seen her.

MAN. You're going straight away, are you?

BELL. I told you, I'm going right away. I'm going now.

Interior. Telephone booth.
His tie in the square mirror.
He is dialling. The number buzzes. No answer.
His hand begins to replace receiver.
A sudden voice in receiver : 'Hullo'.
He holds the receiver still.
The voice : 'Hullo'.
He lifts the receiver and speaks.

STEPHEN. Francesca?

Exterior. Block of flats. Evening.
STEPHEN *walks to door of flats. He stops, walks to*
edge of pavement. Walks past door, stops.
He turns and goes in.

The following sequence with FRANCESCA *is silent.*
The only sounds heard are the voices overlaid at
stated points. The words are fragments of realistic
conversation. They are not thoughts. Nor are they
combined with any lip movement on the part of the
actors. They are distributed over the sequence so as to
act as a disembodied comment on the action.

Interior. FRANCESCA's *flat. Evening.*
Sitting-room.
FRANCESCA *walking towards drink table. She is*
smiling. She is no longer young.
HER VOICE (OVER)
You haven't changed at all!
Not at all!

A silent record turns on the record player.

STEPHEN *standing, looking after her, his eyes narrowed.*
HIS VOICE (OVER) (*gaily*)
Wonderful to see you!
FRANCESCA *brings a glass to him, hands it to him. She smiles tenderly at him.*
HER VOICE (OVER)
I was in my bath when you phoned!
She turns, goes back to drinks.

STEPHEN, *with drink, sitting on sofa.*
HIS VOICE (OVER)
Well, it must be ten years.

FRANCESCA, *at drinks table, concentrating, squirting soda into glass.*
HER VOICE (OVER)
Ten years! It can't be!

Both sitting on sofa, slowly click glasses.
HER VOICE (OVER)
It can't be. It must be.
HIS VOICE (OVER)
It must be.
HER VOICE (OVER)
It is.

FRANCESCA *switching off silent record.*
She walks towards bedroom. As she walks:
HIS VOICE (OVER)
You don't look a day older.
HER VOICE (OVER)
Oh really, I'm ten years older.

FRANCESCA *walking from bedroom with her coat.*
STEPHEN *walks towards her, helps her on with her coat. She leans back, puts her cheek to his, kisses his cheek.*
HER VOICE (OVER)
How's your wife?

Flat door closing. Light goes out.
Sitting-room. Nightlight through window.
The room empty.
HIS VOICE (OVER)
That's a beautiful dress and a beautiful coat. You look marvellous.

Interior. Restaurant. Night.
STEPHEN *and* FRANCESCA *at a table.*
WAITER *pouring wine into glasses.*
STEPHEN *and* FRANCESCA *looking at each other.*
His face, looking.
Her face, looking.
HER VOICE (OVER)
I'm in consumer research. Did you know? It's fascinating.

FRANCESCA *refusing potatoes from* WAITER, *laughing.*

STEPHEN *beckoning the* WAITER *for potatoes, grinning.*
HIS VOICE (OVER) (*softly*)
Remember those times in the car? Do you? Do you?

FRANCESCA *eating.*
HER VOICE (OVER) (*softly*)
Of course I remember.

Both eating, talking.
HER VOICE (OVER) (*softly*)
I remember.

FRANCESCA *accepting cigarette from* STEPHEN.
She looks at him, cigarette in mouth, while he digs in pocket for lighter.
HER VOICE (OVER)
I'm supposed to be on a diet.
I'm too fat.
He lights her cigarette.

HER VOICE (OVER)
So then you'll have three?
Three children. Good gracious.

Exterior. Restaurant. Night.
DOORMAN *opening taxi door for them.* STEPHEN
tips him.
HIS VOICE (OVER)
You're not fat.

Interior. FRANCESCA's *flat. Sitting-room. Night.*
Dimly lit table lamp. STEPHEN *sitting, leaning*
forward.
HER VOICE (OVER)
I'm very happy.

Bathroom door opens. She comes out, walks across
the room to him.
HER VOICE (OVER)
My life is happy.

Interior. Bedroom. Night.
FRANCESCA *and* STEPHEN *in bed, naked. His eyes*
are open. She lies in his arms, eyes closed.
HER VOICE (OVER)
Have I changed?
HIS VOICE (OVER)
You're the same.
HER VOICE (OVER)
The same as I was? The same as I was . . . then?
HIS VOICE (OVER)
The same.

Interior. House. Hall.
STEPHEN *switches light on in hall. He sits down*
heavily at the hall table, holding his head.

Pile of letters on table.
Silence.
Creaks from upstairs.
He looks up sharply.
Another creak.
He stands, tense, looks round for some kind of imple-
ment.
Footsteps along the landing. He stares up.
CHARLEY *looks over the banister. He comes down the*
stairs, sits on a step halfway down. He wears a
dressing gown.

CHARLEY. Hullo.

Pause.

STEPHEN. Hullo. I've just come from London.
CHARLEY. I know.

ANNA *appears at the top of the stairs. She is dressed.*
in sweater and trousers. Bare feet.
STEPHEN *stares up at her.*
Eventually his gaze drops to CHARLEY.

STEPHEN. To see the television people.

ANNA *remains still.*

Silence.

CHARLEY. Did you see them?
STEPHEN. I'm hungry.

STEPHEN *goes along passage to kitchen.*

Interior. Kitchen.
One place is laid for breakfast on the kitchen table.
STEPHEN *goes to the fridge.*
STEPHEN's *face at lighted fridge. He takes out eggs.*
STEPHEN *stands with eggs.*
ANNA *and* CHARLEY *at the kitchen door.* ANNA *is*
whispering to CHARLEY.
STEPHEN *puts eggs in bowl, takes down frying pan.*

STEPHEN. I'm going to make an omelette.

CHARLEY. We don't want anything.

STEPHEN *puts butter in pan.*

ANNA. Shall I cook?

CHARLEY. Can you?

ANNA *sits at table, takes crumpled cigarette packet and matches from trouser pocket, lights cigarette.*

Can I have a cigarette?

She passes packet across table. He lights one.
STEPHEN *heats frying pan and begins to beat the eggs.*

I wrote to you. The letter's out in the hall. You didn't get it.

STEPHEN. I left early.

CHARLEY (*to* ANNA). Get the letter.

She sits still. CHARLEY *grins, goes into hall.*
STEPHEN *empties eggs into pan.* ANNA *smokes.*
CHARLEY *returns with two letters, throws one on table.*

Here it is. (*Looks at other.*) There's another one for you. From my wife. A personal letter from her to you. Open it.

STEPHEN *holds pan handle.* CHARLEY *opens letter and reads.*
Silence.
STEPHEN *twists pan.*

(*Reading aloud.*) De-da-, de-da, de-da, de-da . . . Ah . . . So I just want to beg you that while still being understanding, sympathetic, etc. you don't necessarily show to him you think it's the great thing of his life. You might even hint that sooner or later he'll be bored to death by her. I believe this of course, but naturally am in a wrong position even to hint. I always wondered what this would be like if and when it happened, but I must say it beats everything. Love. Laura. P.S. Don't say I wrote for heaven's sake.

CHARLEY *throws letter on table and grins at* ANNA *and* STEPHEN. STEPHEN *flips omelette on to plate, puts it on table.* CHARLEY *sits down, begins to eat it. Pause.*

ANNA. I thought you didn't want any.
CHARLEY. I didn't.
ANNA. Then why are you eating it?
CHARLEY. Mind your own damn bloody business!

CHARLEY *shoves the plate away.*
STEPHEN *sits at other side of table and continues eating omelette.*
The three sitting at the table.
STEPHEN *pushes plate away and leaves the kitchen.*

Interior. Landing.
STEPHEN *on landing looks down passage into spare room.*
The door is open.
He walks to it, goes in.

Interior. Spare bedroom.
STEPHEN *looks about. The sheets and pillows on the bed are rumpled. The top sheet and blanket falling to the floor.* CHARLEY'S *clothes lie on a chair.* ANNA'S *shoes on floor. Handbag and tissues on dressing table. He leaves room, goes to bathroom.*

Interior. Bathroom.
STEPHEN *looks at his face in mirror, wipes his mouth briskly with towel, looks at towel. He looks round at bathroom. A towel on the floor. Drops of water in bath.*
ANNA *passes bathroom door.*

Interior. Landing.
STEPHEN *on landing looking down passage to spare room.* ANNA *is straightening the bed.*

CHARLEY's *voice from below, on telephone:* 'Hullo. Hullo, yes. This is Palling 146 . . . Hullo.'

Interior. Spare room.
ANNA *bending over bed. She looks up.*

STEPHEN. What are you doing?

ANNA. Making the bed.

STEPHEN. No need to do that. A woman comes in every morning.

ANNA. I can do it.

STEPHEN. Leave it, please.

She stops, goes to handbag, puts tissues into it.

ANNA. We're going.

CHARLEY's *voice from below, raised:* 'Yes. A taxi. Now. To go into Oxford.'

STEPHEN. You might as well stay. It's very late.

ANNA *and* STEPHEN *look at each other.*
CHARLEY's *voice:* 'Straight away. Okay. Right.'
ANNA *and* STEPHEN *remain looking at each other.*
CHARLEY's *voice, ascending stairs:* 'Anna! I've got a taxi.'

Interior. Landing.
ANNA *and* STEPHEN *seen standing in room.*
CHARLEY *walks along passage to room.*

Interior. Spare room.
CHARLEY *at door of room.*

CHARLEY. It's on its way.

ANNA. I'll wait downstairs.

ANNA *goes out.*

CHARLEY. Shut the door, for God's sake.

STEPHEN *shuts the door.* CHARLEY *starts to dress quickly.*

It was her idea, she knew Rosalind was away, she said you wouldn't mind.

STEPHEN. I don't mind. It's got nothing to do with me.

CHARLEY. It's your bloody house!

CHARLEY *struggles into his clothes.*

Anyway, I wrote to you but you didn't get the damn letter.

STEPHEN. When did it start?

CHARLEY. What? Oh, weeks ago. Weeks. We used to go to her room in the afternoon. Didn't even have a lock on the door. Anyone could have come in. Someone did come in once. A girl. Can you imagine?

CHARLEY *pulls at his socks, sitting on the bed.*

I'm sleeping at college most of the time now. I can't take her there, can I? Where can I damn well take her?

STEPHEN. I thought she and William . . . were close friends.

CHARLEY. They are! They're just friends. It means nothing. She's not a whore.

He puts on shoes.

I don't know what to do, you see. I can't have enough of her.

Sound of taxi.
STEPHEN *goes to window, draws curtains.*
Down below he sees taxi drawing up. DRIVER *gets out, goes to front door. A shaft of light from door onto the gravel.*
CHARLEY'*s voice.*

I don't know what to do.

The DRIVER *gets back into taxi, sits.*
STEPHEN *turns from window.*

STEPHEN. Where's your car?

CHARLEY. Laura's got it.

STEPHEN. I'm going to see Rosalind tomorrow. At her mother's. Then I'm going to William's house. I've been invited down there. You can bring her here for the weekend.

Pause.

CHARLEY. Thanks.

He puts on his jacket, combs his hair.

It's the children, you see. I'm never there. They're missing me.

A call from ANNA *from below :* 'The taxi's waiting.'
CHARLEY *shouts :* 'Coming!'
CHARLEY *picks up dressing gown, hands it to* STEPHEN.

This is your dressing gown.
STEPHEN (*taking it*). Can I ask you a question?
CHARLEY. What?
STEPHEN. How did you get in tonight?
CHARLEY. Through the lavatory window.
STEPHEN. You're a bit old for that.
CHARLEY. Yes, I am.
STEPHEN. Here's a key.
CHARLEY. Thanks.

CHARLEY *goes to door.*

STEPHEN. One more question.
CHARLEY (*with fatigue*). What?
STEPHEN. Last Sunday night, when you all stayed, did you sleep with her here?

Pause.

CHARLEY. Of course I did.

Exterior. ROSALIND's *mother's small house, in the country. The garden. Day.*
STEPHEN *and* ROSALIND *lie in deckchairs.*
His eyes are closed. Sun.

ROSALIND (*drowsily*). Did you see anyone in London?
STEPHEN. No.

Pause.

ROSALIND. What happened with the television people?
STEPHEN. Nothing. Wasn't any good. (*He looks at her.*) You look wonderful..
ROSALIND. I feel it. I feel great.

Pause.

I wish you could stay.
STEPHEN. So do I.
ROSALIND. Still, you'll have a good time at William's house, won't you? With all the lords and ladies.

STEPHEN *grunts, sits humped in the deckchair.*
She looks at him.

What's the matter?

Exterior. CHARLEY *and* LAURA's *house in country.*
The garden. Day.
A hose running off lawn into flower beds.
The water spouts.
STEPHEN *from back door comes into garden.*
He walks across it.
LAURA *comes into shot, stops. He waves, walking.*
She watches his approach.
STEPHEN. Hullo, Laura.
LAURA. Hullo, Stephen.
STEPHEN. The door was open. How are you?
LAURA. Fine.

He looks at hose.

STEPHEN. What are you doing?
LAURA. Charley's not here.
STEPHEN. I got your letter.

Pause.

LAURA. I'm just doing the garden.

STEPHEN. What are you doing to it?
LAURA. Caring for it.

Exterior. ROSALIND's *mother's house. Garden.*
STEPHEN *and* ROSALIND.

STEPHEN. I got home from London and found Charley and Anna there.
ROSALIND. Charley and Anna?
STEPHEN. Yes.
ROSALIND. Together? In the house?
STEPHEN. Yes. I got home late, a bit drunk. I was . . . astonished.
ROSALIND. Why were you drunk?
STEPHEN. Oh, I had dinner with Francesca. You remember. You remember Francesca?
ROSALIND. Yes.
STEPHEN. Just gave her a ring, you know. It was quite pleasant.

Pause.

ROSALIND. He's sleeping with her, is he?
STEPHEN. Who?
ROSALIND. Charley. With Anna.
STEPHEN. Of course.
ROSALIND. How pathetic.
STEPHEN. What do you mean?
ROSALIND. Poor stupid old man.
STEPHEN. He's not old.
ROSALIND. Stupid bastard.

Pause.

Does Laura know?
STEPHEN. Yes.
ROSALIND. What about the children? Has he told them?

Exterior. Garden. LAURA's *house.*
LAURA *re-setting hose on flowerbed.* STEPHEN *standing.*

STEPHEN. It'll be all right . . . you know.
LAURA. What will?

She directs hose.

STEPHEN. I know it will.
LAURA. Have you had lunch?
STEPHEN. Yes.

Pause.

Didn't you want me to come?
LAURA. Yes.
STEPHEN. Well, I'm just trying to tell you . . .
LAURA. Do you want some coffee?
STEPHEN. No, I don't want coffee.

She walks along flowerbed. Hose spouting. He follows.

Listen . . . this thing . . . it's nothing. It'll all
fall flat.
LAURA. He says he's in love with her.
STEPHEN. Love! Everyone thinks they're in love!
LAURA. Do you?

Exterior. ROSALIND's mother's garden.
ROSALIND. I've never heard of anything so bloody puerile, so
banal.
STEPHEN. What's banal about it?
ROSALIND. That poor stupid bitch of a girl.
STEPHEN. You just keep calling everyone stupid, what's the
use – ?
ROSALIND. Well, they are. Except Laura. And she's stupid too.

Pause.

You chucked them out, I hope?

Exterior. Garden. LAURA's house.
LAURA and STEPHEN standing middle of lawn.
LAURA. Well . . . don't worry about it.
STEPHEN. I'm not.
LAURA. Thanks for coming.

Exterior. ROSALIND's *mother's garden.*
STEPHEN *and* ROSALIND *in the deckchairs, still.*
Silence.

STEPHEN. I think I'll pop in and see Laura. It's on my way.
ROSALIND. Give her my love.

Interior. LORD CODRINGTON's *country house.*
Evening.
A large stone corridor. High windows. A green baize door at one end. An archway to the main body of the house at the other. Large family portraits on the walls.
About a dozen MEN *are taking off their jackets and hanging them on a stand. They proceed to tuck their trousers into their socks.*
STEPHEN *is watching.* WILLIAM *joins him.*
They stand in archway.

WILLIAM. Anna was coming down, but she's got some of her family over, or something.
STEPHEN. Ah.
WILLIAM. Do you know, I've never thanked you for introducing us.
STEPHEN. I didn't.

A group of LADIES *comes through archway.*
WILLIAM *smiles at them, moves aside with* STEPHEN.

WILLIAM. Haven't you ever played this game before?
STEPHEN. No.
WILLIAM. It's traditional. We all played it at school.
STEPHEN. Ah.
WILLIAM. You'll enjoy it. It's fun.

WILLIAM *goes to side table and picks up a long heavy stuffed shapeless cushion cover.*

This is the ball, you see.
STEPHEN. Uh-huh.

WILLIAM *looks at him.*

WILLIAM. I think you should go in goal.

STEPHEN. Where's that?

WILLIAM. Down there, by that door.

> STEPHEN *looks down corridor.*
> *A few* MEN *are doing limbering up exercises.*
> STEPHEN *turns to* WILLIAM.

STEPHEN. I've got a funny feeling this is a murderous game.

WILLIAM. Not at all.

STEPHEN. Isn't it true all aristocrats want to die?

WILLIAM (*smiling*). I don't.

STEPHEN. What do I do in goal?

WILLIAM. Defend it.

STEPHEN. How?

WILLIAM. Any way you like.

STEPHEN. Can't I just watch?

WILLIAM. No. You're a house guest. You must play. Only the old men watch. And the ladies.

> *Through the archway towards the corridor the* LADIES *walk, talking and laughing.*
> STEPHEN *hangs his jacket on stand and walks uneasily down the corridor, between the men, to the door at the end. He stands by the door.*
> *The* MEN *collect at one wall, under the pictures.*
> STEPHEN *watches them. He bends quickly and tucks his trousers into his socks.*
> *The* MEN *line up by the wall, leaving a space between them and the wall. One* MAN, *at the far end of the row, holds the ball.*
> *The corridor, which has echoed with voices and footsteps, becomes silent.*
> *The row of* MEN *by wall, tense, waiting.*
> *The* MAN *with ball in foreground.*
> *The group of* LADIES, *with a few elderly* MEN, *silent, watching, in the archway.*
> STEPHEN.
> *Long shot of corridor. Utter stillness.*
> *The* MAN *with ball dashes between* MEN *and wall.*
> *The* MEN *fall on him. A scrum.*
> *The* MAN *attempts to break through, gripping the ball*

to him. *The others try to drag it from him. He shoves right and left with his elbows.*

The struggling scrum inches along the wall.

It is silent but for grunts. MEN, *striving, become attached to the backs of others. A communal buggery.*

The MAN *with ball is lifted off his feet from behind.*

WILLIAM *seizes the ball, dashes free towards goal.*

STEPHEN *standing.* WILLIAM *dashing toward him.*

WILLIAM *is tackled by four* MEN, *is trapped at the waist from behind. The others attempt to pull the ball away.* WILLIAM *kicks the* MAN *behind him. He cracks his elbows sharply into the faces of two others and swiftly turning, butts the fourth* MAN *with his head.*

WILLIAM, *free, runs. Others join to chase him.*

He dodges, charges two MEN *down, still holding ball, and again dashes towards* STEPHEN *in goal.*

STEPHEN'*s legs, moving out of goal, bracing, as* WILLIAM *charges down upon him.*

WILLIAM *charges him in the stomach.*

STEPHEN *is carried along a little way on* WILLIAM'*s back.*

He swings off, pressing his fingers on the back of WILLIAM'*s neck.*

STEPHEN *grappling with* WILLIAM, *momentarily.*

They are tackled and surrounded.

A MAN *jumps on* STEPHEN'*s back.* STEPHEN *flings his head back, hitting* MAN *in face. The* MAN *falls, rolls away holding his face.*

The scrum.

WILLIAM, *with ball, trying to force way out.*

STEPHEN *grappling with him, eyes staring.*

Above them a canopy of arms flailing, bodies twisting.

The MEN *fight with each other.*

Elbows in stomachs. Feet kicking. Forearms cuffing.

Hands pulling at ball, which WILLIAM *clutches to him, as he kicks up.* STEPHEN *lashes out at* MEN *above him.*

Top shot of scrum.

It strives forward ponderously, brokenly; a bowel with a gut gone.

WILLIAM's *teeth bared.*
The LADIES, *watching.*
Under canopy of bodies, WILLIAM *grapples with*
STEPHEN.
STEPHEN's *face, teeth bared.*
He savagely knees WILLIAM *in the face.*
WILLIAM's *face, receiving knee.*
STEPHEN *felled from behind. He falls.*
From above.
The scrum, squirming in a circle.
WILLIAM, *bloody, savaged by hands.*
The ball torn from him.

Exterior. Cricket field. Day.
WILLIAM, *batting, hitting ball savagely.*
Vigorous applause.
WILLIAM *wipes his forehead.*
WILLIAM *is immaculate in white.*
The PROVOST, CHARLEY *and* STEPHEN *stand near*
the pavilion, watching the game.

PROVOST. He really is a magnificent athlete.

CHARLEY. Yes, he's a natural, that boy.

PROVOST. I was quite good myself. But not altogether in the
same class. What about you, Stephen? Were you
any good?

STEPHEN (*smiling*). No.

WILLIAM *hooks the ball through the field.*
PROVOST *applauds.* STEPHEN *looks at him.*

I saw Francesca when I was in London.

The PROVOST *looks at him, bewildered.*

Your daughter.

PROVOST. Ah. How is she?

STEPHEN. Very well. She sent you her love.

PROVOST. Ah. Please give her mine when you see her again.

STEPHEN. Oh, I don't know when I'll be seeing her again.

WILLIAM *sends a ball high into the air.*
A FIELDER, *on the boundary, waits for it, catches it.*

Applause, as WILLIAM, *bat raised, runs up steps of pavilion.*
STEPHEN *stands alone under a tree, applauding.*
STEPHEN *turns.* ANNA *is beside him.*

ANNA. Hullo.
STEPHEN. Hullo. Have a nice week-end?
ANNA. Yes, Thank you for your hospitality.

Pause.

I'm getting married.
STEPHEN. Oh. Who to?
ANNA. William.

Pause.
STEPHEN *watches the game, which, in the background, continues.*

STEPHEN. Ah. Have you told him?

ANNA *giggles.*

Well, congratulations.
ANNA. I wonder if you could tell Charley for me.

STEPHEN *looks at her.*

Will you let me know what he says?

WILLIAM *runs up the side of the field to join them.*
WILLIAM *puts his arm round* ANNA.

WILLIAM (*to* STEPHEN). Hullo.
STEPHEN. Well played.
WILLIAM. Thanks. Look, I want to come and see you, have a word with you. Can I come tonight, after this party? I'll be a bit late.
STEPHEN. Sure. What's the trouble?
WILLIAM. No trouble. No trouble at all.
STEPHEN (*to* ANNA). You coming?
WILLIAM. No, I don't want her.

WILLIAM *punches* STEPHEN *on the chest, lightly, but* STEPHEN *staggers.*

I want a man to man talk!

STEPHEN. We can talk when she's in bed. She can sleep in the spare room. Can't you?

ANNA. That would be nice.

WILLIAM. Okay. We'll see you later. Come on!

WILLIAM, *arms round* ANNA's *waist, runs along the edge of the field with her.*
STEPHEN *walks along in their wake.*
He looks down. CHARLEY *is sitting in a deckchair.*
CHARLEY *looks up, winks.*
STEPHEN *looks after them.*
WILLIAM's *face,* ANNA's *face, together, as they run.*

WILLIAM's *face dead at bottom of car.*

ANNA, *head and shoulders rising out of overturned car. Moonlight.*

ANNA *sitting on grass bank. Moonlight.*

ANNA *lying on fourposter bed.*

Interior. House. Bedroom. Night.
STEPHEN *sitting upright on chair by the window. The bedroom.*
ANNA *on bed.* STEPHEN *on chair. Stillness.*
ANNA *sighs in her sleep, rolls on to her side, half sits up, almost falls off bed.*
He goes to her, holds her.
STEPHEN *kneeling at the side of the bed, holding* ANNA's *shoulders on the bed.*

STEPHEN. It's all right.

She stares at him, lost, suddenly frowns, is still, tense, crouched at the edge of the bed.
He lifts his hand to touch her forehead.
She shies away, slides off bed, sits sharply on the floor.
She laughs, stops suddenly.

STEPHEN *bends over her, squatting.*
She looks swiftly up at his body, then down.

Did anyone know you were with him?

She does not look up.
He grips her jaw.

You can hear me.

She moves her jaw in his grip.

Can't you?

He tightens grip, twists her head to him.
Her eyes close, her head jerks back.
Her hands claw at him.
He seizes her hands. Her face jerks from side to side.
She is whimpering.
He thrusts his body between her legs, fixes his elbows
on her arms, and presses his thumbs on her cheeks.
Large close-up.
Her face, pulled out of shape by his thumbs. Her eyes
slits.
His thumbs press her face back against bed.
Top shot.
The two bodies, hardly moving, battling, at the side of
the bed.
The telephone rings from below.
His face, set. His eyes flicker towards sound of
telephone. He concentrates on ANNA.
ANNA's *face, stretched.*
She suddenly becomes limp. The phone stops.
She looks at him. His grip relaxes on her face.

Did anyone know you were coming here with him?

She looks at him calmly. No response.

Was he supposed to have dropped you off at your
room?

Her face, calm, non-committal.
His face.
Her ear. Long hair falling.

His mouth at her ear.

He's dead.

Her head turns to look at him.
Their faces very close.

You had an accident. You crashed.

Pause.

You *were* driving, weren't you?

The telephone rings below. He frowns, hesitates,
stands. ANNA *remains still. He goes to door.*

Interior. House. Landing.
He looks down stairs. Phone ringing.

Interior. House. The stairs.
He starts down the stairs. He is almost at the foot
when the telephone stops ringing.
He stands, then turns back.

Interior. Bedroom.
STEPHEN *at door.*
ANNA *is not by the bed. He turns swiftly.*
ANNA *is standing by the window, holding curtain,*
looking down into garden.
He walks quickly to window, pulls ANNA *away,*
pulls curtain into place, keeping hold of her arm.

STEPHEN. Someone might see you.

He still holds her arm. He looks at her, pulls her to
him suddenly and kisses her.
The kiss is very brief. He draws back.
They stand, apart.
Their bodies standing. Waist level. Not touching.
Their arms.
His hands touch her arms, move up.

He folds her in his arms and kisses her slowly.
She does not resist.
He withdraws from embrace, walks to bedside lamp,
turns it off.
The bedroom door is still half open. Light from the
landing comes into the room.
He stands by the lamp.
She remains by the window.
He is still by the lamp.
Slowly, she walks across the room towards him.
She passes through the channel of light from the door.
Her body, by the bed.
His body, by the bed.
Both of them, standing by the bed, in the dim light.

Exterior. The house. Front door. Morning.
The front door is open. STEPHEN *stands by it, look-*
ing into hall.
ANNA *is sitting in chair in the hall.*

STEPHEN. Right.

ANNA stands, begins to walk to door.

Your handbag.

She stops, turns, picks up her handbag walks, to door,
to him.
The telephone rings.

Interior. Hall.
ANNA *and* STEPHEN *still, at door. Outside, morning*
light. The phone rings. He walks into hall and lifts it.

STEPHEN. Hullo? . . . Yes? . . . Oh, have you? . . . Sorry,
I've been asleep, didn't hear it . . . Yes . . . Ah
. . . I see . . . But she's all right? . . . Yes . . .
I'll get dressed and . . . get there. Thank you . . .
Thank you. (*He lowers receiver, lifts it quickly.*)
Oh, I'm sorry I didn't hear the – (*He replaces re-*
ceiver.)

STEPHEN *walks to the door. They go out. The door closes.*

Exterior. Quiet road in Oxford. Morning.
The road is silent. On one side of it is a tree-lined open space. On the other, a wall.
STEPHEN's *car approaches at far end of road.*
It approaches and slides quietly in to the kerb.
The car, stationary, in long shot.
Early sunshine. Silence.

Interior. Car.
STEPHEN *and* ANNA *sitting. He looks up the road and glances into the mirror.*

STEPHEN. Can you get in . . . without anyone seeing you?

He looks at her.

ANNA. Mmnn.
STEPHEN. No one must see you.

Birds, seen through the windscreen, skim down across the road.
ANNA *gets out of the car.*
ANNA *closes car door quietly and walks along by the wall. She stops and returns.*

Interior. Car.
STEPHEN *leans over and winds passenger window down.*
She leans in at window.
STEPHEN. What?
ANNA. You'll have to help me up.

He grimaces.

I can't get over the wall by myself.
STEPHEN (*muttering*). Why didn't you say so—

Exterior. Car.
He gets out, closes door quietly.

Exterior. Road. The wall.
ANNA *walking by wall, followed by* STEPHEN.
She stops at a part of the wall where a large tree over-
hangs.

ANNA. Here.

STEPHEN *hoists her up.*

Exterior. Women's college grounds.
The other side of the wall. The tree.
ANNA's *head and shoulders rise above wall.*
She clasps branch of the tree, sits on wall, throws
handbag down on to grass.

Exterior. Road. Wall.
STEPHEN *looking up, his hands raised.* ANNA's *left*
leg swings over. She disappears over wall.
His face, glancing sharply up the road.

Interior. Hospital.
Baby in gauze tent. Tubes lead into it.
The baby's mouth is moving. Its eyes are shut.
Camera moves up to see the back of STEPHEN's *head*
going out of ward door.

Interior. Private room. Hospital.
ROSALIND *in bed.* STEPHEN *sitting by bed.*
ROSALIND *speaks very quietly.*

ROSALIND. They phoned you. You weren't there.

STEPHEN. I was asleep. I didn't hear.

Pause.

ROSALIND. He can't breathe. It's difficult for him to breathe.

Did you see that?

STEPHEN. But he is breathing. They're helping him.

ROSALIND. He isn't dead?

Pause.

STEPHEN. No.

Interior. Women's college. Living quarters.
STEPHEN *walking up stone stairway to* ANNA's *room.*
Below him, at foot of steps, sunlight frames in quadrangle arch. His steps echo.
CHARLEY *appears in arch, looks up, calls.*

CHARLEY. Stephen.

STEPHEN *turns on step.* CHARLEY *ascends, reaches him.* STEPHEN *is calm, almost detached.* CHARLEY *is panting.*

I've just heard. About William.

Pause.

You found him.

STEPHEN. Yes.

Pause.

CHARLEY. Does she know?

Pause.

STEPHEN. I don't know.

CHARLEY *looks up to her room.*

CHARLEY. Have you just come to tell her?

STEPHEN. Yes.

Pause.

CHARLEY. It must have been terrible for you.

Pause.

Look, leave this to me, if you like.
STEPHEN. No, it's all right.

They turn up the stairs.

Interior. ANNA's *room.*
There are two cases on the bed.
ANNA *is packing. There is a knock on the door and the*
door opens. CHARLEY *and* STEPHEN *enter.*
She stops packing.
CHARLEY *walks forward, looks at cases.*
CHARLEY. What are you doing?

She does not answer.

You've heard what's happened?

Pause.

ANNA. Yes.

Pause.

CHARLEY. I'm sorry.

STEPHEN *sits down in an armchair.* CHARLEY *turns*
to him.

What happened? Was he drunk? They say there
was whisky all over the car. Was there?
STEPHEN. I didn't notice.
CHARLEY. But you found him.

ANNA *continues packing.*

(*To* ANNA.) How did you hear about it?

He goes to her.

What are you doing? Why are you packing?
ANNA. I'm going home.

STEPHEN *in chair, eyes half closed.*
CHARLEY *stands, bewildered.*
ANNA *bending at suitcase.* CHARLEY *stands.*

CHARLEY. Why?

> ANNA *moves to collect some records, comes back, packs them under dresses.*

Why are you going home?

STEPHEN. They were going to be married.

CHARLEY. Rubbish.

STEPHEN. He told me.

CHARLEY. It's rubbish.

> CHARLEY *moves to* ANNA.

Look, I know it's . . . terrible. But listen . . . there's no reason for you to go home.

> *He touches her shoulder.*
> *Her shoulder. She withdraws her shoulder from his hand quickly.*
> ANNA *continues packing.*
> CHARLEY *grips her arm. She becomes still.*
> STEPHEN, *half-closed lids.*

STEPHEN. Why don't you leave her alone?

> CHARLEY *takes his hand away from* ANNA. *She collects books.* CHARLEY *stands, lost, in the centre of the room.*

CHARLEY. How did she hear about it? I've just heard it from the Provost. Wake up.

STEPHEN. I haven't slept. Sorry. I'm a bit tired.

> ANNA *snaps suitcases shut.*

ANNA. It was kind of you both to come.

> *She goes to the mirror and begins to lipstick her mouth.*
> CHARLEY *bends over* STEPHEN's *chair, whispers.*

CHARLEY (*whispering*). What's the matter with her? She didn't care anything about him. Nothing. What's she going home for? It's ridiculous.

STEPHEN. There's nothing to keep her here.

CHARLEY. She loves me. What are you talking about?

> ANNA *walks to cases.*

ANNA. My taxi should be here.

STEPHEN. Have you got a flight?
ANNA. Yes. I've booked a flight.

> CHARLEY *sits down in a chair.*
> STEPHEN *stands, goes to cases.*

STEPHEN. I'll take these down.

> STEPHEN *leaves the room.*

CHARLEY (*to* ANNA). Why don't you stay for the funeral?

> ANNA *goes to* CHARLEY, *holds out her hand.*

ANNA. Goodbye.

> CHARLEY *looks up at her, grins, does not take her hand.*
> ANNA *goes.*
> CHARLEY *sits quite still.*

> *Exterior. Women's college. Day.*
> STEPHEN *closes taxi door.* ANNA *leans back on the back seat. The taxi drives off.*
> STEPHEN *looks after it, then glances back, through the gate, into the college grounds.*
> *On the college lawn, in long shot,* CHARLEY *stands alone.*
> STEPHEN *standing, from* CHARLEY's *point of view.*
> STEPHEN *walks away.*

> *NOTE: The following scenes until the end of the film are silent except for:*
> *The hum of a car growing on the soundtrack. The sound grows. It includes jamming gear changes and sharp braking.*
> *The sound begins very quietly.*

> *Exterior. Cloister. Day.*
> STEPHEN *walks through cloister towards his study slowly.*

Exterior. House. Day.
(Identical shot as at the beginning of the film).
CLARISSA *and* TED *running over gravel towards front door.* CLARISSA *falls, holds her leg, cries.*
The sound of the car draws closer.
STEPHEN *comes out of house, picks her up, comforts her, carries her into house, her arms around him,* TED *following. The dog runs after them.*
Camera slowly moves back to long shot outside the gate.
It comes to rest.
Sound of the car skidding.
A sudden screech, grind, smash and splintering.
Camera withdraws down the drive to the gate.
The house still, in the sunlight.
Silence.
Sound of ignition, ticking.

The Go-Between

The Go-Between is a World Film Services Production presented by EMI/MGM* with the following cast:

MARIAN	Julie Christie
TED	Alan Bates
MRS MAUDSLEY	Margaret Leighton
MR MAUDSLEY	Michael Gough
TRIMINGHAM	Edward Fox
LEO	Dominic Guard
MARCUS	Richard Gibson
DENYS	Simon Hume-Kendall
KATE	Amaryllis Garnet
CHARLES	Roger Lloyd-Pack
BLUNT	John Rees
STUBBS	Keith Buckley
RECTOR	Gordon Richardson
COLSTON	Michael Redgrave

Directed by Joseph Losey

* *At the time of going to press, the date of first showing was not yet fixed*

The Go-Between

The action of this film takes place during a span of 3 weeks in August in the summer of 1900 except for certain scenes, which take place in the present. The 'present' is any time in the last 20 years.

Exterior. English countryside. A river. Summer. Day.
The river comes out of the shadow of a belt of trees. It flows gently through the weeds and rushes. Heat haze. Steam rising from rushes.
Sound of approaching horses' hooves. A pony carriage drives by on the road, glimpsed only fragmentarily through the leaves. It passes.
Silence.
The camera is still, looking through the leaves towards the silent road. In the distance, a 1900 farm machine, horse drawn, can be seen, moving slowly.
Sound of the flowing river.
The voice of an elderly man, COLSTON, *heard over:*
COLSTON'S VOICE (OVER)
The past is a foreign country. They do things differently there.

Exterior. Gravel road. Long shot.
The pony and carriage trotting. On it are MARCUS, LEO, *a* FOOTMAN *and an* UNDERCOACHMAN. MARCUS *is pointing across the fields.*
From viewpoint of the carriage see Brandham Hall in the distance.
The carriage goes downhill. Brandham Hall lost.

Interior. House. Back stairs.
The back stairs are rambling and narrow. MARCUS
and LEO, *followed by footman, climb up. Doors, other*
passages glimpsed.
They reach MARCUS's *room.*

Interior. MARCUS's *room.*
There is one small window high in the wall. An old
terrier jumps from the four-poster bed as the door
opens and MARCUS *and* LEO *enter.*
The dog jumps up at them.

MARCUS. This is Dry Toast.

Exterior. Front of house. Lawn.
In foreground the shape of a girl lying in a hammock.
The wide lawn falls away before the house on a gentle
slope. Cedars, elms. The hammock, faded crimson
canvas, swings gently. In background figures in white
playing croquet.

Interior. House. Main hall.
A butler carrying a bowl of flowers walks up the
double staircase, which is shaped like a horse-shoe,
and goes out of shot.
MARCUS *and* LEO *appear at the top of the staircase.*
They run down it at different sides. At the foot of it
LEO *turns to look up.*

Exterior. Lawn.
Men in white flannels, white boots and straw boaters,
women in white dresses and hats playing croquet.

Interior. House. Main hall.
LEO *turns from staircase, glances through open double*
doors to a long room with large windows.

The camera pans to see into the room. A long shining mahogany table.

Interior. House. Open front door.
MARCUS *turns from the door.*

MARCUS. Come on, slug.

LEO *moves quickly and threateningly after him to the front of the house.*
Framed in the door a girl in a hammock can be seen, on the lawn, in the distance.

Exterior. Lawn.
Hammock in foreground, the girl in it is still not clearly seen. Indistinguishable shapes of several people lounging in the shade.
In background LEO *and* MARCUS *run out of the house.*
A GUEST'S VOICE (OVER)
Who's that?

Exterior. Derelict outhouses.
LEO *and* MARCUS *wander about derelict outhouses, rubbish heap and disused vegetable gardens, swishing twigs about them. The paths are overgrown. Flies. They walk into denser undergrowth.*

MARCUS. My sister is very beautiful.
LEO. Yes.

They approach a roofless outhouse. In it is a large glossy shrub with bell shaped flowers. They stop. The camera goes before them and stops, regarding the shrub. Their voices over :

LEO. What's that?
MARCUS. It's a deadly nightshade, you oaf!
LEO. Atropa belladonna.
MARCUS. Atropa what?

LEO. Atropa belladonna. It's poisonous. Every part of it
is poison.

Two shot. MARCUS *and* LEO.
MARCUS *thrusts* LEO *towards the shrub.*
MARCUS. Die.
LEO *resists.* MARCUS *runs through the outhouses,*
LEO *following. The camera watches them with the
bell-shaped flowers of the shrub in foreground.*

Exterior. MARIAN *in hammock. Lawn.*
Her eyes are closed in the sun. They open.
LEO *walking alone along grass verge of the garden. He
slowly comes to a halt, looks down.*
MARIAN *in hammock from* LEO'S *point of view.*
Close-up of MARIAN.
Her eyes are half closed.

Interior. House. Back stairs.
LEO *standing in dark passage. Sudden laughter from
servants' quarters.*
LEO'S *point of view. Kitchen door half open.*
*Glimpsed in the kitchen, two women: The cook and
the under-cook, both fat. They are giggling. Steam
from saucepans.*

Exterior. Close-up of MARIAN. *Lawn.*
*Her head turns quickly on her shoulder, her eyes are
open.*

Interior. MARCUS'S *room. Evening.*
LEO *is washing his hands in a bowl. He wipes them
and looks at himself in a small mirror.*

Interior. Hall. Evening.
LEO *descending the stairs. He draws near the half-
open door of the drawing-room and stops. Voices:*

MRS MAUDSLEY. Didn't you say his mother is a widow, Marcus?

MARCUS. I think so. I don't really know very much about him.

MR MAUDSLEY. Seems to be a nice lad.

MARCUS. I do have an impression that he lives in rather a small house with his mother.

MRS MAUDSLEY. Yes. He seems to be a very nice boy. Now – is everyone here?

LEO opens the door and goes in.

Interior. Drawing-room.
LEO at the door.

MRS MAUDSLEY. Ah, Leo. Good evening.

LEO. Good evening Mrs Maudsley.

MRS MAUDSLEY. Now, let us go into dinner.

They all move to the door.

A GUEST. You were in cracking form to-day at croquet, Marian.

MARIAN. Was I?

DENYS. Marian is quite formidable at croquet.

MARIAN. Am I?

Interior. Hall.
The party moving through the hall. MRS MAUDSLEY *with* LEO.

MRS MAUDSLEY. I believe we must be wary of you, Leo, I understand you're a magician. Is that true?

LEO. Well . . . not really . . . only, you know . . . at school.

LEO glances over his shoulder at MARCUS.

Anyway it was supposed to be a secret actually.

Interior. Dining-room. Night.
Candlelight. Glow of silver. The family and guests move to the table.

MARCUS. His curses are fearful. He cast a fiendish spell on two boys at school. They fell off the roof and were severely mutilated.

DENYS. Did they die?

LEO. Oh no. They were just a little . . . you know . . . severely mutilated.

MR MAUDSLEY. Was it difficult to arrange? I mean to get them to fall off the roof without killing them.

LEO. Well, it wasn't a killing curse, you see. There are curses and curses. It depends on the curse.

MRS MAUDSLEY. How frightening.

MRS MAUDSLEY sits. They all sit. MARIAN leans forward.

MARIAN. You're not going to bewitch us here, are you?

LEO. Oh no, I shouldn't think so.

Laughter.

Interior. Bedroom. Night.
MARCUS *and* LEO *in bed.* MARCUS *asleep.* LEO *awake.*
Laughter from the lawn below. A piano playing. A girl's voice singing. LEO *looks up at the high window above his bed. Clear night sky. Voices float in.*

Exterior. House. Disused game larder under a yew tree. Day.
This structure is empty but for a thermometer which hangs on the wall.
LEO *is staring at it. The temperature is eighty-three. He turns.* MR MAUDSLEY *is behind him.*

MR MAUDSLEY. Hello. Enjoying yourself?

LEO. Yes sir.

MR MAUDSLEY. Good. Pretty warm. What does it say?

LEO. Eighty-three.

MR MAUDSLEY. Warm.

MR MAUDSLEY *studies* LEO'*s clothes.*

Suit a little warm, is it?
LEO. No, sir.

MR MAUDSLEY *taps the thermometer.*

MR MAUDSLEY. Enjoying yourself?
LEO. Yes thank you, sir.
MR MAUDSLEY. Good.

Interior. Bedroom. Day.
LEO *wiping his sweating face with a handkerchief.*
LEO. Do you think I should sport my cricket togs?
MARCUS. I wouldn't. Only cads wear their school clothes in the holidays. And another thing. When you undress you mustn't fold your clothes and put them on the chair. You must leave them lying wherever they happen to fall. The servants will pick them up. That's what they're for.

Close-up of DENYS.
DENYS. You are looking hot. Haven't you something cooler to wear?

The camera withdraws to find LEO *and* DENYS *with a group of young people in the hall.*

LEO. I'm not hot, really.
DENYS. Isn't that a Norfolk jacket?
LEO. Yes.
DENYS. Well it's quite appropriate then, isn't it? After all we are in Norfolk.

They move through the open front door on to the lawn.

Exterior. Lawn.
Close-up of large silver tea-pot pouring tea into tea-cups.
The camera shifts to look along the tea table which is laden with watercress, tomato, cucumber and lettuce

*sandwiches, scones, muffins, cream cakes, pastries
etc. Voices over:*

DENYS. Have we a pair of bellows, Mother?

MRS MAUDSLEY. Why?

DENYS. To cool Leo.

MRS MAUDSLEY. Does Leo need cooling?

LEO. I may look hot, but I'm really quite cool underneath.

The camera shifts and settles to look at the gathering.

MRS MAUDSLEY. Did you leave your summer clothes at home?

LEO. I expect Mother forgot to put them in.

Silence. Stirring of cups.

MRS MAUDSLEY. Why don't you write and ask her to send them?

MARIAN. Oh that would take too long, Mama. Let me take
him into Norwich tomorrow and get him a new
outfit. Would you like that, Leo?

LEO. I haven't any money. At least only –

MARIAN. They can be your birthday present from us. When
is your birthday?

LEO. Well . . . it's on the twenty-seventh of this month,
actually. I was born under the sign of Leo.

MARIAN. Good. I can give you a lionskin.

DENYS. Or a mane.

*Close-up of MARIAN.
She is sipping her tea.*

MARIAN. Well, we'll go tomorrow.

*Close-up of MRS MAUDSLEY.
MRS MAUDSLEY raises her eyes and looks at MARIAN.*

MRS MAUDSLEY. Wouldn't you rather wait until Monday, when
Hugh will be here, and make a party to go to
Norwich?

DENYS (OVER). Trimingham? I thought he'd gone to Goodwood.

MR MAUDSLEY
(OVER). Hugh coming?

MRS MAUDSLEY. Yes, I had a letter from him. He comes on Saturday
and stays until the end of the month.

Close–up of MARIAN. *Her eyes are hooded.*
She sips her tea. MRS MAUDSLEY'S VOICE OVER:
Are you sure you couldn't wait until Monday?
MARIAN *looks up and smiles.*

MARIAN. Norwich will hardly be a treat for Hugh, Mama, trailing round the shops. Besides, by Monday Leo will have melted into butter. And all he'll need will be a muslin bag.

Close–up of MRS MAUDSLEY.
She holds her tea–cup faintly smiling.

Close–up of MARIAN.

May we go, Mama?

Close–up of MRS MAUDSLEY.

MRS MAUDSLEY. Yes, of course you may.

Exterior. Country road. Day.
Pony and carriage trotting. MARIAN *and* LEO *on it.*
It trots into the distance.
COLSTON'S VOICE (OVER) (*murmuring*)
You flew too near the sun and you were scorched.

Exterior. Cathedral Square. Norwich.
A footman sits waiting on the carriage. Parcels and boxes are piled up.

Interior. Hotel restaurant. Norwich.
MARIAN *and* LEO *at a table.* LEO *wears a new green suit.*
MARIAN. What did your father do?
LEO. He worked in a bank actually. And he was a pacifist.
MARIAN. Ah.
LEO. Mmm. And he was a book collector. He liked books very much. And so he collected them. That

was his hobby. Mother said they're quite valuable.
We might have to sell them.

MARIAN. Here's your pudding.

The waiter places a large plum pudding in front of
LEO. *He begins to eat.*

What's it like?

LEO. Very good.

MARIAN *is served with coffee. She sips it.*

MARIAN. Used any Black Magic on anyone lately?

LEO (*through food*). Not lately, no.

MARIAN. I envy you your power. What's it like to have such
power at your finger tips?

LEO. Oh it makes you feel fairly good. But I only ever
use it at school, you know.

MARIAN. Can you teach me? I could use it here.

LEO. Would you really want to?

MARIAN. Oh not really. The results might be too alarming.

Exterior. Lobby hotel.
MARIAN *and* LEO.

MARIAN. Would you like to amuse yourself in the Cathedral
for an hour? I have some shopping to do.

LEO. Yes. Certainly.

MARIAN. Can you amuse yourself in a Cathedral?

She giggles.

Exterior. Cathedral.
LEO *wanders through the crowded market and stands
to look up at the Cathedral.*

Exterior. Village street. Long shot. Very still.
Morning.   *PRESENT*
*The sky is overcast. (The sky is constantly overcast
in all present-day shots.)*

The street is more or less deserted. A couple of parked cars.
COLSTON *stands in the distance, looking down the street.*
LEO'S VOICE (OVER)
Well, it wasn't a killing curse, you see. There are curses and curses. It depends on the curse.

The man begins to walk down the street.

Interior. Cathedral.   *PAST*
LEO *looking up at the vaulted roof.*

Exterior. Square. The pony carriage.
The coachman raises his whip in salute. The camera pans to LEO, *who raises his hand and walks towards a statue in the centre of the square where he stands waiting.*
LEO's *point of view. The square.*
Drowsy traffic of carriages. Men and women walking through the market, which is now much quieter.
Suddenly the camera concentrates on a distant corner of the square. MARIAN *is talking to a man, not identifiable. The man raises his hat.* MARIAN *turns and threads her way slowly through the traffic. She suddenly sees* LEO, *waves her parasol and quickens her step.*

Exterior. The river. Afternoon.
Silence.

Interior. The house. Drawing-room.
LEO *is standing on a chair in his new suit revolving. Group of people admiring him.*
AD LIB. Superb! Dazzling! Most impressive! What a splendid green! Remarkably elegant! Most fetching! Charming!

DENYS. Did you get the tie at Challow and Challow?
MARIAN. Of course.
DENYS. And where did you get the shoes?
MARIAN. At Sterling and Potter.
DENYS. What green is this?
MARIAN. Lincoln green.
DENYS. I thought so. I shall dub you Sir Robin Hood.
A GIRL. Do you feel different?
LEO. Yes. I feel quite another person.

Laughter. LEO *gets off the chair.* MRS MAUDSLEY
leads him to the window.

MRS MAUDSLEY. Let me have a proper look at you.

*She feels the material and examines the smoked pearl
buttons.*

Yes, I think it does very well, and I hope your
mother will think so too. Have you written to her,
Leo?
LEO. Oh yes I have.
MRS MAUDSLEY. Good. You've chosen very well, Marian. Did you
do any shopping for yourself?
MARIAN. Oh no, Mama. That can wait.
MRS MAUDSLEY. It mustn't wait too long. You didn't see anyone in
Norwich, I suppose?
MARIAN. Not a soul. We were hard at it all the time, weren't
we Leo?

Pause.

LEO. Yes, we were.

Interior. Platform Norwich Station. Long shot.
                                        PRESENT
COLSTON *walks along the platform carrying a small
case. He declines a porter's help. The camera watches
him move into the ticket hall where a chauffeur in a
peak cap approaches him.*
COLSTON *and* CHAUFFEUR *walk to a car. The
man gets in, the* CHAUFFEUR *puts the case in the boot.*

Over this last shot the following dialogue heard, fragmentarily:

MRS MAUDSLEY. I'm afraid he can't without his mother's permission. Your mother has written to me that you're liable to colds. But you can watch the others bathe, of course.

Pause.

MARCUS. Why are you bringing your bathing suit if you're not allowed to swim?

LEO. Well, it is a bathing party.

MARCUS. But you're not going to swim.

LEO. I know I'm not.

MARCUS. In that case why – ?

The car moves away from the station.

Exterior. The river. Day.   *PAST*
Silence.
Voices heard approaching. Indecipherable chatter. Giggling. Immediately voices are heard the camera moves along the river bank, in front of and at a distance from the characters.
A black peeling construction (a diving pier) is suddenly found. A man emerges from the rushes. The camera stops abruptly. The man is wearing tight woollen trunks. The voices cease. The man climbs onto the platform, stands a moment, and then dives into the river. He swims away.

DENYS'S VOICE (OVER). What cheek! The man's trespassing. What shall we do?

GUEST'S VOICE. Order him off.

DENYS. What cheek!

Exterior. River bank. The group.
MARIAN and KATE are in foreground.

KATE. Who can he be?

MARIAN. I don't know.

KATE. He's a good swimmer. And really rather well built. Don't you think?

MARIAN turns away.

MARIAN. Come on, Kate, we'll go and change.

MARIAN and KATE go towards a small hut among the rushes. The others walk down to the river.

DENYS. Shall we order him off?

Point of view of group. Man swimming in river. The man sees them and swims towards them.

DENYS. It's Ted Burgess.

MAN. Who's he?

DENYS. The tenant of Black Farm. We can't be rude to him. He farms the land on the other side.

MAN. Perhaps you'd better be nice to him.

DENYS. I'll just say how do you do to him. We don't know him socially of course, but I think I should be nice to him, don't you?

MAN. I would say so.

DENYS. In that case I shall. I shall be particularly nice to him.

TED hauls himself up from the water by means of a fixed spiked post. For a moment he appears to be about to impale himself on it. But he jumps onto the bank. DENYS moves forward to shake his hand.

What a way to land! There are some steps over there.

TED. Oh I've always done it this way.

He looks at the group.

I didn't know anyone was going to be here. Just started on the harvest . . . got so hot . . .

DENYS. Don't worry at all, please. We were hot too . . . up at the Hall . . . very hot . . .

Pause.

Trimingham's coming to-night.

TED. Uh. Is he?

Pause.

I won't be long. Just one more header.

DENYS. Absolutely. Absolutely.

TED *raises his hand, turns, runs up to the platform, the camera panning up to watch him, and dives into the water.*
DENYS *turns to the others.*

I think I put him at his ease, don't you?

Exterior. The rushes.
DENYS *and his friend undressing in the rushes. The camera moves to find* MARCUS *undressing,* LEO *watching.* LEO *begins to untie his tie.*

MARCUS. You don't intend to put on your bathing suit, do you? I shouldn't put on a bathing suit if you're not going to bathe. It would look absurd.

LEO *reties the tie, and strolls away, his bathing suit over his shoulder.*
TED *climbing on to river bank.*
DENYS, GUEST *and* MARCUS, *splashing in river.*
LEO *watching.*
MARIAN *and* KATE *pushing each other, giggling.*
They wear long bathing dresses.
LEO *suddenly crouching in rushes.*
Through the rushes glimpse a glistening body, moving. The body sinks to the ground. LEO *raises himself to peer through the rushes.*
TED *lies down in the sun, stretches his arms, and scratches his chest.*
LEO *watching.*
MARIAN'S VOICE (OVER)
My hair's come down! It's all wet!
LEO *turns his head quickly.*
TED *jumps up, pulls on his clothes swiftly, swears as he fastens his leather belt and moves swiftly away.*

Exterior. River bank.
MARIAN *standing holding the long coils of her hair in front of her.*
LEO *runs down to her.*

MARIAN. It's all wet. I shall never get it dry.

She looks at LEO.

Oh you do look so dry and smug. I should like to throw you in the river.

She laughs.

Has that man gone?

LEO. Yes. He went off in a hurry. His name is Ted Burgess, he's a farmer. Do you know him?

MARIAN. I may have met him.

Exterior. Village street. Morning. **PRESENT**
A car appears round the corner and draws slowly to a halt. The engine is cut off. No one emerges. The village street is silent. Over this shot, MARIAN'S *voice:*

MARIAN. It's dripping on my dress.

Exterior. River bank. Twilight. **PAST**
Close-up of LEO.

LEO. Here's my bathing suit. It's *quite* dry. If you fasten it round your neck, so that it hangs down your back, then you can spread your hair on it, and your hair will get dry and your dress won't get wet.

Two shot. MARIAN *and* LEO.
MARIAN *is pinning the bathing suit at her throat.*
LEO *drapes it over her shoulders.*

MARIAN. Spread my hair on it. Take care not to pull it.

LEO *does so. She cries out.* LEO *looks at her in alarm. She smiles.* LEO *drapes her hair delicately.*

Is it well spread?

Exterior. Long shot. Path through the trees.
MARIAN and LEO walking through the lengthening
shadows. The others straggling behind.
MARIAN. Is it dry?

LEO *touches her hair. She cries out.* LEO *takes his*
hand away sharply. She giggles.

What a comfort . . . your bathing suit on my
shoulders. Is my hair well spread?
LEO. Oh yes. It is.

Exterior. Front of house. Evening.
The house is lit. MARIAN *and* LEO *walk up the slope.*
She stops, takes the bathing suit from her shoulders
and hands it to him.
MARIAN. Is it dry?

He touches her hair. She does not cry out.

LEO. Yes.

She touches her hair.

MARIAN (*smiling*). Yes, it is.

Interior. House. Main hall. Morning.
The gong sounds. One or two figures walk across the
hall. LEO *appears at the top of the stairs and bounds*
down.
Camera follows him as he walks swiftly into the
breakfast room. MR MAUDSLEY *is seated at the top*
of the table. All other chairs drawn back and ranged
round the walls. On the sideboard stand the breakfast
dishes.
LEO *makes for a particular chair, sits down on it,*
and moves about to test its creak. It does not creak.
He moves to another chair, sits and does the same. It
creaks sharply. He relaxes in the chair. One or two
guests take their seats. The servants file in and take

theirs. From the servants: 'Good morning Mr Maudsley.' 'Good morning, Mrs Maudsley'.
The servants comprise: An elegant housekeeper, three round cooks, a short elderly gardener, a neat slender butler, a tall footman, two burly coachmen, two very young maids and a skinny pantry maid, even younger. Close shot. LEO *kneeling.*
MR MAUDSLEY *begins to say morning prayers in the background.*
A figure kneels beside LEO. *He looks up. The man is a stranger. His face is scarred.* TRIMINGHAM.
Two shot. LEO *and* TRIMINGHAM.
MR MAUDSLEY *saying prayers in background.* LEO *observes* TRIMINGHAM *sideways.*

Interior. Breakfast room. Men walking about eating porridge.
The ladies are seated. LEO *holds his plate very carefully.*

MRS MAUDSLEY. Now, everybody. Let us decide what we shall do today. Hugh . . . ?

She looks at TRIMINGHAM. LEO *looks at* TRIMINGHAM.

Come, sit down and advise us.

TRIMINGHAM *sits down next to her.*

Now what do you suggest?

Interior. House. MARCUS *and* LEO's *bedroom door. An envelope is fixed on the door, with* NO ADMITTANCE *written on it.* LEO *opens the door and goes in.*

Interior. Bedroom.
MARCUS *is in bed. The dog growls.*
LEO. What's up?

MARCUS. Decent of you to trickle along, but don't come in. I have a headache and some spots. Mama thinks it may be measles.

LEO. Hard cheese.

MARCUS. See Trimingham?

LEO. Is he the man with the face?

MARCUS. Yes. Got it in the war. He was gored by the Boers.

LEO. Hard cheese.

Exterior. Village. Morning.
Church bells.
The house party is passing down the village street on its way to the church.
They pass a cottage. The camera rests momentarily on the cottage.

Exterior. Church. Long shot.
The party, going through the church door.

Exterior. Church door.
LEO *looking into the church.*

Interior. Church. LEO's *point of view.*
Bell ringers at the back of the church, pulling the bell ropes.

Exterior. Cottage. Day.   *PRESENT*
The camera, motionless, looking at the same cottage door.
Church bells heard over.
COLSTON's *back comes into shot.*

Exterior. Village street. Day.   *PAST*
The procession passing the cottage on the way back from church. TRIMINGHAM *joins* LEO.

TRIMINGHAM. I don't think we've been introduced. My name is Trimingham.

LEO. How do you do, Trimingham.

TRIMINGHAM. You can call me Hugh, if you like.

LEO *looks at him.*

Or Trimingham, if you prefer.

LEO. Why not Mister Trimingham?

TRIMINGHAM. I think Trimingham is slightly more in order, if you prefer it to Hugh.

LEO. But why not Mister?

TRIMINGHAM. Well as a matter of fact I'm a Viscount.

LEO. Viscount Trimingham?

TRIMINGHAM. That's right.

LEO. Oughtn't I to call you My Lord?

TRIMINGHAM. No, no. Hugh will do . . . or Trimingham if you like. What's your name?

LEO. Colston.

TRIMINGHAM. Mister Colston?

LEO. Well, Leo, if you like.

TRIMINGHAM. I'll call you, Leo, if I may.

LEO. Oh yes that's quite all right.

High shot. Group walking along lane.
Two shot. LEO *and* TRIMINGHAM.

TRIMINGHAM. Does Marian call you Leo?

LEO. Oh yes. I think she's ripping. I'd do anything for her.

TRIMINGHAM. What would you do?

LEO. Oh anything. Anything.

TRIMINGHAM. Would you like to take her a message for me?

LEO. Oh yes. What shall I say?

TRIMINGHAM. Tell her I've got her prayer book. She left it behind in church.

LEO *runs off.*

Exterior. Village street.   *PRESENT*
Car drawing to a halt. Engine cuts off. Silence.

MARIAN'S VOICE (OVER)
How careless. I forget everything. Please thank him
for me.

Interior. House. Back stairs.   *PAST*
LEO *passes* MARCUS'S *room. He glances at the* NO
ADMITTANCE *sign, pauses, and then goes on to a
green baize door.*

Interior. LEO'S *room.*
LEO *enters and looks at it.*
*The room is very small. Narrow bed. On the side-
board his hairbrush, red collar box. Another largish
locked box. He opens this and takes out two dry sea
urchins, stumps of sealing wax, a combination lock,
twists of whip cord. Under this gradually disclosed a
locked book. He unlocks it, opens first page. We see
'Diary for the year 1900' in copper plate script.
Round this cluster the signs of the zodiac ; The Fishes,
The Crab, The Scorpion, The Ram, The Bull, The
Lion, The Archer, The Virgin and The Water Carrier.*
LEO *studies this page. He then turns the pages of the
diary and stops at a page which contains incomprehensible lettering and in the centre :*

CURSE THREE
AFTER CURSE THREE THE VICTIM DIES!
Given under my hand
and written in my BLOOD!
by order of
THE AVENGER

LEO *shuts the book.*

Exterior. Back of the house. The thermometer.
LEO *staring at thermometer. The temperature is
eighty-four.*

Exterior. Front of house. Lawn.
MARIAN *in hammock. She lies still, gazing up into the trees.*

Exterior. River. The diving pier.
LEO *walks on to pier. Looks down into water.*

Exterior. Cornfield.
LEO *wanders through the corn. The stubble pricks his ankles. He comes to a gate, opens it, the camera with him. He turns into a farm road caked with hard mud and then into a farmyard.*
LEO *looking at a strawstack, a ladder running up it, in the farmyard. He opens the gate and walks into the yard. He stands looking at the height of the stack, and glances towards the silent farmhouse.*
He climbs the ladder to the strawstack, he looks down. He slides. A swift rush through the air. His knee, at the bottom, hits a chopping block. He falls off clutching his knee.

Medium shot TED.
TED *stands at the corner of the farmhouse holding two pails of water. He puts the pails down and strides towards* LEO.

TED. What the hell do you think you're doing? I've a good mind to give you the biggest thrashing you've ever had in your life.

TED *from* LEO's *point of view.*
TED *looking down at him.*

LEO. My knee!
TED. Get up! What the hell are you doing here? Who are you?
LEO. I know you! We've met!
TED. Met?

LEO. At the bathing place. You were bathing. I came with the others.

TED. Oh. You're from the hall.

Pause.

Can you walk?

Wide shot. Farmyard.
TED *helps* LEO *up. They walk.*

LEO. I saw you dive. You did it jolly well.

Interior. Farmhouse.
LEO *is sitting down.* TED *swabbing his knee with carbolic.*

TED. You were lucky. You might have spoiled your suit.

LEO. Miss Marian gave it to me. Miss Marian Maudsley.

TED. Oh did she? Is it stinging?

LEO. Yes.

TED. You're a spartan.

TED *takes out a handkerchief and ties it around the knee.*

LEO. Won't you want that?

TED. I've got plenty more. Try walking.

LEO *hobbles about the kitchen.*

LEO. Thank you very much, Mr Burgess. Is there . . . anything I can do for you?

Pause.

TED. Well, perhaps there is. (*Pause.*) Could you take a message for me?

LEO. Of course. Who to?

Shot across kitchen sink.
TED *approaches sink with bowl of discoloured water, empties it and swills it.* LEO *remains in background.*

TED. How old are you?

LEO. I shall be thirteen on the twenty-seventh of this month.

LEO's point of view. TED *turning to him from sink.* TED *looks at him in silence.*

TED. Can I trust you?

Close-up of LEO.
LEO *looks at him expressionless.*
Close-up of TED.

Can I?

Close-up of LEO.

LEO. Of course you can.

Wide shot. Kitchen.
TED *begins to walk around the room.*

TED. There's a boy, isn't there? A lad of your age.
LEO. He's in bed, with measles.
TED. Oh, is he? (*Pause.*) Are you . . . ever alone with anybody . . . in the house?
LEO. Nobody talks to me much. They're all grown up, you see. Except Marcus and he's in bed. Marian talks to me. Miss Marian.
TED. Oh does she?
LEO. She often talks to me. She talks to me most. When her hair was wet I . . .

Medium shot. TED *sitting at table.*

TED. Are you ever alone with her? I mean, just the two of you in a room, with no-one else.
LEO. Well, sometimes. Sometimes we sit together on a sofa.
TED. On a sofa?

Wide shot of room.
TED *stands, walks about the room.*

Could you give her a letter without anybody else seeing?
LEO. Of course I could.

Close-up of TED.
TED *regards him thoughtfully.*

TED. But can I trust you . . . to keep your mouth shut?

Close-up of LEO.
LEO *looks at him with some disdain.*
Close-up of TED.

Because . . . you see . . . it's a secret. (*Pause.*)
All right. I'll trust you.

Wide shot. Room.
TED *takes pen, ink and paper from the sideboard and
sits down at the table.*

We do some business together.

LEO. Secret business?

TED. That's right. No one else must see this letter. You
understand?

LEO. Yes.

TED. If you can't get her alone don't give it to her. Put
it in the place where you pull the chain.

Interior. House. Tea-time. Sitting-room.
LEO *sitting with handkerchief round his knee.*

MR MAUDSLEY. Yes, Ted Burgess, good-looking chap, rides well,
I'm told. Good to know he was kind to you.

DENYS. Yes, how nice of him to be so nice. But I was very
nice, of course, at the bathing place, wasn't I?
(*To his mother.*) I put him very much at his ease,
you know.

MRS MAUDSLEY. Did you?

MARIAN. I think I'd better dress that knee for you, Leo. It's
looking a bit messy.

Interior. Bathroom.
LEO's *knee under the running tap.* MARIAN *bathing
it. Handkerchief on the edge of the bath.*

MARIAN. Mmmm. There.

She wipes it with towel.
Camera rises as she stands. She collects bandage.
Shot over bath edge.
MARIAN *glances at the handkerchief and bends to fix bandage.*

Is that his?

LEO. Yes. He said he wouldn't want it back. Shall I throw it on the rubbish dump?

MARIAN. Oh I don't know. Perhaps I'll wash it out. It seems quite a good handkerchief.

LEO. Oh he asked me to give you this.

He takes a letter from his back pocket.

It's a bit crumpled.

She snatches the letter, standing.

MARIAN. Oh these dresses.

She tucks the letter up her sleeve.

Now the bandage.

LEO. You've put it on.

MARIAN. Oh yes.

She bends to him.

Now I'll put on your stocking.

LEO. Oh I can do that.

MARIAN. No, no, I'll do it.

Close two shot.
MARIAN *drawing the stocking up.*

You won't . . . tell anyone about this letter will you? You won't . . . will you?

LEO. Of course I won't.

MARIAN's *hand smooths the stocking and touches the bandage.*
Close-up of MARIAN *doing this.*

MARIAN (*softly*). There.

Exterior. Outhouses. The deadly nightshade.
The camera is still, looking at it. It glistens.
VOICES HEARD OVER:
COLSTON'S VOICE
Of course I won't.
MARIAN'S VOICE YOUNG (*softly*)
There.

Exterior. Meadow by stream. Day.
A picnic party. Numerous open hampers. Ladies and
gentlemen sitting on multi-coloured rugs. Footmen
serving food. Ham, cheese, eggs etc.
Over this shot and the next two shots the following
spasmodic dialogue is heard:

A GIRL. But Gussy doesn't dance.
A MAN. Doesn't he really?
GIRL. Not a step.
ANOTHER MAN. Shall you be going to Goodwood?
FIRST MAN. How odd. I thought I saw him dancing at Lady
Mary's.
THIRD MAN. I think I shall go to Goodwood. Shall you?
GIRL. But he doesn't dance a step, I promise you.
SECOND MAN. Yes, I think I shall.

Amber wine being poured from tall bottles into goblets.
LEO *holding glass. A footman bends to him, pours*
fizzy lemonade into it from a bottle with a glass
marble for a stopper.
LEO *drinks lemonade and stands. In the background*
MARIAN *and* TRIMINGHAM *are sitting together. He*
is talking intently to her. LEO *strolls close to them.*
TRIMINGHAM *looks up.*

TRIMINGHAM. Hello, there's Mercury!
MARIAN. Why do you call him Mercury?
TRIMINGHAM. Because he takes messages.

Over the back of MARIAN's *head, rigid, to* TRIMING-
HAM *and* LEO.

MARIAN *turns away.*

You took a message for me, didn't you old chap?
To this young lady, on the way from church. But it
didn't fetch a very warm response.

MARIAN *laughs.*
Three shot. Relaxed.
MARIAN *laughing.*

(*To* LEO.) Do you know who Mercury was?

LEO. Mercury is the smallest of the planets.

TRIMINGHAM. Ah, but before that he was the messenger of the
gods. He went to and fro between them.

Exterior. Picnic meadow. Late afternoon.
LEO *asleep in the grass.* MARIAN *and* MRS MAUDS-
LEY *seen in background. His eyes flicker.*

MARIAN. I think he must be bored to tears, trailing round
with us. He'd be much happier pottering about on
his own.

MRS MAUDSLEY. Do you think so? He's so devoted to you, he's your
little man. Still, I can ask him. It is unfortunate
about Marcus.

MARIAN. If Marcus has got the measles, I suppose we shall
have to put off the ball.

MRS MAUDSLEY. Oh I don't think so. We should disappoint so many
people. You wouldn't want to do that, would you?

MARIAN *and* MRS MAUDSLEY *rise and stroll away.*
LEO *sits up.*
From his viewpoint on the grass :
*The carriages drawn up in the shade. Horses whisking
their tails. The coachmen high up on their boxes, hats
almost touching the branches.*

Exterior. Road. Moving carriage.
LEO *and* COACHMAN BUFF *on the box seats of the
carriage. Below them in the well of the carriage a roof
of parasols.*

Exterior. A small village.
Carriages passing through the village. Children run
along the road as they pass. The COACHMEN *throw*
pennies to them. The children scrabble for them.
Medium shot. LEO *and* COACHMAN.
LEO *is watching the children. He turns abruptly to the*
COACHMAN.

LEO. Do you know Ted Burgess?

BUFF. Ted Burgess? We all know him. He's a bit of a lad,
Ted Burgess.

LEO. What do you mean by a lad? I should have said he
was a full grown man.

The carriage has reached the top of a steep hill.

BUFF. Hold on, hold on. Here we go!

The descent begins, the coachman grinding the brakes
the horses' hindquarters sweating. LEO *clutches the*
rail and turns sharply to look behind him up the hill.
His face into the camera.

Quick Cut. Close shot. A car door bangs shut.

PRESENT

Long shot.
COLSTON's *back standing by car in village street. He*
begins to walk down the street away from the camera.

MARIAN's *skirt glimpsed flashing quickly by through*
weeds.

The thermometer.
The marker points to ninety-four.
LEO *staring at it. His hand to his mouth.*
A voice behind him.

MR MAUDSLEY. Enjoying yourself?

LEO. Oh yes thank you, sir.

MR MAUDSLEY. Miss your mother?

LEO. Yes, sir – I mean . . . no, sir. A little, sir.

MR MAUDSLEY *peers at the thermometer.*

MR MAUDSLEY. Pretty hot today.

LEO. Is it a record?

MR MAUDSLEY. I shouldn't be surprised. I shall have to look it up. Hot weather suit you?

LEO. Yes sir.

Exterior. Back of house.
LEO *looking back at game larder.* MR MAUDSLEY'*s back is bent towards the thermometer.*

Exterior. The derelict outhouses.
Camera, still, looks through tangled bush towards the half-hidden outhouses.
Flies. Silence.

Exterior. Front of house. Lawn.
LEO *walking past in foreground. In background figures strolling.*
TRIMINGHAM *turns in background and calls:*

TRIMINGHAM. Hi! Mercury! Come here! I want you.

Shot over TRIMINGHAM *to* LEO, *strolling in the distance.*
TRIMINGHAM *walks towards* LEO. *They meet in the centre of the lawn.*

Trying to sneak past in dead ground. (*Pause.*) Where were you off to?

LEO. Nowhere.

TRIMINGHAM. Ah. Nowhere. Well, would you like to go somewhere?

LEO. Well, yes . . . where?

TRIMINGHAM. That's up to you.

LEO. Oh.

TRIMINGHAM *laughs.*

TRIMINGHAM. I want you to find Marian. We need her to make a four at croquet. No idea where she is. Can you find her?

LEO. I don't know.

TRIMINGHAM. No one else could. But you can. Will you do that?

LEO. Yes.

> LEO *turns and begins to trot away.*
> TRIMINGHAM *calls after him.*

TRIMINGHAM. You must bring her back dead or alive!

> *Exterior. Back of the house.*
> LEO *wandering along, looking vaguely about, picks up a stone, throws it. Suddenly stops.*
> MARIAN *is walking along the cinder track from the outhouses.*
>
> *Close-up of* MARIAN.
> *She stops.*

MARIAN. What are you doing here?

LEO'S VOICE. Hugh asked me to find you.

MARIAN. Why?

LEO'S VOICE. He wants you to play croquet.

> MARIAN *does not reply. She moves away.*
> *Silence.*
> LEO *stands a moment, and then follows.*
> *Two shot.*

He said I was to bring you back dead or alive.

MARIAN. Well, which am I?

> *They laugh and begin to walk slowly towards the house.*

We're going to luncheon with some neighbours to-morrow. They're very old and mossy. I don't suppose you want to come, do you?

LEO. Oh no. I can stay here.

MARIAN. What will you do?

LEO. Oh . . . anything.

MARIAN. But what?

LEO. I might go for a walk.

MARIAN. Where to?

> *They stop.* MARIAN *sits on a bench.*

LEO. I might slide down a strawstack.

MARIAN. Oh. Whose?

LEO. Farmer Burgess.

MARIAN. Oh, his. Oh well, Leo, if you go that way perhaps you'd give him a letter for me.

LEO. I was hoping you'd say that.

MARIAN. Why? Because you like him?

LEO. Yes. But there's another reason.

MARIAN. What is it?

LEO. Because I like you.

Close-up of MARIAN.
She smiles.

MARIAN. That's very sweet of you.

Exterior. Cornfield. Day.
TED *riding on a reaper, horse drawn, cutting corn. Three labourers binding the sheaves.* LEO *appears, walks beside the reaper. The reaper and* LEO *go through the corn.*
Medium shot of REAPER.
TED *stops the horse and gets down.* LEO *gives him a letter.* TED *opens it, reads it, stuffs it into his pocket.*

TED. Tell her it's all right.

Interior. House. Long corridor. Evening.
MARIAN *walking alone. She pauses, looks at a painting on a wall.* LEO *walks towards her, speaks quietly to her. She walks on.*

Exterior. Cornfield. Day.
TED *standing with gun, pointed at a small area of uncut corn.* LEO *watches from a distance. A labourer moves through the corn calling 'sshoo'.*
Close-up of TED *with gun.*
He shoots.
Close-up of rabbit.

The rabbit is flung into the air.
Close-up of LEO.
Two shot.
TED *holds out his hand for the letter. His hand is smeared with blood. He takes the letter from the envelope. The letter is smeared with blood.*

LEO. Look what you've done.

TED *stuffs the letter into his pocket.*

TED. Tell her it's no go.

Interior. Passage. Door of MARCUS's *room.*
Sign on door 'Safe entry'. LEO *opens door, peeps round it.*

MARCUS. You may enter boldly. My disease has fled.
LEO. You don't look better.
MARCUS. Of course I'm better. I shall be down this afternoon. You can bore me with your life story.

LEO *standing alone at the top of a flight of stairs in the back of the house. He runs down it.*

Interior. Front of house.
LEO *walking quickly down a passage.*

Interior. Writing room.
MARIAN *sitting at desk writing. She puts the letter in an envelope.* LEO *enters quickly, closes the door.*

LEO. Marian, Marcus is –

The latch clicks. She slips envelope into his hand, he slips it into his pocket. TRIMINGHAM *enters.*

TRIMINGHAM. Ah! A conspiracy. A love scene. May I seize you from this fortunate fellow?
MARIAN. Is seize an appropriate word?

TRIMINGHAM. Gather then. (*He holds out his hand to her.*) May I gather you from this fortunate fellow?

MARIAN (*to* LEO). Do you mind if I'm gathered, Leo?

LEO. Oh no, not at all.

TRIMINGHAM *bows to* LEO *and leads* MARIAN *out.*

LEO *alone in writing room.*
He takes the letter from his pocket and looks at it.
It is unsealed.

Exterior. Side of the house. A part of the lawn.
Sounds of croquet. Smack of the mallet on the ball.
Taps of the balls hitting each other. Voices in the distance:

A GIRL. Charles! Do come over here. Look at this beautiful bird.

CHARLES. What is it?

GIRL. Isn't is pretty? Look at the pretty colours.

CHARLES. Never seen one like it, I must admit.

LEO *passes quickly through the shot.*

Exterior. Woods.
LEO *walking towards farm.*
He stops, takes the unsealed envelope from his pocket, looks at it, puts it back.
He continues walking, stops, sits on a hillock, thinks.
He stands, walks, stops to look down into a valley.
Close-up of LEO.
He takes out the envelope and looks at it. He turns it to the open flap. Handwriting can be discerned on the paper. He looks at it upside down and swiftly turns it right side up. The camera concentrates on the writing on the paper.
The words exposed are:
Darling, Darling, Darling,
Same place, same time, this evening.

But take care not to –
Close-up of LEO, *his mouth open.*
LEO *sits down by a tree.*
His expression is one of utter disappointment and disbelief. He leans on his elbow. He grimaces.
He emits a number of short noises, grunts, and 'hahs', hollow laughs. He sits baffled. Looks at the words again.
He sighs, stands, seals the letter. He walks on, uttering further short noises. The loudest of these alarm some birds. They fly up.

Exterior. Farmyard gate.
In foreground LEO *is crouching looking into the farmyard. In background* TED *can be seen emerging from the stable door.* LEO *watches him move across the yard.*

Exterior. Farmyard. Reverse shot.
In background LEO *stands up.* TED *stops.*
TED. Hullo, how's the postman?
LEO. Very well, thank you.
TED. Brought anything for me?

LEO *hands him the letter.* TED *reads it.*

LEO. I'm afraid I shan't be able to bring you any more letters.

TED *stares at him.*

TED. Why not?
LEO. Marcus has got over his measles. I'll be with him all day. You said he wasn't to know. If he came here with me he would know.
TED. Have you told Miss Marian this?
LEO. No.
TED. She won't know what to do. Nor shall I.
LEO. What did you do before I came?
TED. Well . . . it wasn't so easy then.

Interior. Farmhouse. Kitchen.

The door opens. TED *comes in.* LEO *appears on the threshold, and stands in the doorway.* TED *walks about the room.*

TED. She likes you doesn't she? You want her to like you, don't you? You wouldn't want her to stop liking you. No . . . you wouldn't. (*Pause.*) She won't be the same to you, if you don't take the letters. That's the truth. They're not just ordinary letters. She'll miss them. So shall I. She'll cry perhaps. Do you want her to cry? (*Pause.*) It isn't hard to make her cry. She used to cry, before you came along.

LEO. Did you make her cry?

TED. She cried when she couldn't see me.

LEO. How do you know?

TED. Because she cried when she did see me.

LEO *walks into the room and sits down.*

Silence.

(*To himself.*) I've been busy. Smiler's going to have a foal. She's ill.

LEO. Why does she have it then if it makes her ill?

TED. She hasn't much choice.

LEO. What made her have one?

TED *looks at him.*

TED. What?

LEO. What made her have one?

TED *is silent for a moment, then laughs.*

TED. Between you and me she did a bit of spooning.

LEO. Spooning? I didn't know horses could spoon.

TED. Oh it's a silly word really.

LEO. What does it *mean*?

TED. You seem to know something about it.

LEO. I don't know anything about it. That's the point. It's all this kissing, isn't it? That's what it is. All that silly kissing. I've seen it on postcards at the seaside. You can't tell me horses do that.

TED. No, horses don't do that.

LEO. Well, what do they do? What does anyone do? There's more to it than just kissing, I know that. But what?

TED. You'll find out.

Pause.

LEO. Could you marry someone without ever spooning with them?

TED. Spooning's a silly word.

LEO. Well whatever the word is. Could you marry someone and never do . . . whatever it is?

TED. You could. But it wouldn't be a very lover-like thing to do.

Pause.

LEO *stares at him.*

LEO. Lover-like?

TED. That's enough questions anyway.

LEO. But you haven't told me anything.

TED. All right. Let's make a bargain. I'll tell you all about it on the condition you go on being our postman.

Close-up of LEO.

LEO. All right.

Interior. House. Drawing-room.
MARIAN *is arranging flowers by the window.*
LEO *runs in in cricket flannels.*

MARIAN. Hello. Don't you look marvellous? Are you in the team?

LEO. Well, not exactly. I'm twelfth man. Marcus, you see, is convalescent.

MARIAN. What's twelfth man?

LEO. First reserve.

MARIAN. Ah. Well maybe someone will drop dead and then you can play. (*She pricks her finger on a thorn.*) Blast!

LEO. I've got a message for you from Hugh. He wants to know if you'll sing at the concert.

MARIAN. Oh, does he? Well, tell him . . . that I'll sing
. . . if he sings too.

Exterior. Village street. Day.   **PRESENT**
The back of COLSTON *crossing the street towards a*
young man who glances at him.
TRIMINGHAM'S VOICE (OVER)
But I don't sing.

Exterior. Lane.   **PAST**
The house team walking to the ground, dressed in
white. The camera finds LEO *and* MARCUS.
LEO. Why did you say I couldn't wear my cap?
MARCUS. Because it's a school cap. If it was an England cap,
or a county cap, or a club cap, then, of course, you
could wear it. But to wear a school cap in a private
match simply isn't done.
LEO. Stomach pump!

Exterior. Cricket pavilion.
The village team stands in a line. TRIMINGHAM
leads LEO *along it.*
TRIMINGHAM. Burdock, this is our twelfth man, Colston.

BURDOCK *and* LEO *shake hands and mutter 'how do*
you do'. This formula is repeated in all cases, with the
following men : STUBBS, MERSHAM, TOMS, BLUNT,
HOLLYOAK, BATES, HANDSON, THORBURN,
BOLT *and lastly* TED BURGESS.
Close-up of LEO.
Three shot.
TED *smiles.*
TED. Oh we know each other, m'lord, Master Colston
and I, he comes to slide down my strawstack.
TRIMINGHAM. Of course. He's told us all about it.
LEO. Are you a good batsman?
TED. No, not me. I'm not much of a cricketer, really.

TRIMINGHAM. He can be very dangerous, Leo. We've got to get him out quickly.

TED. I'm not a cricketer. I just hit.

TRIMINGHAM. Well, we're going to get you out before you get the chance.

Exterior. Cricket ground.
Four old men sitting on a bench smoking pipes. The camera pans from them to see the ground filling up with spectators.
TRIMINGHAM *and* BURDOCK *on the field.* BURDOCK *spins a coin.* TRIMINGHAM *calls 'heads'. The coin lands. He looks at the coin, turns to the pavilion, and makes a gesture of batting.*

Exterior. Pavilion.
LEO *jumping across a bench to* MARCUS.
LEO. He's won the toss! We're batting!

Exterior. Ground scoreboard.
A boy approaches the scoreboard with two mugs of tea and hands them to the scorers.
A shout from the spectators. The scorer looks up and takes down the last batsman's score from the board.

Exterior. Pavilion.
The ladies of the house, including MRS MAUDSLEY *and* MARIAN, *walk to the pavilion to their seats. The gentlemen standing. They settle in their seats. The rector sits beside* MRS MAUDSLEY.
MARIAN *sits in front of them with* KATE. TRIMINGHAM *comes out of the pavilion, inclining his head to the ladies as he passes them. Applause.*
The camera pans from the ladies to find DENYS *with* LEO *and the rest of the team.*
DENYS. He's a pretty bat. A very pretty bat. I have great confidence in him.

Exterior. The pitch.
TRIMINGHAM *driving gracefully.*
MARIAN *applauding.*
DENYS *and* LEO.

DENYS. Isn't he fine? Such command and elegance. Don't you think he's fine?

LEO. Yes, I do.

A shout. They lean forward, shocked.
TRIMINGHAM *leaving the wicket. His stumps are down.*
MARIAN *applauding vigorously as* TRIMINGHAM *returns to the pavilion.* MR MAUDSLEY *comes out of the pavilion. Applause.*
DENYS *turns to* LEO.

DENYS. We're in trouble. There's only me to come. I mean that's any good, quite frankly.

Exterior. The pitch.
MR MAUDSLEY *tapping his bat on the ground, waiting for the ball. It is bowled. He places it calmly between two fielders and runs.*
MR MAUDSLEY *steering the ball calmly off his legs. He runs.*

Exterior. Pavilion.
DENYS. He's in some command. But he mustn't tire himself.

A shout. DENYS *jumps up.*

That's me. It's absolutely up to me. But I mustn't tire him. He's not young.

Exterior. Pitch.
MR MAUDSLEY *leaning on bat waiting.* DENYS *comes to arrive at the wicket.*

Shot over DENYS *to* MR MAUDSLEY *batting.*
MR MAUDSLEY *plays the ball and starts to run.*
DENYS's *hand shoots up.*
DENYS (*loudly*). No!

MR MAUDSLEY *looks at him with irritation.*
Long shot. Ground.
MR MAUDSLEY *plays the ball and starts to run.*
DENYS *flings up his hand.*
DENYS (*loudly*). No!

Exterior. Ground. LEO *and* MARCUS.
LEO. Why does he keep saying no?
MARCUS. He wants to save my father's strength. Which is a little unnecessary I think.

Exterior. Pitch.
MR MAUDSLEY *plays the ball and begins to run.*
DENYS *flings up his hand.*
DENYS. No!
MR MAUDSLEY (*shouting*). Come on!

MR MAUDSLEY *runs up the pitch.* DENYS, *late, begins to run. The ball is thrown in.* DENYS *stumbles, falls headlong, flat on his face. The ball has hit the wicket. He is out. He stands, dusts himself, and walks away.*
Close shot. MR MAUDSLEY.
He stands calmly, his hands on his hip.

Interior. Pavilion.
The teams are having tea. The camera tracks down the table.
TRIMINGHAM. Beautifully played, sir.
MR MAUDSLEY. Thank you very much. Now we have to get Burgess out.

The camera tracks. Sandwiches, buns etc.

LEO. What about Burgess? Isn't he dangerous?

DENYS. He's a strong hitter, I grant you. But he's no sense of culture or discipline. Trimingham will be far too cunning for him.

Exterior. Cricket pitch.
TED *hitting six.*
A tree.
The ball soars into a tree.
Close-up of LEO.
In foreground MARIAN *intent. In background* MRS MAUDSLEY *intent.*
They are both watching the game.
TED *hitting six.*
LEO *applauding suddenly. He stops. Looks about him. The camera looks with him towards* MARIAN. *She is biting her lip.*
The back of MRS MAUDSLEY's *head in foreground. The back of* MARIAN's *head in background. They are both still.*
Close shot. TED.
He hits the ball hard.
A FIELDER *half stops the ball with his hand, falls. The ball careers on.*

Exterior. Pavilion.
The ball hurtling into the pavilion. It lands near the ladies' seats. MRS MAUDSLEY *jumps up with a cry.* MARIAN *puts her hand to her mouth. The other ladies jump up.*

RECTOR. Mrs Maudsley! Are you all right?

MRS MAUDSLEY. Yes, yes. Perfectly all right.

RECTOR. That was a close shave.

KATE. What a shock. He's terribly savage.

Close shot. LEO *picking up the ball. He looks up.*

TRIMINGHAM'S
VOICE. Where's our twelfth man?

Two shot. MRS MAUDSLEY *and* MARIAN.
MRS MAUDSLEY *leans over.*

MRS MAUDSLEY. Are you all right, Marian?
MARIAN. Yes, Mama. Thank you.
MRS MAUDSLEY. The ball didn't hurt you?
MARIAN. It didn't touch me, Mama.

Exterior. Pitch.
TRIMINGHAM *walking with* LEO.
TRIMINGHAM (*muttering*). We've got to get him out or he'll beat us on his own.

TRIMINGHAM, *tossing the ball, walks to the bowler's end. The camera with* TRIMINGHAM *looks down the wicket at* TED. TRIMINGHAM *runs up to bowl. Bowls.* TED *swings, the ball beats him but misses the wicket.* TRIMINGHAM *flings up his arms.* TED *grins. The ball is returned to* TRIMINGHAM.
Close-up of LEO *watching.*
Close-up of TRIMINGHAM *turning.*
Close-up of TED *waiting for the ball.*
TRIMINGHAM *bowls.*
TED *drives.*
The ball landing in the crowd.
LEO *standing. Biting his thumb.*
TRIMINGHAM *bowls fast.*
Shot over LEO's *shoulder.*
In background TED *swings. Hits the ball. It hurtles through the air towards* LEO. LEO *jumps up and catches it.*
LEO *on his back on the grass. The ball in his hand. Applause.* TRIMINGHAM *comes into the shot, helps him up, pats him on the back.*
TRIMINGHAM. Magnificent catch.

Shot from behind MRS MAUDSLEY *and* MARIAN. *Their backs are still. In background the players are returning to the pavilion.*
The players.
LEO *runs to* TED *who is walking alone.*

LEO. I didn't really mean to catch you out.

TED. It was a damn good catch. (*He laughs. Then murmurs.*)
I never thought I'd be caught out by our postman.

Applause grows. TED *goes forward. Shouts of his name. He goes into the pavilion alone.* TRIMING-HAM *stops the team at the pavilion gates and ushers* LEO *in alone. Applause for* LEO. *As the team follows* LEO *up the steps the camera rests on* MARIAN. *She is still. Her head is bent.*

Exterior. Cricket field. Evening.   *PAST*
The field is silent. As we have just seen it, but empty. Long shadows across it.

COLSTON'S VOICE (OVER)

Isn't it dull for you to live here alone?

MARIAN'S VOICE OLD (OVER)

Alone? But people come in shoals. I'm quite a place of pilgrimage.

Interior. Village hall.
The concert.
Union Jacks, paper streamers etc. Food, wine. MR MAUDSLEY *on the platform.*

MR MAUDSLEY. And last but not least, except in stature, our young David, Leo Colston, who slew the Goliath of Black Farm, if I may so describe him, not with a sling but with a catch.

Close shot of TED. *In high starched collar.*
He winks at LEO.
LEO *surrounded by applause.*
MR MAUDSLEY *on platform.*

And now, I believe, it is time for the music. Who I wonder will be prepared to give us the first song?

The assembly.
A proportion of the assembly is slightly drunk, particularly BLUNT *and* STUBBS. *A number of people turn to look at* TED *and call for him.*

BLUNT. Ted's the one! He's the big hitter!

STUBBS. And he's the best shot with a gun!

BLUNT. But is he the best singer?

Calls of 'Yes, come on, Ted' 'Ted's the one' and 'Give us a song'.

TED stands boldly. A shout of acclaim from the audience. TED walks with confidence up to the platform. Shouts of 'Good old Ted'.

The platform.

TED puts his music down on the piano and grins. He suddenly looks at the piano stool, goes to it and lifts it up, looking at it carefully. He turns to the audience.

TED. I can't see the pianist.

The audience.

Some of the audience laugh and then a murmur begins. Voices: 'Where's the pianist?' 'What's happened to him?' etc.

VOICE. He's in bed. Ill.

Cries of 'In bed?' 'He should be here'.

He's caught a fatal finger disease.

A laugh and then sudden silence falls on the assembly.

TRIMINGHAM. We can't manage without a pianist.

The platform.

TED holding piano stool uncertain.

The audience from TED's point of view.

BLUNT. Come on, Ted. Don't be shy. You don't need music.

STUBBS. Yes, give us a song.

BLUNT. But take your collar off first! It's going to strangle you!

Medium shot. TED.

He puts the piano stool down and stands dogged and unhappy. He shakes his head.

Close-up of MRS MAUDSLEY.

She sits with a very faint smile in her eyes.

BLUNT'S VOICE (OVER)
Come on, be a gentleman. You're dressed up like one.

STUBBS. A sheep in wolf's clothing.

A sudden rustle. Silence. A murmur from the audience.
The audience from TED's *point of view.*
MARIAN *moving swiftly down the aisle towards the platform. Applause from the audience.*
The platform. Long shot.
MARIAN *climbing the steps to the platform.* TED *still. He moves abruptly to help her up. Ironic applause from some members of the audience. She goes to the piano stool and sits down. She picks up the top sheet of music and holds it up to* TED *questioningly.* TED *nods miserably. She places it on the music rest.* TED *turns to the audience.*

TED *(very low)*. Take a pair of sparkling eyes.
BLUNT. What did you say? Speak up.
TED. Take a pair of sparkling eyes.
STUBBS. Well, cheer up it isn't a funeral.

Close-up. TED *begins to sing.*
Close-up of MARIAN *playing the piano.*

Interior. Cottage. The sitting-room. Long shot.

PRESENT

COLSTON *standing with his back to the camera. A maid comes into the room. She says something unheard.* COLSTON *shakes his head. The maid leaves the room.* COLSTON *stands.*
Over this TED's *voice singing 'Take a pair of sparkling eyes'.*

Interior. Village hall.
Audience clapping.
Close-up of LEO *clapping.*
Shouts of encore.

PAST

TED *and* MARIAN *on platform.*
TED *begins to leave the platform. Shouts of encore.*
TRIMINGHAM *smoking, looking up at the platform.*
MR MAUDSLEY *looking across at* TRIMINGHAM.
He glances down.
Applause. MARIAN *rises from her stool. She bows to*
TED. *He jerks his head towards her and away. The*
audience laughs. He slowly turns towards her and
bows. Then they bow to the audience.

Exterior. Cricket field. Early evening. **PRESENT**
The field is silent. A modern mower stands in the
centre of the field. The shot is held in silence. Suddenly
MARIAN's *voice :*
MARIAN'S VOICE. Well, Leo, what's it to be?

Close-up of LEO. *Quick cut.*   *PAST*
LEO *is now on the platform.*
Platform. Long shot.
LEO *approaches the edge of the platform. The audience*
is still. He sings :

Angels! Ever bright and fair,
Take, oh take me to your care.
Speed to your own courts my flight
Clad in robes of virgin white
Clad in robes of virgin white.

During this song the camera gently cuts between
STUBBS *and* BLUNT, *totally sober and attentive,*
TRIMINGHAM, MR MAUDSLEY, MRS MAUDSLEY
and TED. *Close-ups of* MARIAN *and* LEO. *Gleam of*
MARIAN's *white arms and neck from* TED's *and*
LEO's *point of view.*
The final shot of this sequence of shots is from the back
of the hall as LEO *finishes the song, the audience quite*
still, before the applause.

Exterior. Lane. Moonlight. Night.
The party walking back to the house. MARCUS *and*
LEO *straggling behind.*

MARCUS. Well, thank goodness we've said good-bye to the
village for a year. Did you notice the stink in that
hall?

LEO. No.

MARCUS. What a whiff! I suppose you were too busy mooing
and rolling your eyes and sucking up the applause.
Still, toadstool, I must admit you didn't do too
badly.

LEO. Oh thank you.

MARCUS. Except that it was rather horrific to see your slimy
serpent's tongue stuck to the roof of your mouth
and your face like a sick cow.

LEO *seizes him.*

LEO. You po-faced pot-bellied bed wetter!

MARCUS. Pax! I'll tell you a secret.

LEO. What?

MARCUS. Marian's engaged to marry Trimingham. It'll be
announced after the ball. Are you glad?

LEO *lets him go.*

LEO. Yes, I am. I'm sure I am.

Exterior. House. The long shot. Lawn. Day.
MARIAN *and* TRIMINGHAM *playing croquet. They*
play slowly and with concentration. He moves to-
wards her and whispers something to her. They laugh.
The camera suddenly observes that LEO *is watching*
them.

Interior. House. The hall looking through to dining-
room.
The end of luncheon. The house party sitting at the
long table eating peaches.
MARCUS *and* LEO *come out of the dining-room.*

MARCUS. Are you going out?

LEO. Yes. Shall we?

MARCUS. I'm afraid I can't.

LEO. Why not, sewer rat?

MARCUS. Nanny Robson isn't well. She lives in the village. Marian says I have to spend the afternoon with her. Isn't it boring? Marian said she was going herself after tea. What will you do? Where will you drag your evil smelling carcase?

LEO. Oh I might hang round the rubbish heap for a bit. And then –

MARCUS. Well, don't get carted away by mistake.

The boys tussle in the hall.

Exterior. Back of house.
LEO *strolling away from the thermometer. He turns in the direction of the rubbish dump.* MARIAN's *voice stops him:*

MARIAN. Hello, Leo. Just the man I was looking for.

She comes into shot.

Will you do something for me?

LEO. Oh yes. What?

MARIAN. Take this letter.

She holds out the letter.
LEO *looks at it and then at her.*

LEO. But . . . who to?

MARIAN. Who to? Why to the farm. You silly.

Close-up of LEO.
He stares at her.
Two shot.

What's the matter?

LEO. But I can't.

MARIAN. Can't? Why not?

Pause.

LEO. Because of Hugh.

MARIAN. Hugh? What has Hugh to do with it?

LEO. He . . . might be upset.

MARIAN. What has Hugh got to do with it? I told you, this is
a business matter between Mr Burgess and myself.
It has nothing to do with anyone else, no one else in
the world. Do you understand? Or are you too
stupid?

Close-up of LEO.

LEO. But you and Hugh . . . you and Trimingham
. . . you . . .

Close-up of MARIAN.

MARIAN. What are you talking about? You come into this
house, our guest, a poor nothing out of nowhere,
we take you in, we know nothing about you, we
feed you, we clothe you, we make a great fuss of you
– and then you have the damned cheek to say you
won't do a simple thing that any tuppeny-ha'-penny
rag-a-muffin in the street would do for nothing!

Long shot.
MARIAN *and* LEO *alone on the path.*

Nothing!

She raises her hand. LEO *starts back. They are still.*
Close-up of MARIAN.

You want paying, I suppose. I see. How much do
you want?

Two shot.
LEO *snatches the letter and runs.*

Exterior. Country lane. Very high shot.
LEO, *a tiny figure in the landscape, walking, kicking*
a stone.
MARIAN'S VOICE OLD (OVER)
So you met my grandson?

COLSTON'S VOICE (OVER)
Yes. I did.
MARIAN'S VOICE OLD (OVER)
Does he remind you of anyone?
COLSTON'S VOICE (OVER)
Of course. His grandfather.
MARIAN'S VOICE OLD (OVER)
That's it, that's it. He does. Yes, he does.
The stone is kicked against a gate.
Shot over farmyard gate to LEO.
His face is stained with tears.

Interior. Farm. Kitchen.
TED *is sitting alone holding a gun between his knees.*
His chest is naked. The barrel is pressed against it.
The muzzle just below his mouth. He is peering down
the barrel.
The shot holds.
Sound of a knock and a door opening.
TED *looks up.*

TED. Hullo! It's the postman!

Shot of kitchen.
TED *stands.*

How are you?

He comes closer to LEO *and peers at him.*

You've been crying. What's the matter?

TED *takes out a handkerchief and gives it to him.*

Would you like to have a shot with my gun? I was
just going to clean it but I can do that afterwards.

LEO *shakes his head.*

Come and watch me then. There's some old rooks
round here that could do with a peppering.

Exterior. Farmyard.
TED *standing in the yard. Gun at his shoulder.* LEO *by*
the door.

TED *shoots.* LEO *starts.*
LEO's *point of view.*
The bird twirls slowly to earth. TED *picks it up and throws it into a bed of nettles.*
The sky.
Rooks wheeling away.
TED'S VOICE. They won't come back in a hurry.

Interior. Scullery.
TED *putting the kettle on to boil on the grate.*
TED. Have you got a letter for me?

Interior. Kitchen.
TED *walks in with tablecloth and drapes it over the table.* LEO *hands him the letter.*
TED. Looks as though you've been sleeping on it.

TED *reads it quickly, puts it away.*

You'd like some tea, wouldn't you? I'm on my own to-day. My daily woman doesn't come on Sundays.
LEO. Oh, do you have a woman every day?

TED *looks at him.*

TED. No. I told you she doesn't come on Sundays.
LEO. Have you any message for her?
TED. Who?
LEO. Marian.
TED. I might have, but do you want to take it?
LEO. Not very much. But she'll be angry if I don't.

TED *lights a cigarette.*

TED. So it was her. (*Pause.*) It isn't fair to ask you to do it for nothing. What can I do to make it worth your while?

Close-up of LEO.

LEO. The last time I was here you said you'd tell me something.

Close-up of TED.

TED. Did I?

LEO. Yes, you said you'd tell me about . . . spooning.

Close-up of LEO.

I don't know any other word. Is there another word?

The kitchen.
TED *goes to the dresser, brings some teacups and saucers and puts them on the table.*

You'd said you'd tell me.

TED (*collecting plates*). Yes. But now I'm not sure that I shall.

LEO. Why not?

TED. It's a job for your dad, really.

LEO. My father's dead. And I'm quite sure he never did it!

TED. Are you?

Pause.

LEO. You can't break your promise.

Pause.

TED. Well . . . it means putting your arm round a girl, and kissing her. That's what it means.

LEO *jumping out of chair.*

LEO. I know that! But it's something else too. It makes you *feel* something.

TED. What do you like doing best?

LEO. Oh . . .

Hissing of the kettle from the scullery.

TED. The kettle's boiling.

TED *goes into the scullery.* LEO *stands.* TED *comes out with a teapot and a jug of milk and puts them on the table.*

It's like whatever you like doing best, and then some more.

Close-up of LEO.

LEO. Yes, but *what more*? What is lover-like? What does it mean? What is a lover? What does a lover do? Are you a lover? What do you do? You know. I know you know. And I won't take any more messages for you unless you tell me!

TED *from* LEO's *point of view.*
TED *towers above him, and moves towards him.*

TED. Clear out of here quick.

LEO's *back darts out of shot.*

Interior. Cottage. Hall and front door. PRESENT
The back of COLSTON *walking through the hall, down a step into the sitting-room. The maid closes the door and follows. She leaves the room by another door.* COLSTON *stands.*
Over this LEO's *voice :*
LEO'S VOICE (*as if writing*).
Dear Mother, I am sorry to tell you I am not enjoying myself here. I would like to come home.

Exterior. Road outside farm.   PAST
LEO *running away from farm.* TED *waving and shouting at farmyard gate, receding into the distance.*

Interior. House. Tea. The silver teapot.
The camera withdraws to find MARIAN *presiding over tea.* TRIMINGHAM *sits beside* MARIAN, *on a low stool, half in shadow. She regards her guests with a smile, pouring milk in one cup, a slice of lemon in another and lumps of sugar into some. The cups and plates of cakes are passed round. When it is* LEO's *turn for tea* MARIAN *drops four lumps of sugar into his cup, giggling.*

This shot is silent. Over the shot hear MARIAN's *voice as an old lady.*

MARIAN'S VOÏCE (OLD)

I rarely went to parties. People came to see me, of course, interesting people, artists and writers, not stuffy country neighbours. There *are* stuffy people, aren't there? No, no, interesting people came to see me. Artists and writers. Modern people with modern views.

Interior. House. Hall. Brass postbox.
LEO *popping letter into the postbox.*

Exterior. Back of the house. Early evening.
LEO *and* MARCUS *pushing each other.*

MARCUS. What shall we do? Where shall we go?

LEO. What about the rubbish dump?

MARCUS. Oh no, it's so boring. What about those mysterious outhouses?

LEO. Good idea.

MARCUS. Not that there's anything worth seeing, apart from a lot of dreary old outhouses.

LEO. There's the deadly nightshade.

MARCUS. Oui, le belladonne.

LEO. You mean atropa belladonna.

They begin to walk towards the outhouses. MARCUS's *voice receding.*

MARCUS. I don't mean that at all. I mean deadly night-shade.

MARCUS *and* LEO *walking through the tangled undergrowth.*

Mama is ill in bed.

LEO. Why?

MARCUS. I don't know.

They walk on.

What do you think of my mother?

LEO *glances at him.*

LEO. I think she has a lot to look after . . . with the house and everything, and organizing the ball and everything.

MARCUS. She has, yes. She undoubtedly has.

They walk on.

My sister is very beautiful, isn't she?

LEO. Yes. She is very beautiful.

They walk on.

MARCUS. She's going to London tomorrow.

LEO. What for?

MARCUS. Firstly to buy a dress for the ball, you oaf. The engagement ball, you oaf, and then to get something for you.

LEO. What do you mean?

MARCUS. A birthday present, frog-spawn. Now shall I tell you what it is or shall I not?

LEO. Do you *know* what it is?

MARCUS. Yes, but I don't tell little boys.

LEO *grapples with him and holds him in a firm grip.*

Well swear that you won't tell anyone I told you.

LEO. I swear.

MARCUS. It's a bicycle.

LEO *lets* MARCUS *out of his grip.*

LEO (*with great pleasure*). What?

MARCUS. Do you know what colour it is? It's green, green, you imbecile. Bright green. And do you know why? Because you are green yourself. It's your true colour, Marian said so.

LEO *standing with* MARCUS *dancing round him.*

Green. Green. Green!

LEO. Did she say that?

MARCUS. But of course.

MARCUS continues to dance around LEO.

Green. Green. Green!

Close-up of LEO.

LEO (*violently*). Do you know where Marian is at this moment?

Two shot.
MARCUS *stops still.*

MARCUS. No. Do you?
LEO. Yes.
MARCUS. Where?
LEO. I don't tell little boys.

LEO *dances round* MARCUS.

Little boy, little boy, wouldn't you like to know?
MARCUS. Pax!

LEO *walks away.*
LEO *and* MARCUS *walking.*

Do you really know where she is?
LEO. Ah-hah!

They walk on in silence, kicking stones as they go.
Suddenly LEO *stops.*
The deadly nightshade.
It has grown out of its door, and spread. It emerges over the roofless wall. It is heavy, purple, oppressive.
MARCUS'S VOICE
Shall we push past it into the shed?
Close-up of LEO.

LEO. No, you mustn't.

Suddenly the low murmur of a man's voice heard.
MARCUS *and* LEO *freeze. The voice is insistent, cajoling, tender. The words are indecipherable.*
MARCUS *whispers to* LEO.

MARCUS. A loony talking to himself. Shall we go and see?

A second voice heard, low, toneless, light.

There are two of them. They're spooning. Let's go and rout them out.

Quick close-up of LEO.

LEO (*hushed whisper*). No! It would be too boring!

Exterior. Outhouses.
LEO *walks away.* MARCUS *stands a moment, looking back, and then follows. He joins* LEO *in foreground.*

MARCUS. What confounded cheek. Why should they come here? This is private property. I wonder what Mama would say.

LEO. Oh, I shouldn't tell her. What's the point?

MARCUS. What confounded cheek!

They disappear from shot.
The camera holds on the view of the outhouses, including the deadly nightshade.

Interior. House. Hall. The postbox.
LEO *looks through the pane into the postbox. He sees his letter. He fingers the door. It opens. He takes the letter out, looks at it, puts it back quickly. Closes the door.*
The camera pans to watch him run up the centre stairs.

Interior. House. Corridor. First landing.
LEO *appears and sees* TRIMINGHAM *going into the smoking-room. The door closes.*
LEO *hesitates, then walks to the smoking-room door, hesitates, knocks at the door, opens it.*

Interior. Smoking-room.
TRIMINGHAM *picking up a newspaper.* LEO *pokes his head round the door.*

TRIMINGHAM. Hello.

LEO *hesitates at the door.*

Come in.

LEO *closes the door.*

Never been in here before?

LEO. No.

TRIMINGHAM. Sit down. Cigar?

LEO. No thank you.

TRIMINGHAM *sits down and lights a cigar.*

Can I ask you something?

TRIMINGHAM. You can.

LEO. I was reading a book. And in this book . . . two men fought a duel . . . over a quarrel . . . about one of the men's wife. And then . . . in this duel . . . the wife's husband . . . the husband . . . was shot.

TRIMINGHAM. Mmn-hmnm. (*Pause.*) What's your question?

LEO. Well, I thought . . . when I read it . . . that it was probably the lady's fault, but she didn't have to fight the duel and I just thought that it was a little unfair.

Close-up of TRIMINGHAM.

TRIMINGHAM. Nothing is ever a lady's fault.

Close-up of LEO.

LEO. Oh.

Close-up of TRIMINGHAM.

TRIMINGHAM. Does that answer your question?

Shot across TRIMINGHAM *to* LEO.

LEO. Yes.

TRIMINGHAM. Any other questions?

LEO. Er . . . what do you think of Ted Burgess?

TRIMINGHAM (*ruminatively*). What do I think of Ted Burgess? (*Pause.*) He's a powerful hitter.

LEO *chuckles.*

But you had the measure of him.

LEO *smiles*.

You defeated him, didn't you? (*Pause.*) Yes, Ted Burgess is quite a decent fellow. A bit wild.

LEO. Wild? Do you mean he's dangerous?

TRIMINGHAM. He's not dangerous to you or to me. He's a bit of a lady-killer, that's all.

LEO (*baffled*). A lady-killer?

The door opens. MR MAUDSLEY *comes in.*
TRIMINGHAM *and* LEO *rise.*

MR MAUDSLEY. Sit down, please sit down. Ah! A new recruit to the smoking-room. Have you been telling him some smoking-room stories?

TRIMINGHAM *laughs.*

Or showing him the pictures? (*He turns to* LEO.) Have you looked at the pictures?

MR MAUDSLEY *indicates a row of small dark canvases, set deep in heavy frames.*
LEO *turns to look at the pictures.*
Men sitting on tubs, drinking. Women serving them. One woman leaning on the back of a man's chair watching the card game. The chair back pressing against her breasts, which bulge over its rim.
LEO *turns away from the pictures.*
Close-up of MR MAUDSLEY.

He doesn't like them.

Three shot.

TRIMINGHAM. Teniers is an acquired taste, in my opinion. We were talking about Ted Burgess when you came in. I told Leo he was a lady-killer.

MR MAUDSLEY. He has that reputation, I believe.

TRIMINGHAM. I've been talking to him about joining the army. A likely man. Single. No ties. And a pretty good shot too with a rifle, by all accounts.

MR MAUDSLEY. He has that reputation, I believe. (*Pause.*) Do you think he'll go?

TRIMINGHAM. I think he may. He was quite interested.

MR MAUDSLEY. He won't altogether be a loss to the district.

TRIMINGHAM. Why?

MR MAUDSLEY (*vaguely*). Oh, what you were saying just now.

> MR MAUDSLEY *goes to the cabinet to pour sherry from a decanter.*

They say he's got a woman up this way.

LEO. I know.

> *Close-up of* MR MAUDSLEY.
> MR MAUDSLEY, *in the act of pouring sherry, stops and looks over his shoulder at* LEO.
> TRIMINGHAM *and* MR MAUDSLEY *looking at* LEO.
> *Close-up of* LEO.

But she doesn't come on Sundays.

> TRIMINGHAM *and* MR MAUDSLEY.

TRIMINGHAM (*to* MR MAUDSLEY). Cigar?

> *Exterior. Cornfield. Long shot. Day.*
> LEO *stands in foreground looking across the field.*
> TED *is driving the reaper.* LEO *waves.* TED *does not see him. A labourer sees* LEO *and signals to* TED.
> TED *stops the horse and dismounts. The labourer gets up on the reaper and continues the work.*
> TED *walks slowly across the fields towards* LEO. *The camera moves with* LEO *as he walks towards* TED. *They stop at a short distance from each other.*
> *Silence.*

TED. I didn't think you'd come again. (*Pause.*) I'm sorry I shouted at you. I didn't mean to. I just didn't feel like telling you – what you wanted to know – that's all. But I'll tell you now if you like. (*Pause.*) Do you want me to tell you? Because I'll tell you now. If you want me to.

> *Close-up of* LEO.

LEO. No, no. I wouldn't dream of troubling you. I

know someone who'll tell me. As a matter of fact I know several people who can tell me.

Two shot.

TED. As long as they don't tell you wrong.
LEO. How could they? It's common knowledge, isn't it?

Pause.

TED. What are you doing with your bathing suit?

They begin to stroll along the edge of the cornfield.

LEO. I told Marcus you were going to give me a swimming lesson. I've come to say good-bye, you see.

Long shot. Across cornfield.
LEO and TED walking along its rim. Their voices:

TED. Oh, you're off are you?
LEO. Yes, I'm expecting to hear from my mother by Friday at the latest. I think I really should go home. She does miss me, you know.
TED. I'm sure she does.

Pause.

LEO. Is it true you're going to the war?
TED. Who told you that?
LEO. Lord Trimingham. (*Pause.*) Did you know Marian was engaged to him?
TED. Yes. I did.

Close two shot. TED *and* LEO *stopping.*

LEO. Is that why you're going?
TED. I don't know that I *am* going. That's for her to say. It isn't what I want, but what she wants.

Close-up of LEO *staring at him.*

Two shot.

LEO. Well, good-bye.
TED. So long, postman.

They shake hands. LEO *turns, turns back.*

LEO. Shall I take one more message for you?

Close-up of TED.

TED. Yes. Say tomorrow's no good, but Friday at half-past five, same as usual.

Close-up of MARIAN.

MARIAN. Did you miss me?

LEO'S VOICE. Well . . . I've been quite busy.

MARIAN. That's the first unkind thing I've ever heard you say.

Two shot MARIAN *and* LEO.
They are sitting in a small writing room.

MARIAN. I've been to London on a special mission.

LEO. Did you enjoy yourself?

MARIAN. No.

LEO. I'm sorry.

MARIAN. No you're not. You couldn't care less if I dropped dead in front of you. You're a hard-hearted boy, but then all boys are.

LEO. What about men?

MARIAN. You're all alike, blocks of granite. Or the beds here. They're *really* hard.

LEO. Mine isn't.

MARIAN. You're lucky. Mine is, harder than the ground.

LEO. I know a boy who slept on the ground once. He said it made his hips sore. Did you find that?

MARIAN *looks at him.*

MARIAN. What makes you think I've slept on the ground?

LEO. Because you said your bed was harder.

MARIAN. Well, so it is. (*Pause.*) I'm sorry I was so nasty to you the other day. I'm not really nasty. I'm a good natured girl, really.

Close-up of LEO.

LEO. Do . . . soldiers have to sleep on the ground?

MARIAN. Yes, I suppose so.

LEO. Will Ted have to?

Close-up of MARIAN.

MARIAN. Ted?

LEO. Yes, when he goes to the war.

MARIAN. Ted going to the war, what do you mean?

Two shot.

LEO. Hugh told me. Hugh asked him to join up and he said he might.

MARIAN. Hugh? Hugh! Do you mean that Hugh has persuaded Ted to enlist?

She stands and goes to the window.
MARIAN *foreground. Window.* LEO *background.*

(*Quietly.*) No. No he won't, he won't go to the war. I'll see to that. I'll tell Hugh . . . that it's out of the question. One word would do it.

LEO *comes to her at the window.*

LEO. No, you mustn't say any word. You see, Hugh doesn't *know*.

MARIAN. Doesn't know? Then why does he want Ted to go to the war?

LEO. He's patriotic. (*Pause.*) Perhaps he *wants* to go.

MARIAN. He couldn't.

Pause.

LEO. Why don't you marry Ted?

MARIAN. I can't . . . I can't. Can't you see why?

LEO. But why . . . are you marrying Hugh?

MARIAN. Because I must. I must. I've got to.

Wide shot. Room.
MARIAN *suddenly cries quietly.* LEO *stares at her and then begins to cry himself.*

They stand, crying. They hold each other. LEO *forces himself to stop.*

LEO. I have a message for you.

She looks up.

Friday at 5.30.

MARIAN. Yes.

LEO. But can you be back in time?

MARIAN. For what?

LEO. For my birthday. For cutting the cake.

MARIAN *takes his hand.*

MARIAN. Of course. Of course.

Exterior. Village street. **PRESENT**

COLSTON *standing by the car. At the far end of the village the figure of a young man appears. He slowly draws nearer on the other side of the street.* COLSTON *moves a few steps, stops and watches the young man. As the young man comes closer,* COLSTON *begins to cross the street towards him.*

Zoom in to young man's face turning sharply, seeing COLSTON *approach.*

LEO'S MOTHER'S VOICE *over this (as if writing):*

LEO'S MOTHER'S VOICE.

I think it would be ungrateful to Mrs Maudsley after all her kindness to you if you were to leave so suddenly. I think it would be a mistake.

Interior. LEO'S *room. Night.* **PAST**

LEO *at the writing table, erecting a structure like a small altar. Four books form the framework. Within stand four candles, a soap dish drainer rests on the books, on the drainer a silver cup, four boxes of matches, a water bottle and a damp sponge, set at precise intervals on the table.* LEO *looks at his clock. It is 11.15.*

Over this shot the woman's voice continues:

LEO'S MOTHER'S VOICE.

The ten days will soon pass, my darling, and then you'll be home. We can't expect to be happy *all* the time, can we?

He puts on his slippers and his dressing gown over his nightshirt and opens the door.

Interior. House. Staircase. Night.
Through the closed door of the drawing room sounds of a piano and singing. MARIAN *is singing 'Roaming in the Gloaming'.*
The front door is open. LEO *creeps down the main staircase, hesitates a moment and then goes out the door.*

Exterior. Back of the house. LEO *running through the bushes.*
The sky, cloudy, through moonlight.
The outhouse.
LEO *stops dead.*
LEO's *point of view. The deadly nightshade.*
LEO *walks towards it slowly. When he is close to it, he stops.*
He touches it. He moves quickly past it and into the outhouses.

Interior. Outhouse.
Close-up of LEO. *The twigs of the deadly nightshade about him.*
He shifts his position. A berry touches his face. He whimpers, tries to force his way out, hits a wall, turns, nightshade flowers around his face.
LEO *begins to tear at the nightshade. Branches rip and crack. He stumbles, still pulling, out of the outhouse, pulling at the main stem. Leaves fall, the main stem cracks. Roots creak. He pulls with all his might to unearth the plant and suddenly it gives way.*
He falls on his back clutching the stump.

High shot. LEO *lying with stump.*

LEO. Delenda est Belladonna.

Interior. LEO's *room. Close shot silver cup on writing table. Night.*
Diary open beside it. Incomprehensible writing seen.
LEO *is crushing a leaf, flower and two berries from the deadly nightshade in the cup, pouring boiling water into it with his left hand.*
LEO'S VOICE (*whispering*).
Delenda, delenda, delenda.

Interior. Lavatory.
LEO *pouring the mashed contents of the cup into the lavatory.*
COLSTON'S VOICE.
Delenda est Belladonna.
LEO *makes a gesture of exorcism.*

Exterior. House. Lawn. Rain. Day.
The rain sweeps over the lawn and through the cedars.
Close-up of MRS MAUDSLEY.
MRS MAUDSLEY. And now today . . . is Leo's day.

She smiles.
The camera tracks back to find MRS MAUDSLEY *and the others at the breakfast table. In front of* LEO *are opened envelopes and packages. Cards, ties etc.*

You've opened your presents. At seven o'clock you'll cut your birthday cake, and receive a rather special present, so I believe. Now how would you like to spend the day? Unfortunately the weather . . . has changed, but if it clears perhaps you would like to go for a drive to Beeston Castle, after luncheon? You haven't seen it, have you?

LEO. That would be very nice.
MRS MAUDSLEY. Well, we shall do that, if the weather clears. We shall decide at luncheon.

DENYS. What if the weather doesn't clear, Mama?

MRS MAUDSLEY. Then we shall have to think again. We shall make our decision at luncheon. Don't you think, Hugh?

TRIMINGHAM. Quite a fair plan, I should say.

DENYS. But it may not clear.

Exterior. Village street. Over COLSTON *to the young man.* **PRESENT**
The young man steps back to point to a cottage at the far end of the village. COLSTON *nods to the young man. They shake hands and part.*
Over this the following dialogue:

MR MAUDSLEY. I think it will. The rain seems to have stopped. For the moment anyway.

DENYS. So it has.

MRS MAUDSLEY. There you are then. It seems that all will be well for Leo's birthday.

DENYS. There's still a lot of dark cloud about.

MR MAUDSLEY. What's your opinion, Hugh?

Interior. Hall. Morning. **PAST**
Guests passing through the hall. MARIAN *stops, alone, and turns.*

MARIAN. Leo, come with me and tell me what the weather means to do.

Exterior. Front of house.
MARIAN *and* LEO *emerge and look up at the sky. They walk along the path and turn by the side of the house into the rhododendrons, the camera watching them.*
MARIAN *and* LEO *amid the rhododendrons.*

LEO. Do you think the summer is over? It's one of the hottest summers on record. You know.

MARIAN. Of course it isn't over. Tell me, would you like to walk?

LEO. Oh yes! Where shall we walk?

MARIAN. I can't, I'm afraid. It's this kind of walk.

Close shot of MARIAN's *hand touching* LEO's. *A letter in* MARIAN's *hand.*
Close-up of LEO.

LEO. Oh no!

Close-up of MARIAN.

MARIAN (*laughing*). Oh yes!

Two shot.
MARIAN, *laughing, tries to thrust the letter into* LEO's *hand.* LEO *resists. They begin to dodge and feint and lunge, both now laughing.*

MRS MAUDSLEY'S
    VOICE. Marian! Leo!

They stop still. The camera moves towards them.

What were you fighting about?

MARIAN. Oh I was just teaching him a lesson –

LEO *whose hands are at his sides, suddenly drops the letter.*
The camera dips slowly to look at it. It lies on the ground, crumpled.
LEO *looks sharply into camera.* MARIAN *remains composed.*
Close-up of MRS MAUDSLEY.

MRS MAUDSLEY. Was that the bone of contention?

Three shot.
MARIAN *picks up the letter and puts it into* LEO's *pocket.*

MARIAN. Yes it was, Mama. I wanted him to take this note to Nanny Robson to tell her that I will go and see her some time this afternoon. And would you believe it, Leo didn't want to! He pretended he had something on with Marcus.

LEO *looks at her.*

Yes you did!

MRS MAUDSLEY. I shouldn't let it worry you, Marian. You say she often doesn't remember whether you've been or not. She is certainly growing old, poor Nanny Robson. I think it's about time Leo and I took a walk in the garden. (*She takes* LEO's *hand*.) Come along Leo. I don't believe you've seen the garden properly, have you? (*She turns to* MARIAN.) You can spare Leo now, can't you Marian?

MARIAN. Oh, yes.

Long shot.
MRS MAUDSLEY *with* LEO *walks away from* MARIAN.

LEO. Would you like Marcus to come with us?

MRS MAUDSLEY. Oh no. Marcus isn't interested in flowers. You are though, aren't you?

LEO. Yes, I am.

The backs of MRS MAUDSLEY *and* LEO *walking through the garden.*
They arrive at the flower beds.

MRS MAUDSLEY. The rain has certainly stopped. (*Pause.*) Well, now, here's the garden. What kind of flowers truly interest you?

LEO. Poisonous ones really.

MRS MAUDSLEY. I don't think you'll find many of those.

LEO. Oh there is one in the out –

Two shot.
MRS MAUDSLEY *stops.*

MRS MAUDSLEY. In the what?

LEO. Well . . . I've seen . . .

MRS MAUDSLEY (*smiling*). What have you seen, Leo?

LEO. Well, there is a deadly nightshade in one of the outhouses.

MRS MAUDSLEY. Oh, you mean where the old garden used to be.

LEO. Yes, somewhere there . . .

MRS MAUDSLEY. Do you often go to the outhouses?

LEO. Oh no, not often.

They stop by a magnolia.

MRS MAUDSLEY. This always reminds me of Marian. How sweet of you to say you'd take her note to Nanny Robson. Does she often send you with messages?

LEO. Oh no, just once or twice.

MRS MAUDSLEY. It rather worries me that I stopped you going just now. Perhaps you would like to go? You know the way, of course?

Pause.

LEO. Well, not quite but I can ask.

MRS MAUDSLEY. You don't know the way? But I thought you had taken messages there before.

LEO. Yes, well, yes I have.

MRS MAUDSLEY. But you don't know the way. (*Pause.*) I think perhaps the note should be delivered. You have it in your pocket, haven't you? I'll call one of the gardeners and ask him to take it.

LEO. Oh no, really. It's not a bit important. Please don't bother.

MRS MAUDSLEY. It is important in a way, you see. Stanton, could you come here a minute.

A gardener puts down his tools and comes towards her and into the shot.

We have a note here for Miss Robson, rather urgent. Would you mind taking it?

STANTON. Yes 'm.

LEO *digs his fingers into his pocket.*

LEO. I've . . . lost it. I haven't got it. It must have fallen out of my pocket.

MRS MAUDSLEY. Feel again.

LEO *does so.*

LEO. I must have dropped it.

MRS MAUDSLEY. Very well, Stanton.

STANTON *moves away.*

Close-up of MRS MAUDSLEY.

Take your hands out of your pockets. Has no one

ever told you not to stand with your hands in
your pockets?

Close-up of LEO *taking his hands out of his pockets.*

Two shot over LEO *to* MRS MAUDSLEY.

MRS MAUDSLEY. I could ask you to turn your pockets out. But I
won't do that. I'll just ask you one question. You
say you have taken messages for Marian before?

LEO. Well I –

MRS MAUDSLEY. I think you said so. If you don't take them to
Nanny Robson –

Exterior. Village street. No cars. Day.
                                    TIME NEUTRAL
Exterior. House. Garden. Long shot.
MRS MAUDSLEY *and* LEO *standing.*

Interior. House. Lavatory.
LEO *sitting on lavatory lid.*
MRS MAUDSLEY'S VOICE (OVER)
– to whom do you take them?

Exterior. Village street.   *PRESENT*
Across COLSTON *to the young man. The young man
is listening to* COLSTON.

*Exterior. House. Garden. Rain sweeping over the
garden.*   *PAST*
No one in sight.

Interior. Cottage.   *PRESENT*
COLSTON *ushered into the room by the maid.*

Interior. House. Lavatory.   *PAST*
LEO *sitting.*
MARIAN'S VOICE OLD (OVER)
So you met my grandson.
COLSTON'S VOICE
Yes, I did.
MARIAN'S VOICE OLD (OVER)
Does he remind you of anyone?
COLSTON'S VOICE
Of course. His grandfather.
MARIAN'S VOICE (OLD)
That's it, that's it. He does.

Close-up of COLSTON.   *PRESENT*

(*NOTE: In the following shots we see the faces of* COLSTON *and* MARIAN *old for the first time.*)

COLSTON. It must be a comfort for you to have him near you.

Close-up of MARIAN *as an old lady.*   *PRESENT*

MARIAN. Yes. But he doesn't come to see me very much. I think he has a grudge against me.

Close-up of COLSTON.   *PRESENT*

COLSTON. Oh surely not.

Close-up of MARIAN.   *PRESENT*

MARIAN (*old*). They tell me that he wants to marry a girl – a nice girl – but he won't ask her . . . he feels . . . I think he feels . . . that he's under some sort of spell or curse, you see. That's just plain silly. Now this is where you come in.

COLSTON. I?

MARIAN. Yes, you. You know the facts, you know what *really* happened. Tell him, tell him everything, just as it was.

Close-up of COLSTON.   *PRESENT*
Shot over COLSTON *to* MARIAN   *PRESENT*

Every man should get married. You ought to have got married. You're all dried up inside, I can tell that. Don't you feel any need of love? Speak to him, tell him there's no spell or curse except an unloving heart.

Interior. House. Hall. Evening.   *PAST*
MRS MAUDSLEY *descending the stairs.*
MARIAN'S VOICE OLD (OVER)
Tell him that.
MRS MAUDSLEY *walks to the door of the drawing-room and opens it.*
From her point of view. See a collection of people standing at windows looking out.
Distant thunder.
Interior. Drawing-room. The windows. LEO. *He turns.*
MRS MAUDSLEY *moving into the room.*

MARCUS. We're watching the lightning, Mama.

TRIMINGHAM. Rather good luck we didn't set out for Beeston Castle.

MRS MAUDSLEY. Yes, it would have been rather a damp expedition.

The gathering clusters round the tea-table.

Sit here please, Leo, dear. (*She indicates a place.*) Do you see what's in front of you?

Across table at LEO. *Sitting.*
In foreground a birthday cake with twelve candles. Crackers, flowers. A smaller cake with one candle.
Over LEO *to* MRS MAUDSLEY.
You see I don't like the number thirteen – isn't it silly of me? So we've put twelve candles round the big cake, and then when they're blown out, you shall light this one, and blow this one out.

MRS MAUDSLEY's *hands.*
Over MRS MAUDSLEY *to* LEO.

LEO. When will that be?

MRS MAUDSLEY. When Marian comes. She has a rather special present for you. She wants to give it to you herself, naturally.

Long shot. Room.

Let's all sit down.

Everyone does so.

Marian should be back at about six o'clock from Nanny Robson.

TRIMINGHAM. I haven't seen Nanny Robson for years. How is she?

MRS MAUDSLEY. Remarkably well. Isn't it time that Leo cut the cake?

MARCUS. Yes! If he can do it.

MRS MAUDSLEY. That's unkind. Of course he can do it. He's a man of great capabilities.

TRIMINGHAM. Considerable. And well loved. Didn't you know he was Marian's cavalier?

LEO *blowing the candles out.*
Cries of encouragement. Applause.

MARCUS. He's done it!

The SERVANTS *handing round portions of the cake.*

DENYS. Leave a piece for Marian.

TRIMINGHAM. She ought to be here now.

MR MAUDSLEY. It's still raining. (*Pause.*) We'd better send the carriage down to fetch her. Why didn't we think of it before?

Table in foreground.
MR MAUDSLEY *talking to butler at door in background.*

Exterior. House. Rain. Evening.
The carriage going into the distance down the drive.

Interior. Drawing-room.
Everyone eating cake.
Silence.

TRIMINGHAM. She should be with us in five minutes now.

A GUEST. She may be walking up in the rain. Poor darling, she'll be soaked.

Pause.

MARCUS. What about your thirteenth candle?

TRIMINGHAM. We must light it first.

It is lit.

LEO *blowing the candle out.*

DENYS. Now you must cut a piece for yourself.

LEO *does so.*

He'd rather have his cake than eat it.

DENYS *laughs. No one else does.*
Close–up of LEO.
He nibbles a little at his cake.
Silence.
The room.
Silence.

MR MAUDSLEY. Let's have a round of crackers. Here, Leo, come pull one with me.

LEO *does so. Everyone, with the exception of* MRS MAUDSLEY, *finds partners.*

Now all together!

They pull the crackers. They all put on paper hats and blow whistles.
Medium shot of LEO *turning to look for a cracker.*
A cracker is thrust into his hand. He looks up.
LEO'*s point of view.* MRS MAUDSLEY *with cracker.*
Over MRS MAUDSLEY *to* LEO.
They pull. The cracker cracks.
Back of BUTLER *at door.*
The assembly turns to him. MRS MAUDSLEY *in the forefront.*

BUTLER. Excuse me, Madam. The carriage has come back but not Miss Marian. She wasn't at Miss

Robson's. And Miss Robson said she hadn't been all day.

The BUTLER *goes out.*
Silence.

DENYS. Where can she be?

Pause.

MR MAUDSLEY. Well, all we can do is wait for her.
DENYS. I've just found a wonderful riddle. Listen to this.

MRS MAUDSLEY's *chair scraping back. Her skirt.*

Close-up of MRS MAUDSLEY.

MRS MAUDSLEY. No. We won't wait. I'm going to look for her. Leo. you know where she is. You shall show me the way,

Long shot. Room.
MRS MAUDSLEY *seizes* LEO's *hand. A chair falls.*
She takes him to the door.
Close-up of MR MAUDSLEY.

MR MAUDSLEY. Madeleine!

Interior. Hall.
MRS MAUDSLEY *and* LEO *going through hall. They pass a green bicycle standing in the hall, and go out the door.*

Interior. Room.
Silence. Everyone still.

Close-up of TRIMINGHAM *sitting quite still.*

Exterior. House. Night.
MRS MAUDSLEY *and* LEO *come out of the front door. The* BUTLER *follows them swiftly and offers* MRS MAUDSLEY *a lantern and an umbrella. She ignores them both.* MRS MAUDSLEY *and* LEO *walk along the path, she leading. It is raining heavily.*

Exterior. House. Garden. Rain. Night.
MRS MAUDSLEY *and* LEO *moving past the rho-dodendrons towards the outhouses.*

Interior. Cottage.   **PRESENT**
COLSTON *and* MARIAN *sitting. Long shot.*
She is speaking, but the words are unheard.
Over this voices:
MARIAN'S VOICE (YOUNG)
You won't . . . tell anyone about this letter.
You won't . . . will you?
LEO'S VOICE.
Of course I won't.

Exterior. House. Garden. Rain. Night.   *PAST*
MRS MAUDSLEY *and* LEO *moving past rhododen-drons towards outhouses.*

Exterior. Outhouses. Rain. Night.
MRS MAUDSLEY *and* LEO *approach the outhouses.*

Exterior. Cottage. Through window.   **PRESENT**
MARIAN *and* COLSTON *sitting. She is talking, words unheard. Over this voices:*
MARIAN'S VOICE (YOUNG)
Tell me. Would you like a walk?
LEO'S VOICE
Oh yes! Where shall we walk?
MARIAN'S VOICE (YOUNG)
I can't, I'm afraid. It's this kind of walk.

Exterior. Outhouses. Rain. Night.   *PAST*
MRS MAUDSLEY *and* LEO *approach the outhouses.*
Medium shot. Stump of deadly nightshade lying on the path. Camera still. Rain.

Interior. Deadly nightshade. Outhouse.
MRS MAUDSLEY *standing.* LEO *behind her.*

MRS MAUDSLEY. Not here.

Close-up of LEO *whimpering.*
MRS MAUDSLEY's *face comes into the shot.*

No, you *shall* come.

She pulls him after her.

MRS MAUDSLEY *dragging* LEO *towards the row of outhouses. Rain.*
Light flickering. Their faces.
They stop.

Interior. Outhouse.
A lantern on the ground.
A shadow moving on the wall like an umbrella opening and closing.
Close-up of LEO *mystified.*
The shadow.
Close-up of MRS MAUDSLEY.
The shadow.
Close-up of MRS MAUDSLEY.
Her face contorts. She lets her breath out in a long exhalation and groan.
The shadow ceasing to move.
Close-up of MRS MAUDSLEY. *Her face contorted. No sound.*
Close-up of LEO.
The faces of TED *and* MARIAN *on the ground.*
They are still. TED's *head is buried in* MARIAN's *shoulder.* MARIAN *looks up through half-open eyes.*

Exterior. Lawn. Front of houses. Day.
In foreground a shape of a girl lying in a hammock.
The wide lawn falls away before the house on a gentle slope. Cedars, elms. The hammock, faded crimson

canvas, swings gently. In background figures in white playing croquet. Over this MARIAN's *voice.*
MARIAN'S VOICE (OLD)
You came out of the blue to make us happy. And we made you happy, didn't we? We trusted you with our great treasure. You might never have known what it was, you might have gone through life without knowing. Isn't that so?

Close-up of COLSTON *listening.* **PRESENT**
MARIAN'S VOICE (OLD)
But you see you can tell him, Leo. You can tell him everything, just as it was.
The camera holds on COLSTON.

Medium shot of TED *dead.*

He is slumped in his chair, his gun against his leg. His shirt is bloody. His head cannot be seen.
Near the end of this shot MARIAN's *voice begins:*
MARIAN'S VOICE (OLD)
Hugh was as true as steel, he wouldn't hear a word against me.

Close-up of MARIAN OLD. **PRESENT**
MARIAN. But everybody wanted to know us, of course. I was Lady Trimingham, you see. I still am. There is no other.

Interior. Car windscreen. Moving towards Brandham Hall. **PRESENT**
MARIAN'S VOICE OLD (OVER)
Remember how you loved taking our messages, bringing us together and making us happy. Well

this is another errand of love and the last time I
shall ever ask you to be our postman.
The car goes down an incline and begins to rise.

Interior. Car. COLSTON's *face impassive.*

                                          PRESENT

MARIAN'S VOICE OLD (OVER)
Our love was a beautiful thing, wasn't it? Tell him
he can feel proud to be descended from our union,
the child of so much happiness and beauty. Tell
him –
The sound stops abruptly.
The car comes to the top of the hill.

Exterior. Road. Day.   *PRESENT*
*The south west prospect of Brandham Hall springs into
view.*
The elms have been cut down.
The car stops.
Brandham Hall.
A cloud of dust from the car slightly obscures the view.